Wholehearted Cooking

Wholehearted Cooking

Simply Delicious Low-Fat Recipes

Terry Joyce Blonder

Camden House Publishing
A division of Telemedia Communications (USA) Inc.

Camden House Publishing

Ferry Road

Charlotte, Vermont 05445

Library of Congress Cataloging-in-Publication Data

Blonder, Terry Joyce.
Wholehearted cooking: simply delicious low-fat recipes / Terry Joyce Blonder.
     p. cm.
Includes Index.
ISBN 0-9444475-45-0 (h/c) : $22.95. — ISBN 0-9444475-46-9 (s/c) : $17.95
     1. Low-fat diet—recipes. I. Title.
RM237.7.B563 1993
641.5'638—dc20

93-17813
CIP

Editorial Director: Julie Stillman
Copy Editor: Barbara Jatkola
Cover and interior design: Susan Romanoff
Photography: Becky Luigart-Stayner
Food Styling: Kate Hays
Illustrations: Elayne Sears

Trade distribution by

Firefly Books Ltd.

250 Sparks Avenue

Willowdale, Ontario

Canada M2H 2S4

Printed and bound in Canada by

D.W. Friesen & Sons

Altona, Manitoba

Contents

Introduction

*t*he recipes and style of cooking in *Wholehearted Cooking* are not a deviation for me. This is the way I live, full-time. I am not a food writer cashing in on a trend. And I am not a classically trained chef, steeped in the French tradition of butter, cream and labor-intensive recipes, looking for a way to pare down that cuisine. Rather, my approach to food is based on a love of fresh, basic ingredients that are the foundation for a healthy diet. Instead of reducing fat from a fatty diet, I build up, by taking inherently healthful, low-fat, nutrient-dense foods, such as vibrant vegetables, satisfying grains, ripe fruits and tender chicken, and creating flavorful meals with them. Although I am conscientious about what I eat, eating remains a pleasure for me. Cooking and dining are activities that I pursue without guilt, trepidation or calculator in hand. Because I enjoy my food, my healthy habits never seem like a diet forced on me; I never feel as if I have to cheat. If I occasionally desire French fries or ice cream, I eat them, knowing full well that a serving now and then won't have me succumbing to full-fat ways. I do not look nostalgically back to foods that I no longer eat. I have replaced them with others that I like equally well, if not better.

Also, my cooking style lends itself to simple recipes that use only a few ingredients prepared in a straightforward manner. This ease in the kitchen is essential, for recipes are worthwhile only if a person wants to use them. Few people, myself included, have the time to make elaborate meals, especially as a part of an everyday diet. My hope is that you will want to try the recipes in *Wholehearted Cooking* and that this book will encourage and enable you to wholeheartedly embrace healthful cooking and eating as a part of your daily life.

Wholehearted Nutrition

The cornerstone of what we used to consider healthful eating—the four food groups, with an emphasis on meat and animal products—has been discarded, but many people are not sure what to replace it with. Instead of embracing something sensible and equally simple, people dissect their meals into grams of nutrients and agonize over the smallest details. The link between food and health has prompted people to treat eating as a dangerous activity and food as medicine to be consumed. The media feed this myopic view by hyping each new nutrition study. Rarely are the findings critiqued or kept in perspective. Additionally (or maybe partially because of this), cooking and eating are low on our priority list. We begrudge any time spent in the kitchen, eat on the run and rarely sit down to communal meals. Instead of mealtimes being nourishing, relaxing interludes in our busy days, they are fraught with anxiety or approached with a devil-may-care attitude—neither of which makes for enjoyable or healthful dining.

My aim in *Wholehearted Cooking* is to give you

the ability to approach food without confusion and nit-picking. There is a solid and growing consensus that a high-carbohydrate, high-fiber, low-fat diet makes sense. This way of eating provides all the calories, protein, fiber and essential vitamins and minerals that the average person needs, while minimizing foods linked with disease and obesity. The principles of this diet are easy to understand. Meat, though not banned, yields center stage to low-fat foods that come from plants. Complex carbohydrates, or what used to be called starches, fill the plate instead of a thick steak. These complex carbohydrates (not to be confused with simple carbohydrates, also called sugars, which contribute only empty calories) include potatoes, grains, pastas and beans. Starches are good foods because they are nutrient dense, provide energy (calories) and fiber, and are naturally filling. Fruits and vegetables also are emphasized for many of the same reasons. They also contain essential antioxidants and other vitamins and minerals and are so important to good health that it is recommended that a person eat at least five servings of them a day.

Concern about excessive fat consumption motivated the biggest change from the former four food groups. Before, fat-laden foods like whole milk and marbled steaks were promoted. Now that fat is kept to a minimum; lean meats and low-fat dairy products have replaced their heavier cousins. Thus, skinless chicken, fish and low-fat ricotta have a place on the table where cream sauces and roasts used to sit. Getting enough complete animal protein is no longer a worry. In fact, too much meat has been implicated as a cause of heart disease and other illnesses. So lean meats are part of the diet, but only in moderation.

Nutritionists suggest that less than 30 percent of a person's daily consumption of calories comes from fat. Many think that 20 percent is a more desirable goal. This doesn't allow for fried foods or cheese sauce on broccoli, but there is leeway for the cook to use small quantities of fat-containing foods like nuts, oils and Parmesan cheese. These ingredients contribute to gustatory pleasure—which is as important to maintaining a healthy diet as is sticking strictly to the dietitian's numbers.

The way I design a recipe is simple. I don't number-crunch grams of this and that. I just take ingredients that fit within my taste and nutritional parameters and combine them in ways that emphasize their inherent flavors. I figure that if everything going into the recipe is good for you, the outcome is bound to be equally wholesome. The nutritional analysis that follows each recipe proves that the details do indeed fall into place. For recipes that give a range for the number of servings, the nutritional analysis is based on the first number of servings given.

Along with the nutritional guidelines, I have other criteria for choosing ingredients. They must taste good and be of excellent quality. Imitations and second-rate substitutions, even if they meet my nutritional standards, have no place in my kitchen. Thus, you won't find margarine, soy cheeses, egg substitutes or artificial sweeteners in my pantry. I use only the freshest, most aromatic, most full-flavored foods. If it doesn't look or taste right going into the recipe, it will be no better in the finished product.

But good ingredients aren't worth a thing if you aren't willing to get into the kitchen and cook with them. I want you to be able to quickly and confidently put together a meal that is savory and promotes well-being. Eating well doesn't have to be a big production, but all too often cooking with basic, low-fat, wholesome ingredients seems too daunting to become a part of everyday life. Assembling a meal centered on fresh and unprocessed foods takes not only preparation but also thinking time—unfamiliarity with ingredients and cooking techniques can make the task overwhelming. That is why all my recipes are clear and easy to follow. I rely on uncomplicated cooking techniques and troubleshoot potential problems within each recipe. Many of my recipes take less than 30 minutes to make, and most rely on ingredients found in supermarkets. The introduction to each chapter and explanatory sidebars will help you cook efficiently and with assurance. Producing healthy, satisfying home-cooked meals requires knowledge of only a few basic cooking skills, an efficiently organized kitchen and an understanding of your ingredients.

Reducing Fat But Not Flavor

Healthy foods have a reputation for being boring. Certainly, rice cakes, celery sticks and plain broiled chicken prove that point. You expect those foods to be dull, and they are. But what really disappoints a cook is when he or she attempts to go beyond those minimalist foods and still comes up with bland results. This often happens when fat is omitted from a recipe without adequate compensation. Fat has many roles, including providing texture and flavor and interacting with other ingredients. A cook has to understand what he or she has taken away from a recipe before he or she can make another dish as appealing without it.

Often one of the first places that a recipe calls for fat is in sautéing, a cooking technique that is the starting point for many dishes. Sautéing entails cooking foods in a thin layer of oil or butter. A fat-conscious person might think that an obvious step toward healthier eating would be to substitute a liquid, such as water or stock, for the oil. But that doesn't work. The reason that foods are sautéed, and not boiled or steamed, is that foods sautéed in oil brown. Browning creates complex flavors that cannot be obtained in any other way. Think of how sweet, rich and aromatic sautéed onions are compared to boiled onions, and you will understand how browning improves flavor.

Browning is a chemical reaction that needs temperatures near or above 300 degrees F. Water (or wine or stock) cannot brown foods because water boils at around 212 degrees F. Once it is boiling, it can't get any hotter, no matter how high the heat is, and so it cannot cause the browning reaction. Browning also can't happen in a dry pan because the ingredients will shrivel up and burn before getting nicely browned. Moisture and heat are needed, and the only medium that provides moisture and attains the proper temperature is fat. If you take out all the fat, you can't brown your ingredients. If your ingredients don't brown, your food will taste flat.

This doesn't mean that large quantities of fat are needed for sautéing. There are ways to brown foods using a minimum of fat. You can use oil instead of butter or lard to avoid saturated fat. And you don't need much oil to brown an onion. A teaspoon or two to coat the bottom of the pan is usually all that you need, rather than the tablespoon or more often called for in recipes.

A smaller amount of oil is enough to brown foods, but not always enough to cook them through and soften them. A nonstick pan helps by keeping the foods from scorching. Also, vegetables exude liquid as they cook. If you keep the lid on between stirrings, you will trap moisture and steam the food at the same time that it is browning. Ingredients that require further cooking after sautéing can be simmered in any number of nonfat liquids, such as juices, stocks, water, wine and vegetable purees.

Many other cooking techniques rely on fat for myriad purposes. Casseroles use fat for moisture. In this case, an equal amount of liquid substituted for fat will make things mushy. Sometimes using a thick tomato sauce or layering vegetables helps. Remember that watery liquids evaporate out faster than fat, so you'll have to keep a closer eye on the oven and perhaps reduce the temperature and cover the casserole for most of the baking time. When substituting a lower fat dairy product for cream or cheese, keep in mind that its flavor is less rich and often milder. Compensate by heightening flavors elsewhere. Also, fat binds foods together. Egg whites and low-fat cheeses can help keep the casserole together. I've used all these tricks in my recipes. Once you get the feel for it, you'll be able to adapt some of your own recipes too.

Fat also is used to impart flavor. Although but-

ter is a rich-tasting fat, I don't use it in my recipes because of its high saturated fat content. To keep flavor in, use a flavorful oil. For example, use extra-virgin olive oil in Mediterranean dishes and sesame oil for Asian recipes. Most of these oils contain a lot of flavor in just one teaspoon.

Fat also affects the flavors of other ingredients. Without fat, many seasonings seem to disappear. That is because fat binds flavors to the foods. It also melds flavors together. Without fat, sweet foods taste sweeter, vinegars taste sharper, and spices taste more distinct. It is easier to create a harmonious whole when cooking with large quantities of cream or butter. But it is still possible to do so with only a little fat. You just have to take greater care when balancing sweet and sour, salty and pungent, mild and hot flavors.

Fat hides flaws. In low-fat cooking, not only do your proportions need to be carefully balanced, but the basic ingredients also must be the best. A cream-based pasta primavera will taste wonderful even if the vegetables are out of season, but a stir-fry made with tired, wilted vegetables will be inedible. So start with the best ingredients, season carefully and cook attentively.

How to Make the Most of Time Spent in the Kitchen

The kitchen is the hub of the household. It is where we socialize with neighbors, the kids do their science projects and the mail is sorted and read. But it is the activity of putting meals together and the lure of food that make the kitchen the heart of the home. As much as we like spending time in the kitchen, however, we don't have all day to cook. We want to minimize meal preparation time, for if we spend all our time cooking, something else won't get done.

Relying on nutritionally and gustatorily deficient processed foods or forgoing communal dinners (which are often the only chance the family has to be together) is not the solution to this time crunch. Cooking fresh, healthy foods doesn't have to take a lot of time or effort. Many simple yet flavorful recipes require only that you buy some good ingredients and combine them before cooking. But even the most basic recipe isn't easy if you don't have the right tools, or the knowledge or setup to use them.

A large, fancy kitchen is not necessary. A well-lit, comfortable work space encourages and aids home cooking. It should have a work surface at the right height. I am short and use my kitchen table instead of the counter. When I work on a high counter, my shoulder hurts. Tall people get back pains from bending over low sinks. If you are uncomfortable, you will avoid cooking. Short of remodeling your kitchen, try to make the surface height right by using thick or thin cutting boards, wearing clogs or working at a table.

Keep the work surface open. Having to clear an area each time you want to cook is an unnecessary hassle. The work area should be large enough to give you room to work. A cramped area slows all tasks. If your kitchen is small or narrow, get a portable cart so that you'll have extra space when needed. Just having a convenient place to set down a bowl can make the difference between liking and disliking cooking. Set your garbage can (and perhaps the compost bucket) near your workstation before you begin. Carrying trash across the kitchen is messy and takes time.

Frequently used tools should be easy to reach. If utensils or appliances are kept in crowded, out-of-the-way cabinets, you'll avoid using them, or you'll be annoyed after trying to untangle them from the rest of the clutter. Keep your equipment in good condition. Buckled pans and rusted spatulas make tasks more difficult. Dull knives can be dangerous. Pot holders are tools too. Keep them hanging by the stove so that you can grab them in case of an emergency (such as an overflowing pot or burning cookies). Having the right tools where you need them takes much of the stress out of cooking and reduces time spent in the kitchen.

Although cooking does take energy and effort, the tasks required to put a meal on the table will proceed smoothly and take on their own rhythm if you are organized and have a feel for the food and the job at hand. If you haven't cooked much, with each additional hour spent in the kitchen, you will become more competent and your job will become more enjoyable. But even experienced cooks benefit from efficient work habits and a well-thought-out approach to each meal.

Think through your menu. (For some suggestions, see page 17.) Once you settle on which recipes to cook, read them all the way through. Make sure you have all the ingredients in the house. A last-minute shopping trip is an avoidable aggravation. Get out the pots and utensils that you'll need. Make sure they're large enough. Mixing things together in too small a bowl is messy and impossible to do well. Stirring an overflowing pot is a lesson in frustration. Preheat the oven and adjust the oven racks if necessary. Assemble the ingredients at your workstation.

Next, think through the tasks at hand. Do all chores of a similar nature together. This saves a great deal of time because often there is more work in setting up for a task and cleaning up afterward than in doing it, and having to do it once instead of several times is much more efficient. Also, work takes on a smoother rhythm if a job is not interrupted. For example, if you have several vegetables to peel and chop, peel them all and then chop them. Don't peel one and chop, then peel another. If two recipes call for chopped onions, do all the chopping at one time.

If your stove is a distance from your work area, put the prepared ingredients in a bowl to carry them over to the stove. Carrying them by handfuls is time-consuming (although my dog likes it because I invariably drop some).

Most importantly, remember that cooking is a craft that stimulates your senses. Enjoy it. Take a moment to smell a simmering soup. Enjoy the feel of kneading dough. Appreciate the colors of ripe fruit. And taste as you cook. Not only is that one of the perks of being the chef, but you will learn a lot from it. Snack on pieces of vegetables, get familiar with variations and adjust the recipe accordingly. Taste a soup when you first add the seasonings, then try it again in half an hour. Add more salt and see what happens. Try a piece of broccoli when it is partially steamed and when it is done. Attentiveness to the ingredients and an enjoyment of the process make a good cook.

Following is a list of the most useful kitchen equipment. Don't be daunted by its length. You probably own most of these things. The hand-held items are small and can fit into two drawers or stand upright in a couple of canisters. If you have not cooked much or have a disorganized kitchen, you might want to pull out all the items listed. If they are hard to get at, think about rearranging shelves so that the most used tools are close at hand. If the equipment is in poor condition, think about replacing it. Most of the tools are inexpensive. Some of my favorite muffin tins, casseroles and cast-iron pots were flea market bargains. However, it does pay to purchase high-quality knives and excellent pots.

Appliances

Stove top: Know your burners. Know how long each takes to bring a pot of water to a boil. Know if any of them heat unevenly. Match the pot's bottom to the size of the heating element. Like most professional chefs, I prefer gas. But this entire book was written using electric stoves. One was old and defective, and it made me cross to work with it. I burned many pots of rice because it took forever to bring a pot of water to a boil, and once at that high heat, it took forever to reduce it down to a simmer. The newer stove works fine. Only when sautéing, when I want fine-tuned temperature control, do I miss the gas stoves that I've used in restaurants.

Oven and broiler: Note where the hot and cold spots are so that you know where to place your baked goods and when to rotate them. Convection ovens blow the hot air around with a fan, and thus the temperature stays more even throughout and recipes take less time to cook. But the blowing can dry out some foods.

Microwave: I use this appliance mostly for heating up leftovers. It is also useful to cook sauced chicken parts. It is possible to use the microwave for more complicated recipes, but most of them require several steps. I find it awkward and dangerous taking hot casseroles in and out of the microwave. Besides, I miss being able to smell and watch my dinner cook. There is no standardization in wattage and power among manufacturers, so it is difficult to give microwave directions. With that said, you can adapt many of my recipes for microwave use. When doing so, taste and adjust the seasonings.

Grill and griddle: Some stoves have these, or you can buy separate appliances. They do not have to be elaborate, but they should be large enough to be useful and efficient.

Electric mixer: The hand-held ones are inexpensive, conveniently portable and easy to clean, but they tend to burn out after a while and are not powerful enough for some jobs. Still it is worthwhile having one around. The old, heavy-duty mixers are terrific workhorses, and if you can find one at a tag sale or can afford a new one, buy it, although it is not necessary for the recipes in this book.

Food processor: It grates faster and cleaner than any other tool. It is worth having just for this function. It also finely minces large quantities of herbs, blends doughs and chops nuts. It gives you more control than a blender for chopping and mixing. Although I prefer to use my chef's knife for slicing, a food processor can do this task as well, and it's fast. Processors can be a pain to wash, as foods stick to the plastic bowl. Try to rinse it out right after you use it; when you go back later to clean it, it won't be such a chore. If you don't own a processor, you'll be able to make most of the recipes in this book.

Blender: Blenders puree better than food processors. A good feature is that you can carry around the filled, detached bowl, which is difficult to do with a processor. Blenders also are inexpensive. Keep one on your counter, and you'll find ways to use it.

Pots and Pans

Pots are made from a wide variety of materials. The choice can be confusing. However, the most important trait for all quality cookware is how well the material absorbs and then radiates heat. This allows for steady, even cooking. Regardless of the material, if the bottom of the pot is so thin that it buckles or has heat spots, the pot will be difficult to work with.

Glass is the poorest conductor, as it does not absorb heat. Instead, the heat passes right through the glass and into the food. Ovens and burners generally have hot and cold spots, and glass will exacerbate that problem. Foods will cook faster and dry out more quickly in glass casseroles because no time is taken up by the pan absorbing the heat. To compensate for this, reduce your oven temperature by about 20 degrees F when using glass. Better yet, use a different type of casserole. Pottery is a good choice because it absorbs and conducts heat well. Since white reflects heat, I cook chicken in a white ceramic casserole, which seems to keep the meat moister.

Copper might be pretty and an excellent conductor of heat, but it is difficult to care for. Because copper interacts with food, it needs to be lined with another metal, usually tin. Cast-iron cooks food evenly, and if seasoned and cared for, it can be almost nonstick. Also excellent are cast-iron pots lined with enamel. However, iron is heavy, so it is not appropriate for everyone. Stainless steel is light, doesn't interact with food and is easy to clean, but it does not conduct heat well and is appropriate only for the interior of pots. All-aluminum pots aren't good be-

cause although aluminum is a superb heat conductor, it pits, discolors and interacts with many foods. Some of the best pots combine aluminum bottoms with stainless-steel interiors. New alloys are being introduced that conduct heat well and don't interact with food. Some are excellent.

Nonstick cookware not only reduces the amount of fat needed but also speeds cleanup. Older nonstick surfaces scratch and peel. The newer surfaces are melded into the pan and remain nonstick even if scratched. Nonstick pans still must have thick, conductive bottoms.

You need only five pots and a few casseroles to make all the recipes in this book:

6- and 10-inch nonstick sauté pans with lids: These are for all your sautés and quick sauces and for plenty of other jobs. People cooking for large families might want a deep 12-inch sauté pan.

1½- to 2-quart saucepan with lid: This is for small simmering jobs, cooking rice or steaming a few vegetables.

4- to 5-quart saucepan with lid: This is for everything from soups and stews to boiling pasta. It is best to have two of these.

Stock pot: This big pot is for simmering stock or any other large job. It's necessary only if you cook for a crowd or plan to make stock.

Casseroles: Have about four in different sizes.

Roasting pan: A must for poultry. An inexpensive enamel one works fine. Have a poultry rack that fits inside it.

Cookie sheets, jelly roll pans (jelly roll pans have small sides), muffin tins: I get along with a couple of each, most of which I picked up at flea markets (the old muffin tins have pretty designs).

Tools and Utensils

Cooling racks: Use these for cooling off cookies or as trivets when taking hot things out of the oven. They allow air to circulate underneath the hot pans or baked goods.

Rolling pin: Find a wooden one that is weighty but not too heavy. It is necessary only if you plan on baking or making something with pastry, such as knishes.

Whisk: Get one that is stainless steel and of medium size. In many cases, a whisk does the job as well as an electric mixer.

Four-sided grater: This is useful for small grating tasks.

Cutting boards: There are three essential boards. The most important is a large one (at least 12 by 20 inches), on which most foods are cut. A cutting board that is too small will slow you down more than anything else I can think of. It cramps your cutting rhythm, as you have to make small, constrained strokes. Chopped vegetables roll off, and large ingredients don't fit and are awkward to work with. Use one side of the cutting board for onions, garlic and foods that you don't mind tasting like onions and garlic. Use the other side for fruits. My board is made of wood (which I like much more than plastic) and is designed for carving roasts. One side has a gully that captures meat, fruit and vegetable juices.

A small board does have a place in the kitchen. It is useful for quick tasks like cutting cheese or bread.

Another board is needed for meat and fish. It is very important not to cut foods that will be eaten raw on the same surface that meats are cut on.

Stainless-steel and glass work bowls: Have several in all sizes from large to small.

Salad spinner: This is used for cleaning and drying fresh herbs and keeping washed lettuce crisp. Al-though you can get along without one, it is an inexpensive piece of equipment well worth the cost and the shelf space to store it.

Vegetable steamer insert: This stainless-steel item sits in any size pot and keeps foods out of the water. It costs only a couple of dollars.

Measuring cups and spoons: Dry and liquid measurers are entirely different. The dry ones can be leveled off. Have a set of them, as well as a glass measuring cup for liquids. Have a set of measuring spoons.

Vegetable peeler: Find one that you like to use. Replace it when it gets dull.

Small rectangular grater: Also called a cheese grater, this is the ideal kitchen tool. It fits in your hand, has no moving parts and is useful for several tasks. Use it to grate Parmesan cheese, citrus peel and fresh ginger.

Zester: You can get by with the small rectangular grater, but a zester peels long, thin strips off of an orange or lemon. A delightful gadget for under $10 (see additional note on page 127).

Can opener: I still prefer the rubber-handled, mechanical model. It stores out of the way when not in use and works fine. For those with arthritis or other hand-mobility problems, an electric can opener is a godsend.

Rubber grip: This circular piece of rubber can give you the traction you need to open a recalcitrant jar.

Bag clip: These are sold as potato chip bag clips, but I use them for everything from brown sugar to raisin bags.

Wooden spoons and spatulas: Have a container of these on your countertop right next to the stove.

Metal spoons, slotted spoons, metal spatulas, ladles: Have another container filled with these.

Plastic cake decorating spatulas and rubber spatulas: Put these in with the wooden spoons. Having one the right size and shape to scrape a bowl makes any task easier.

Salad bar tongs: These spring-loaded tongs are useful for everything from moving a hot casserole around in the oven, to turning baking chicken legs, to serving pasta. Stainless-steel salad bar tongs are far superior to any other type.

Colander: Use this for washing vegetables, draining pasta and myriad other uses. Have one that fits in your sink and is easy to clean. I prefer plastic because it doesn't get too hot to handle when boiling water is poured through it.

Fine wire mesh strainer: I use a medium-size strainer to sift flour, drain tiny pasta and rinse rice. A small sifter that fits over a cup is good for straining freshly squeezed lemon juice.

Kitchen towels: Towels are needed to mop up spills, keep a work surface clean, double as an oven mitt and squeeze liquids out of foods. A professional chef is never without one tucked into his or her apron.

Knives: Do not compromise on your knives; they are your most important tools. Knives must be sharp and of high quality. They should sit comfortably in your hand and be so well balanced that they feel almost weightless. Only three knives are essential:

6- or 8- inch chef's knife: Its blade is long and high enough to allow you to cut and slice vegetables very quickly and with little effort. This knife is not flexible, which makes it perfect for cutting hard vegetables. Such a large knife might intimidate some people who are not used to working with one, but it is actually safer to use a large knife when cutting through large, dense vegetable because one downward push takes care of the job.

Paring knife: The small blade can be used to pare fruits and vegetables, do delicate trimmings, cut eyes out of potatoes or mark a design on a pie crust.

8- to 10-inch serrated knife: It cuts bread and tomatoes better than a straight edge.

Knife sharpener: Much to my chagrin, I have not been able to master the art of sharpening a knife on a stone. Instead, I use a preset ceramic stick, which sharpens the blade, and a diamond steel, which puts the edge back on. Use the steel each time you set to work; use the sharpening stone or stick whenever the knife feels dull. Besides keeping knives sharp, take other precautions to keep them in their best shape. Store them in a special knife rack in a drawer or on the countertop. Never place them loose in a drawer. Not only will they dull and perhaps chip, but it is extremely dangerous to have their edges exposed. On that note, never put them in the sink, especially if it is filled with water and dishes. Instead, always place them carefully, in full view, to the side of the sink and wash them individually with care.

Guide to Ingredients

The ingredients used in *Wholehearted Cooking* have a chance to show off their textures and flavors because they aren't hidden or changed by complicated cooking techniques or a lot of fat. Because each ingredient shines through and contributes to the whole, it is important to select the highest-quality ingredients at the market. Most people are aware that a vegetable bought one week can be very different from one bought the next week, but fewer people realize that the staples in their pantry, such as milk and oil, also can vary widely and that differences in quality profoundly affect the outcome of a recipe.

You can find most of the ingredients discussed here in a supermarket, but I encourage you to venture away from the chain supermarkets and go to a farmers' market, a local fishmonger or a bakery.

These places carry versions of the same foods found in supermarkets, but you are likely to get better service and a fresher, tastier product. At the same time, you'll be supporting small businesses and local agriculture.

Oils

Most brands of oil in the supermarket have been filtered and deodorized. This removes flavor and some nutrients in exchange for a very long shelf life. I prefer to buy oil at a natural food store. Often called "cold pressed" or "minimally processed," these oils retain some fat-soluble vitamins as well as flavors distinctive of their ingredients. Corn oil still tastes like corn and peanut oil like peanuts. Keep these oils in a cool, dark place, such as the refrigerator, so that they don't get rancid.

I use a variety of oils. I don't worry about the monounsaturated fat content differences between oils because I use so little. I figure that the health benefits of one type over another are minimal when you're using only 1 tablespoon in a recipe that serves six. That small amount of oil can, however, affect a recipe's flavor, so I carefully choose the oil for how well it works with the other ingredients. The taste difference between sesame oil and canola oil is tremendous.

When my recipes call for "vegetable oil," it is all right to use any mild-flavored oil, such as canola or a vegetable oil blend. But when I request that you use a specific oil, such as peanut, that oil's flavor is important to the overall flavor of the dish.

Olive oil: Until recently, olive oil tasted like olives. But now that olive oil has been mainstreamed into the American diet and is being used in recipes where olive flavor isn't welcome, much of the olive essence has been removed. Most of the olive oil sold in supermarkets has been deodorized and filtered to make it taste as neutral as corn or canola oil. It is still possible to buy flavorful olive oils, but some knowledge is necessary to make the right choice.

Olives absorb other flavors and are especially sensitive to handling. Good olive oil starts with fruits that have been picked at optimum ripeness and carefully handled. Immaturity and bruises mar the oil's flavor. Quality olive oil starts with only the best unblemished olives. (Less than perfect olives go into the lower grades of olive oil.) It is labeled "cold-pressed" or "first-pressed" because a paste made of washed olives is squeezed between stones that extract the oil. The stones stay comparatively cool. This is in contrast to oil extracted by metal rollers in large commercial presses that operate at high speeds. These get hot as the oil is removed, and heat is detrimental to flavor.

Olive oil that has the ideal golden color, olive aroma and flavor, and less than 1 percent free oleic acid (a fatty acid that ruins the flavor) is labeled "extra virgin." It is possible that it was cold-pressed, but there is no guarantee unless it is stated on the label. Oils with too much oleic acid and those made from poorer-quality olives are further refined. In some cases, the olives are pressed again to extract more oil, and solvents are used to remove the oleic acid and other impurities. Oil at this stage of manufacture is bland. Some producers add back a touch of extra-virgin oil for its olive flavor. This oil is called "pure." Bottles labeled simply as olive oil also are "pure." Olive oil marked "virgin" is in between extra virgin and pure.

Extra-virgin olive oil is costly, which is understandable because it takes more time and labor to produce. Some of these oils are prohibitively expensive and are not worth the price. Olive oil varies from year to year, like wine. The major commercial brands tend to have a consistent product but lack character and robustness. In contrast, some of the smaller purveyors sell products that are overly fruity and useful in only a handful of recipes. The rule that the darker green the color, the stronger the flavor holds true most, but not all, of the time. The manager of a gourmet store should be able to tell you about the oils he or she has for sale. For most uses, from sautés to salad dressings, a lighter-colored, lightly flavored extra-virgin olive oil is appropriate. These are found in supermarkets. Fruity oils are most suitable for salads and as seasoning. They are costly, but you will not need much.

All olive oils can be stored for up to a year in an airtight container in a dark cupboard. If refrigerated, the oil will cloud and thicken (as will dressing made from it), but it will liquefy again at room temperature.

Sesame oil: The nomenclature on this ingredient is inconsistent and confusing. The sesame oil I use, and the one that packs the most flavor, is made by toasting the sesame seeds and then extracting the oil. Sometimes it is called Asian sesame oil, dark sesame oil or toasted sesame oil. Sometimes it is just called sesame oil. No matter, it is easily distinguished from the less flavorful untoasted oil. Oil that hasn't been toasted is lightly golden in color. Although much milder than toasted sesame oil, is is still more intense than vegetable oils, with a faint sesame aroma and a mild sesame flavor. In contrast, toasted sesame oil is a dark caramel color, smells strongly of sesame and contributes a strong roasted sesame flavor to recipes. A little goes a long way. Think of it and use it as a seasoning.

Dairy Products

The dairy aisle in your supermarket probably takes up the length of the store. It contains the basic milks, specialty dairy drinks, familiar and gourmet cheeses, spreads, butters, yogurts and sour creams. Except for imitation dairy products—margarines, fake creamers and soy cheeses—all of these products have one thing in common: They began with milk that came from the mammary gland of a lactating mammal. In this country, we rely mostly on Holstein cows, but we also use rich milk from Jersey and Guernsey cows, sheep and goats.

Milk, being an animal product, starts out containing saturated fat and cholesterol, which are easily removed, resulting in healthful, low-fat dairy products with ample supplies of protein, vitamins and minerals, especially calcium. I use these foods

throughout the book, especially low-fat milk, part-skim mozzarella, low-fat ricotta and low-fat yogurt.

I also cook with some high-fat dairy products. When used in the moderate amounts I suggest, they contribute invaluably to the recipe and do not raise the fat content beyond a prudent level. When I occasionally indulge in high-fat dairy products, I eat them in a way that gives me their full impact. I savor a wedge of ripe Brie on a slice of pear, a pat of butter on toast or a dollop of fresh whipped cream on pie. I don't use high-fat dairy products to bind casseroles together, add liquids (as in soups) or provide the base flavor of a dish. Such roles can be accomplished just as well with more healthful low-fat ingredients.

I never use imitation foods. They tend to substitute artificial flavors, colors and binders for a few very simple natural ingredients. I'd rather eat the real thing in moderation than a lot of a fake product. All too often, the imitation isn't that much healthier. Margarine is a perfect example. It has been marketed as being better than butter. It doesn't contain cholesterol, but dietary cholesterol isn't such an important thing to avoid anyway. Margarine still contains plenty of fat—as much as butter (unless air or water is whipped in)—and it contains saturated fat. (Don't be fooled. Once polyunsaturated vegetable oil is hydrogenated, it is saturated.) Imitation foods rarely work as well as the ingredients they're trying to copy. For example, fake cheeses have less flavor and don't melt well, and nondairy creamers have a chemical aftertaste. Also, some studies suggest that foods like margarine or coconut oil-based milk substitutes have a negative impact on health. I keep them out of my recipes.

Low-fat milk: Across the country, a few small dairies sell fresh milk from one well-cared-for herd. That milk tastes better than you can imagine. If you can find some, try it, if only to experience what really good milk tastes like.

Buy 1 percent or skim milk. The percentage refers not to the proportion of fat to calories (which is what nutritionists are concerned about), but to the percentage of fat per weight. Actually, the percentage correlates fairly closely and accurately with the grams of fat per ½ cup. Whole milk (4 percent) has about 4 grams of fat per ½ cup (or 50 percent of its calories come from fat). Two percent milk has 2 grams of fat per ½ cup (about 35 percent of its calories come from fat). Low-fat milk (1 percent) has 1 gram of fat per ½ cup. Skim milk contains less than 1 gram of fat per ½ cup.

Most people can switch easily from whole to 1 percent milk in about a week. It is harder to switch to skim milk and isn't worth it if the milk doesn't taste right to you. In cooking, that little bit of fat in low-fat milk can make a difference. When a recipe specifies low-fat milk, don't use skim.

Buttermilk: Buttermilk was so named not because it had butter in it, but because it was the liquid that remained after cream was churned into butter. Unlike low-fat milk, buttermilk is not thin. Instead, like yogurt, it is a cultured, thickened, soured product.

In the past, airborne bacteria were used to produce buttermilk, but today's manufacturers rely on sophisticated, sanitary and consistent techniques. Buttermilk is no longer a by-product of butter making, but begins when a carefully chosen culture is added to skim or low-fat milk and then continues to ferment in a controlled environment.

Buttermilk does more for baked goods than just impart a tangy, rich taste. It adds body, too. Substituting skim milk for cream is little better than using water. But buttermilk provides a thick, low-fat, full-flavored liquid for baking. Buttermilk also helps to leaven and soften baked goods. Buttermilk lasts several weeks in the refrigerator. Many recipes in this book use it, so a quart shouldn't go to waste.

Yogurt: When manufacturers remove the fat from yogurt, they use a number of methods to retain the flavor and a thick, smooth consistency. Some add artificial flavors. Avoid those. Some add gelatin. Avoid those. Some start with quality milk, use live cultures and perhaps add natural gums to get the desired consistency. That is the product you want.

Parmesan cheese: I rely on Parmigiano-Reggiano, a hard Italian grating cheese with a sharp flavor. Parmesan Reggiano is imported, expensive and worth it. So far, no domestic cheese maker has produced a Parmesan with as much character and depth of flavor as this cheese aged in caves in Italy. If you use the milder, less costly brands, you'll end up using a lot more cheese to make up for the lack of flavor.

Buy a piece of Parmigiano-Reggiano in a size that you can use within about a month. Try getting a chunk from the center of the wheel that doesn't have any of the hard exterior rind attached. Keep the cheese tightly wrapped in plastic in your refrigerator. Grate only as much as you need for a recipe, or if you're serving it as a garnish, grate it right over the individual dish.

Romano cheese is similar to Parmesan, but it is stronger because it is made from sheep's milk. This can be used in addition to or instead of Parmesan.

Mozzarella: Mozzarella is a mild melting cheese. Whole-milk mozzarella has about 15 grams of fat per serving. When made with part skim milk, the fat content is reduced to 10 grams, which is still high but is fine when baked into a low-fat recipe. Some companies are now making a "lite" version and bringing the fat down to about 3 grams. Some of these brands are palatable and meltable; others are not. The cheese will melt better if grated instead of sliced. The nutritional analyses of my recipes were calculated with part-skim, so if you can't find a good "lite" cheese, the recipe is still within healthy parameters.

Ricotta: Ricotta, a soft-curd cheese similar in looks to cottage cheese, is available in whole-milk, part-skim and low-fat versions. Part-skim ricotta still contains quite a bit of fat, but it has up to 40 percent less fat than the whole-milk version. Truly low-fat ricotta is sometimes too dry or bland to work well in a recipe. Only one company out of three in my area does a good job with its low-fat ricotta. When I can find it, I buy it.

Substituting cottage cheese is not a good idea. Cottage cheese exudes moisture, has a different flavor and doesn't bind ingredients together.

Vinegars

The success of many a recipe hinges on the cook's ability to balance sweet and sour flavors. Vinegar often is used as one half of that equation. Vinegar is made by taking an alcoholic liquid, such as wine or hard cider (although any sugar-containing fermentable liquid will do), and adding bacteria that break down the alcohol and convert it into acetic acid. The vinegar retains the flavors from the original liquid. Throughout the world, there are regional vinegars: rice vinegar from Japan, red wine vinegar from France, cider vinegar from the United States. Each type of vinegar lends its own unique flavor to a recipe.

The best vinegars start with liquids that are good enough to drink (which is why white distilled vinegar is suitable for cleaning projects but not for eating). Commercial vinegars are made in a matter of days, or sometimes even hours, using high temperatures and aerators. The resulting vinegar is clarified and then pasteurized. Although this method quickly and inexpensively produces a consistent and shelf-stable product, it does not produce one with depth of flavor.

Other vinegars are made over the course of weeks, which allows nuances of flavors to come through in the final product. Sometimes the "mother" (the bacterial starter) is left in. It will grow slowly and eventually form a jellyfish-like blob in the bottle. It is ugly but not harmful. If it bothers you, pour it off. (Some cooks save it and use it to make their own vinegars.)

Unopened bottles of vinegar can last for years. Once opened, use the vinegar within months. Some-times vinegar is infused with herbs, hot peppers or other seasonings. These make lovely salad dressings, but if some of the vinegar is used and the herbs are exposed to the air, they can turn moldy, so remove them once they appear above the level of the vinegar in the bottle.

Until recently, balsamic vinegar was not for sale. This Italian vinegar was passed from generation to generation as part of dowries and inheritances. Balsamic vinegar starts with a thick must of grape juice. It is stored in wooden casks in attics and moved from barrel to barrel over the years. As it progresses, it gets thicker and sweeter. After a number of years (at least 12, but sometimes as many as 50), it is ready to be decanted. Traditional balsamic vinegar is so mellow and syrupy that you can drink and savor it as you would a fine brandy. A drop or two heightens the flavors of any dish. Very little of this vinegar gets to market, and a small bottle costs well over a hundred dollars.

Other versions of balsamic vinegar are more affordable. Some are very good; others are sharp and no different from wine vinegar with caramel added. Although traditional balsamic vinegar is never used for cooking, commercial balsamic vinegar can be used in salad dressings, poultry glazes and pasta dishes. A quality commercial balsamic vinegar tastes woodsy, herbal and a bit sweet. Brands change from year to year, so you'll have to try them yourself and see which you prefer.

Herbs

In general, herbs are the leafy green parts of plants. In recent years, it has become easier to find fresh herbs in the supermarket. Many home gardeners cultivate their own, and even those without a yard find them easy to grow in windowsill pots. Fresh herbs have more aroma and a lighter, greener taste than dried herbs. But high-quality dried herbs that are less than 9 months old are fine for cooking. Dried herbs are convenient and available at most supermarkets, so unless otherwise specified, the recipes in this book call for dried herbs. But if you have fresh herbs, use them. A general rule of thumb is that 1 teaspoon dried equals 1 tablespoon fresh (this is because dried is more concentrated than fresh).

When buying dried herbs, look for a bright green color and fresh aroma. A dull olive color and musty smell indicate an old, flavorless herb.

Spices

I like gutsy, interesting recipes. I look to other cultures to find creative spice and seasoning combinations. I do not replicate authentic recipes; instead I use ideas from other traditions to enliven familiar foods. A few of the spices in these recipes might be new to you. Urban supermarkets might carry some of them, but you will have to purchase others at a natural food store or gourmet shop.

Spices come from the seeds or other parts (such as the bark) of a plant. Whole spices last a long time. Black peppercorns stay fresh for 100 years. Once ground, however, spices lose their potency. Some, like pepper, deteriorate rapidly after grinding. Others remain strong and distinctive for several months. For this reason, many people grind their own spices right before use. Certainly, pepper is best right from a pepper mill. Cardamom and nutmeg are two other spices that are best if freshly ground.

Powdered spices are convenient and will work fine if purchased when fresh and aromatic. Unfortunately, many of the spices in the supermarket are already old when you purchase them. Some gourmet, ethnic and natural food stores sell very high-quality ground spices. Most ground spices last up to nine months. If the store sells fresh spices, you'll have plenty of time to use yours up. Fresh spices are bright in color and have a sharp, clear aroma. Some stores sell spices by the ounce; others sell them already bagged. Once you have them home, put them in glass jars to prevent one spice's aroma from penetrating another. Remember to label the bottles. Do not keep them on the counter next to the stove, as light, heat and moisture are detrimental. Store them in an easy-to-access cupboard.

Salt

Salt plays a very important role in flavoring foods. This became clear when people on sodium-restricted diets complained about how bland their meals were. Luckily, very few of us have to eliminate salt from our diets or even live on a severely restricted ration. (Only 5 to 10 percent of the population is sodium sensitive.) Eating well without exceeding a reasonable amount of salt (the American Heart Association suggests 3,000 mg, or 1 to 2 teaspoons, a day), is not hard to do, especially if you avoid processed foods.

Salt's importance goes beyond the salty flavor it imparts. It also affects how we taste other flavors. It makes sweet flavors sweeter and balances pungent flavors like vinegar. It disguises bitter foods and compensates for bland flavors, as in bean soups. Cold foods need extra seasoning and are especially bland without salt. (For this reason, always taste and adjust the seasonings after foods have chilled.) Salt accomplishes its many tasks in an easy and economical manner. A teaspoon or less of salt can improve most recipes.

Regular table salt has additives to keep it loose and pourable. Some has iodine added. I find regular salt to be bitter and have a chemical aftertaste. Instead, I use kosher salt, which has a pure, almost mellow salt flavor. I have conducted taste tests in my cooking classes, and my students are always amazed that salt can vary so much in flavor. Kosher salt crystals are much larger and more jagged than table salt crystals, so they adhere to foods better. They will stick together if it is humid, but you can loosen them with a spoon. If you want smaller crystals, you can grind the salt in a mill. Kosher salt comes in a large box. I transfer a small amount to a glass jar with a tight cover for regular use.

Garlic

I don't know anyone who enjoys peeling garlic cloves. This task is especially tedious when the paper-like skins stick to your fingers or cling to the cloves. Nonetheless, the job is essential. Dried, granulated garlic won't do, nor will jarred, oil-packed minced garlic, which tastes bitter and sour. Restaurants know how to resolve this quandary. They assign someone (it is usually the person lowest in the pecking order) to peel a dozen or so bulbs. The cloves are then put in a jar and refrigerated for future use. Or the restaurant buys peeled cloves, in quart-size or larger containers, from produce purveyors. These peeled cloves are not in special packages, and have no preservatives, yet the cloves remain fresh for weeks.

Like a restaurant, you too can have peeled cloves at the ready in your refrigerator. When a recipe calls for garlic, peel the entire bulb. In the long run, doing this chore all at once will save a lot of time, as you will have to set up and clean up after this task only once. The next time you need garlic, all you'll have to do is open a jar.

Garlic is easier to peel if you're starting with a bulb that is heavy for its size and has dry, papery skin and solid, fat cloves. Begin by rubbing off and discarding the papery skin. Then break apart the bulb so that all the cloves separate. One prep person with whom I worked had huge hands and accomplished this task by making a fist and pounding down on the garlic. The bulbs flew apart. I was always jealous of this ability.

The next step is to cut off the end of each clove where it was attached to the bulb. Then, with the flat side of a chef's knife, give each clove a gentle whack. This splits the skin and loosens it from the clove, easing its removal. Some skins can be squeezed off, some rubbed off and some pried off. It's too frustrating to try to peel tiny cloves; save them for stock. Your hands will smell like garlic. If that bothers you, rub them with lemon juice and then wash well.

Store the cloves in a glass jar. Don't use plastic, as it absorbs and leaks aromas. Peeled garlic cloves stored in the refrigerator will remain fresh for at least a month. I've had garlic for two months and couldn't detect any deterioration.

When you are about to cook with the garlic,

take as many cloves as you need out of the jar and mince them in a food processor or with a chef's knife. I don't use a garlic press because I find it wasteful. Not enough of the garlic squeezes through those little holes, and too much ends up as a skin to be discarded.

Fresh Ginger

Fresh gingerroot adds a sharp, clear, somewhat sweet pungency to recipes. It is spicy without being hot and warms you up without burning your mouth. It blends well in complex curries but also can be the most important seasoning in a simple noodle dish.

Just as garlic powder bears little resemblance to fresh garlic, so does ground ginger have little in common with fresh gingerroot. The basic flavor is there, but not the full range of expression. There is no reason to cut corners and use ground ginger, as fresh ginger is as easy to use as fresh garlic.

Start by purchasing a shiny beige piece of gingerroot. It should be free of wrinkles, dark spots and soft areas. Ginger grows in segments; break off as much as you need at the store. You don't have to buy the entire piece, which can sometimes be very large. The inside of the root should be a warm yellow color and smell fragrant.

Ginger deteriorates in the refrigerator from the moisture and cold. It also will turn moldy if wrapped in plastic. It stores best, like onions, in a cool, dark, dry place. A basket in an out-of-the-way corner of your kitchen is a good storage spot.

Don't worry about the exposed surface where you break it off from the rest of the root or where you cut off a slice for cooking. It quickly dries and seals off the inside, which will remain fresh and moist for 2 to 3 weeks, depending on how fresh it was when purchased.

Most recipes call for minced ginger. This is easily accomplished even though the root is hard and fibrous. First, cut off however much you need from the main root. Then peel off the skin. Use a small cheese grater (a hand-held tool with small holes) to grate the ginger. Quality ginger will exude juice. Catch it by working over a bowl. Older and tougher ginger will leave fibers on top of the grater as the softer ginger falls into the bowl. Discard the fibers. Don't try pushing ginger through a garlic press. I've had firsthand experience that it will break the press.

Although storing ginger in sherry is often suggested, I think that it becomes milder and tastes too alcoholic. I also don't like the flavor of frozen ginger. Stick with the fresh root. Stored properly and with the use of a grater, having fresh ginger for your recipes is no hassle at all.

Carbohydrates

See the *Grains, Pastas, Beans & Potatoes* chapter for information about these foods. Each carbohydrate is discussed prior to the recipes featuring it.

Sugars

Details about the sugars used in *Wholehearted Cooking* appear in the *Desserts & Beverages* chapter.

Following the Recipes

Recipes are like chemistry formulas in that individual ingredients are combined to create a new entity. To get the final result, chemists and cooks use scales and measuring cups, heat and cold, and machines to whip, grind and emulsify. Chemists, like cooks, rely on smells and visual clues to determine how the process is going. But whereas chemists usually experiment with pure ingredients in very controlled environments, the home cook relies on foods that change with the season, age, humidity and brand. Home ovens have cold spots, and pots have hot spots. And the end result for a cook is not a provable, objective equation, but something whose success is judged using emotional and cultural criteria. A recipe that one person loves another finds unpalatable. A recipe that was welcome in the winter is too heavy for the summer. A recipe that tasted great with local strawberries tastes bland with imported fruits.

Because of this, following a recipe at home requires flexibility that would be inappropriate in a chemistry lab. Feel free to substitute an in-season food for a less flavorful ingredient. Be prepared to add more salt, to reduce liquids and to taste and adjust flavoring according to your own senses. Work with the recipe until it feels, looks and tastes right.

Having said all that, I have put great effort into making the recipes as consistently reproducible as possible. I have tested them with various ingredients, in different pots, at different times of the year. I've included information and advice so that you can solve problems if they arise. I have tried to make the recipes as clear, simple and straightforward as possible. To this end, I have written the recipes in specific and precise ways. Ingredients are listed in the order in which they are used. The cooking method is divided into numbered steps, which makes a recipe easier to follow. In some recipes you will see the ▦ symbol. This refers you to other recipes or helpful information elsewhere in the book.

To avoid recipe clutter, I have assumed certain things about the ingredients. All vegetables should be washed well and have inedible ends and bruises trimmed off. All herbs should be dried unless fresh is specified. Garlic is fresh and peeled unless otherwise noted. Eggs are large.

Cooking times are for the average home electric or gas range. Start timing when the pot comes to the temperature requested in the recipe. For example, if a soup is supposed to simmer for 30 minutes, start counting once bubbles appear, not before. Some stoves take so long to raise the temperature of a liquid that unless you take that into account, you might undercook the recipe or serve a meal much later than planned. Restaurant stoves are much more powerful, and if you are fortunate enough to have one, remember that foods heat faster on them, sautés lose liquid more quickly and commercial broilers can get up to twice the temperature of a home stove.

Menus

The first three menus are for people who haven't cooked much or who have very little time to spend in the kitchen. The cooking skills and equipment needed are minimal, and the ingredients are all readily available in any supermarket.

Dill Poached Fish (page 82)

Orange Rice (page 127)

Steamed Broccoli with
Honey-Poppy Seed Vinaigrette (page 59)

Honeyed Pineapple (page 214)

Pecan Baked Chicken (page 68)

Sweet Potato Spears (page 157)

Sage Tomatoes (page 167)

Tossed Salad (page 57)
with Creamy Herb Dressing (page 59)

Strawberry Sauce (page 210)
over low-fat frozen yogurt

African Peanut Sauce (page 116) over pasta

Tossed Salad (page 57)
with dressing of choice

Grand Oranges (page 208)
or Fruit Salad (page 209)

Celebratory Meals:

For people who enjoy cooking and have the time, and for occasions when there are helping hands in the kitchen, here are a few menus to enjoy.

A Summer Meal

Tropical Gazpacho (page 20)

Golden Fish (page 85)

Asparagus in a Gingerly Citrus
Dressing (page 163)

Tiny Pasta with Almonds (page 147)

Honey of a Lemonade (page 223)

Blueberry-Peach Cobbler (page 216)

For a Winter Evening

Barley Vegetable Soup (page 27)

Oven-Baked Ratatouille (page 90)

Herb Roasted Chicken (page 74)

Double-Corn Polenta (page 135)

Glazed Baked Pears (page 212)

A Thanksgiving Feast

Gingerly Pumpkin Soup (page 25)

Lemon Roasted Chicken (page 74)

Mashed Potatoes
with Roasted Garlic (page 154)

Beet & Orange Salad (page 37)

Oven-Roasted Brussels Sprouts
& Carrots (page 172)

Hot Mulled Cider (page 223)

Dried Fruit & Ginger Compote
with low-fat frozen yogurt (page 210)

Gingersnaps (page 221)

recipes

Soups

althought there's a different soup for every occasion, all soups have some things in common. Cooking takes place in one pot, easing preparation and cleanup. Timing isn't crucial; soups sit and simmer and are fine without receiving a lot of attention. Soups are easy to expand if more people than expected come to dinner. Soups appreciate creative impulses; add a new ingredient or adjust them to the season, and they get better. They are forgiving and can be fixed when you make a mistake. Many soups are better as leftovers. The soups in this collection are a diverse lot, but they all live up to the ideal soup's characteristics of being nourishing, straightforward to make and a pleasure to smell as they simmer.

Tropical Gazpacho

This soup is festive, sweet, pungent and cooling.

SERVES 8 TO 10

1 quart	tomato juice		¼ cup	lime juice
1 20-ounce can	crushed pineapple packed in its own juice		¼ cup	lemon juice
½	cantaloupe, peeled, seeded and cut into large chunks		2 teaspoons	kosher salt
			¼ teaspoon	freshly ground pepper
1	cucumber, peeled and seeded		⅛ teaspoon	Tabasco or other hot pepper sauce
1	green bell pepper, trimmed		1 tablespoon	minced fresh parsley or cilantro
1	papaya, peeled and seeded		½ tablespoon	minced fresh mint

1. Puree the tomato juice, pineapple (including the juice from the can) and cantaloupe.
2. Dice the cucumber, green pepper and papaya.
3. Put the puree and diced vegetables and papaya in a large bowl. Stir in the lime and lemon juices, salt, pepper, Tabasco and herbs.
4. Let the soup rest for 1 hour, preferably in the refrigerator, before serving. You can serve this soup the next day, but the flavor will not hold more than 2 days.

101 CALORIES PER SERVING: 2 G PROTEIN, 0 G FAT, 26 G CARBOHYDRATE; 920 MG SODIUM, 0 MG CHOLESTEROL

Watermelon Soup

I came up with this recipe after I'd bought a big watermelon on sale and then realized that no one but me would be home all week to eat it.

SERVES 4 TO 6

6 cups	seeded, cut watermelon (about 4-6 pounds)		1 tablespoon	Grand Marnier or other orange-flavored liqueur
1	orange		¼ teaspoon	ground ginger
¼ cup	chopped fresh mint		¼ teaspoon	ground allspice
3 tablespoons	lime juice		⅛ teaspoon	ground cinnamon

1. Getting the seeds out of the watermelon flesh is easy (page 209). After seeding, cut the flesh into chunks.
2. Peel the orange with a sharp knife to remove the skin and the white pith underneath (page 208).

Cut the orange in half along its equator. Remove the seeds.
3. Puree the watermelon, orange, and remaining ingredients in a blender or processor.
4. Chill the soup before serving.

110 CALORIES PER SERVING: 2 G PROTEIN, 1 G FAT, 24 G CARBOHYDRATE; 7 MG SODIUM, 0 MG CHOLESTEROL

Stock

*f*or some recipes that require a liquid for cooking, such as stews and soups, water just won't do. Water dilutes flavors, and sometimes, no matter how much you increase the other seasonings, the dish will taste weak. That's when stock is called for. Stock is made by simmering savory ingredients in water until their flavors transfer to the liquid. Think of it as a type of tea. Just as you discard the tea bag, so you discard the vegetables and chicken bones used to infuse the stock with flavor.

Stock freezes well. Store it in 2-cup containers for use in grain dishes and small quantities of soup. Freeze it in ice cube trays, then put the cubes in a freezer bag so that you have small amounts for sautés.

Vegetable Stock

Many different vegetables, such as mushroom stems, squash and beans, can go into a vegetable stock. I am cautious about adding any assertively flavored vegetables. For example, cabbage, broccoli and asparagus make bitter, odoriferous stock. Also, sweet vegetables like carrots, parsnips and yams make sweet stock. I don't use peelings or vegetables that are going bad, as their off flavors will come through. This is a basic vegetable stock. Add to it as you wish.

MAKES ABOUT 3 QUARTS

3 ribs	celery, with leaves		2	yellow onions, unpeeled, quartered
1	leek			
1	summer squash		4	peppercorns
3	carrots		2	bay leaves
3 cloves	garlic, unpeeled, crushed		½ teaspoon	kosher salt
stems	from 1 bunch parsley		¼ teaspoon	thyme
			3 quarts	water

1. Wash all the vegetables well, especially the leek. Cut the celery, leek, squash and carrots into chunks about 2 inches long.
2. Put all the ingredients in a big pot. Bring the stock to a boil, then reduce to a simmer. Skim off and discard any sediment that foams to the surface.
3. Cover and cook for 30 minutes or longer—the longer, the stronger.
4. Discard the vegetables. Strain the stock through a fine sieve or cheesecloth.

Chicken Stock

To have enough chicken bones to make a full pot of stock, I save the carcasses from roast chicken and the bones from boned breasts in freezer bags. When I have the required 2 pounds, I make stock. I like a light chicken stock that adds flavor to a recipe without overwhelming it. I keep this recipe simple so that its uses can be as varied as possible.

MAKES ABOUT 4 QUARTS

6 quarts	water		1 small bunch	parsley
2 pounds	chicken bones, with some meat left on		1 rib	celery, cut into 2-inch pieces
3 cloves	garlic, crushed		2	carrots, scrubbed and cut into 2-inch pieces
1	large Spanish onion, halved, peeled and cut into big slices		3	bay leaves
			8	peppercorns

1. In a big stockpot, bring the water and the chicken bones to a boil. Reduce to a simmer. Skim off the brownish foam that rises to the surface.
2. Add the rest of the ingredients. Gently simmer, uncovered, for at least 2 hours.
3. Allow the stock to cool enough so that you can handle it. (Big pots are awkward, and you want to avoid splashing hot stock on yourself.) With a slotted spoon, remove and discard the bones and vegetables. Then pour the stock through a fine wire mesh strainer, preferably lined with cheesecloth.

4. Chill the stock in the refrigerator for 1 day until the fat rises to the surface and solidifies. Skim off the fat, then store the stock in the freezer. I put it in well-marked 2- and 4-cup containers. You can store stock in the refrigerator, but chicken stock is a magnet for bacteria and should not be kept for more than 2 days. Bring it to a rolling boil before use. If you are in a rush to use the stock as soon as it is made and want to avoid the fat, use a turkey baster to suck up the stock under the fat floating on top.

Bread Soup

This recipe, of peasant origin, turns scraps of stale bread, herbs and tomatoes into a wonderful meal. All the ingredients need to be fresh and carefully chosen. I use basil and tomatoes from my garden. Canned tomatoes, hard pink tomatoes, even winter plum tomatoes won't do. A hearty bread is a must. I make a special trip to a small shop to get bread for this soup.

SERVES 4 TO 6

1 tablespoon	olive oil
2 cloves	garlic, minced (1 teaspoon)
2	shallots, minced (2 tablespoons)
2	bay leaves
2-3	large beefsteak-style tomatoes, peeled and seeded , then chopped (3½ cups)
1 cup	fresh basil (lightly packed), coarsely chopped

2½ cups	defatted chicken or vegetable stock or water
½-1 teaspoon	kosher salt
¼ teaspoon	freshly ground pepper
2 cups	stale, hearty bread, cut into 1-inch cubes
2 cups	fresh spinach, torn or cut into large pieces
	freshly grated Parmesan cheese for garnish (optional)

1. Heat the oil in a soup pot over low heat. Sauté the garlic, shallots and bay leaves in the oil. Cover and cook over low heat for about 10 minutes until the vegetables are soft and golden. Take care not to let them brown or scorch.

2. Add the tomatoes, basil, water, salt and pepper. Simmer, covered, for 15 minutes. You can store the soup up to this point until the next day.

3. Ten minutes before serving, bring the soup to a boil. Stir in the bread cubes and spinach. Turn off the heat. If you're using an electric stove, take the pot off the burner. Cover the pot and let the soup rest for 10 minutes.

4. If desired, garnish with grated Parmesan cheese.

150 CALORIES PER SERVING: 5 G PROTEIN, 5 G FAT, 24 G CARBOHYDRATE; 401 MG SODIUM, 0 MG CHOLESTEROL

 page 110

Garlic Vegetable Soup

An entire bulb of roasted garlic is pureed with golden chicken stock to form the base for this soup. This simple yet rich combination can be the start of many other soups. Instead of the ingredients I've listed, use an equal amount of other vegetables, perhaps from the late summer bounty of your garden or an inspired trip to a farmers' market. This soup is thick with vegetables. For a lighter soup, reduce the amount of kale and corn or add more stock.

SERVES 6 TO 8

1 bulb	roasted garlic
5 cups	defatted chicken or vegetable stock
1½ teaspoons	olive oil
1	medium yellow onion, chopped (1 cup)
1	small zucchini, chopped
2 ribs	celery, with leaves, chopped
2	carrots, peeled and chopped
½ pound	kale, deribbed and chopped
2 cups	corn kernels
2 tablespoons	chopped parsley
1 teaspoon	oregano
1 teaspoon	kosher salt
¼ teaspoon	freshly ground pepper
	croutons and Parmesan cheese for garnish (optional)

1. Squeeze the garlic out of its skin and put the cloves in the blender along with 1 cup of the stock. Puree into a thin, smooth paste.
2. Heat the oil in a large soup pot. Cook the onion, zucchini, celery and carrots in the oil. Keep covered; the vegetables will sweat out liquid and become lightly browned over low heat.
3. Pour the remaining stock and garlic puree into the soup pot. Add the remaining ingredients. Simmer, covered, for 15 minutes. Add more salt to taste if you wish.
4. If desired, serve with croutons and grate Parmesan cheese over each serving.

112 CALORIES PER SERVING; 6 G PROTEIN, 2 G FAT, 21 G CARBOHYDRATE: 386 MG SODIUM, 0 MG CHOLESTEROL

page 179

Gingerly Pumpkin Soup

This is one of those recipes that makes even noncooks look as if they know their way around the kitchen. As long as you can chop an onion, you can make this impressive soup. For a festive presentation, serve it in a pumpkin tureen or in individual acorn squash.

SERVES 4

2 teaspoons	vegetable oil	2 cups	defatted chicken or vegetable stock
2	large shallots, minced (2 tablespoons)	1 teaspoon	kosher salt
1	small yellow onion, chopped (½ cup)	1 teaspoon	orange zest
½ tablespoon	grated fresh gingerroot	½ teaspoon	freshly ground pepper
2 cups	pumpkin puree	⅟₁₆ teaspoon	ground cloves
1 cup	orange juice	2 tablespoons	minced fresh parsley
		¼ cup	toasted pumpkin seeds (optional)

1. Heat the oil in a soup pot over low heat. Sauté the shallot, onion and ginger in the oil until the onion is soft and golden. Be careful not to scorch the ginger.

2. Add the pumpkin, orange juice, stock, salt, zest, pepper and cloves. Simmer for 10 minutes over medium heat.

3. Garnish with parsley and pumpkin seeds (if using).

112 CALORIES PER SERVING; 6 G PROTEIN, 2 G FAT, 21 G CARBOHYDRATE: 386 MG SODIUM, 0 MG CHOLESTEROL

page 127

The Pumpkin Tureen

*W*hen soup is offered at a buffet and will be sitting out for a while, it is fun to present it in an unusual tureen. A hollowed-out, partially baked pumpkin not only holds any quantity of soup (simply select the size pumpkin you need), but it also keeps the soup warm and doesn't need to be washed out later (discard it in your compost pile).

To make a tureen, you need a squat, round pumpkin that sits solidly without moving. Wash it well, then pat it dry. Cut off the top. Cut off a wider opening than you would for a jack-o'-lantern. Pull out the strings and seeds. Then take a metal spoon and scrape the inside walls until only hard pumpkin flesh remains.

Bake in a preheated 350 degree F oven for about 30 minutes to rid the pumpkin of its raw aroma, but you don't want the pumpkin to soften and crumple. I've known people who bake soups in pumpkin tureens. I don't think that's a good idea. Not only does the soup taste too strongly of pumpkin, but if overcooked, the pumpkin also looks on the verge of collapse, and diners approach it with more worry than delight.

Mandarin Soup

The first step in making this soup not only makes the soup stock but also cooks the chicken. This takes time but not much effort. The resulting soup has intense, complex flavors with a balance of sweet and salty, pungent and smooth. This soup reheats well. I know because after the final recipe test, my husband ate it for lunch three days in a row—and was sorry when there was none left on the fourth day. If fresh shiitakes are not available, you can use dried, although their flavor will be more pronounced. To slice the dried mushrooms, soak them in warm water until they are soft and you are able to cut them.

SERVES 4

4	large fresh shiitake mushrooms (½ cup)	5	scallions, sliced
2 cloves	garlic, peeled and crushed	½ cup	snow peas, de-stringed and cut into thirds
2	chicken thighs, skinned and fat removed	½ cup	mung bean sprouts
6 cups	water	⅛-¼ teaspoon	freshly ground pepper
1	leek, chopped	1 tablespoon	dry sherry
1 tablespoon	minced fresh gingerroot	1 11-ounce can	mandarin oranges packed in light syrup, drained
3-4 tablespoons	soy sauce		

1. Snap the stems off the mushrooms. Reserve the caps. Put the stems in a pot with the garlic, chicken, water and leek, and simmer for 45 minutes.
2. Strain the stock. Discard the vegetables. Set the chicken aside. Put the stock back in the pot. It will have been reduced by about one-third, to 4 cups.
3. Take the chicken off the bones and cut it into small pieces. Add the meat to the pot.

4. Add the ginger, soy sauce, scallions, snow peas, bean sprouts, pepper and sherry to the soup.
5. Slice the mushroom caps. Add them to the soup.
6. Puree the mandarin oranges. Stir them into the soup.
7. Bring the soup to a gentle simmer. Cook for 10 minutes. Check the seasonings. Add more soy sauce and pepper if desired.

129 CALORIES PER SERVING: 9 G PROTEIN, 3 G FAT, 17 G CARBOHYDRATE; 809 MG SODIUM, 25 MG CHOLESTEROL

Barley Vegetable Soup

The nice thing about hearty soups is that they are so easy to make. This one does require some cutting and chopping of vegetables, but after that you can sit back and enjoy the wonderful aromas coming from the simmering pot. The barley will thicken the soup to the consistency of stew by the second day. Thin it with stock if desired. This soup freezes well.

SERVES 4 TO 6

1½ teaspoons	vegetable oil
2 cloves	garlic, minced (1 teaspoon)
1	leek or small yellow onion, chopped (½ cup)
1 rib	celery, chopped
1	carrot, peeled and chopped
½ cup	barley
6 cups	defatted chicken or vegetable stock
1 cup	sliced mushrooms, preferably a dark, fancy variety
½ cup	green beans, cut into short pieces
1½ teaspoons	kosher salt
½ teaspoon	freshly ground pepper
½ teaspoon	sage

1. Heat the oil in a soup pot over low heat. Sauté the garlic, onion and celery in the oil. Keep covered. (While watching the pot and occasionally stirring it, this is a good time to chop the other vegetables.) Cook until the leeks are soft and golden.

2. Add the remaining ingredients. If you're using shiitake mushrooms, remove and discard the woody stems before slicing. Bring the soup to a boil. Reduce to a gentle simmer and cook, covered, for 1 hour.

157 CALORIES PER SERVING: 8 G PROTEIN, 3 G FAT, 25 G CARBOHYDRATE; 806 MG SODIUM, 0 MG CHOLESTEROL

Housewarming Soup

This recipe made its debut at a potluck housewarming party. The kettle of soup was kept warm on the back burner of an antique gas stove. It was out of the way and a distance from the buffet table, but during the evening, word spread among the guests. Many asked me what was in it, thinking that it was a fancy recipe. I was pleased to tell them that it was simply beans and greens.

SERVES 6 TO 8

½ tablespoon	olive oil
2 cloves	garlic, minced (1 teaspoon)
1	medium yellow onion, chopped (1 cup)
1 cup	uncooked white beans, soaked in water for at least 4 hours
3	small carrots, peeled and cubed (1½ cups)
½ pound	white-ribbed Swiss chard, chopped (4 to 5 cups)
1 rib	celery, chopped
6 cups	defatted chicken or vegetable stock or water
2	bay leaves
½ teaspoon	freshly ground pepper
2 tablespoons	minced fresh parsley
½ teaspoon	sage
1 teaspoon	kosher salt
2 tablespoons	freshly grated Parmesan or Romano cheese

1. Heat the oil in a soup pot over low heat. Sauté the garlic and onion in the oil until the onion is soft and golden. Keep the lid on between stirrings.
2. Drain the beans from the soak water. Pick out any discolored beans or pebbles. Add the beans and the remaining ingredients, except the salt and cheese, to the pot.
3. Bring the soup to a boil. Reduce to a simmer and cook, covered, for 45 minutes to 1 hour, or until the beans are thoroughly cooked. You'll know they are done when you can easily squish one between your fingers.
4. Stir in the salt. If the salt was added earlier it would have prevented the beans from softening. Add more salt to taste if desired.
5. You can puree this soup completely or only half-puree it. Pureeing will give it a smoother texture but a slightly greenish cast. In fact, the reason that I ask you to use white-ribbed and not red Swiss chard is that red chard will turn the soup a light purple color.
6. Stir in the cheese or use it as a garnish on top of each serving.

186 CALORIES PER SERVING: 13 G PROTEIN, 3 G FAT, 29 G CARBOHYDRATE; 538 MG SODIUM, 2 MG CHOLESTEROL

Two-Pea Soup

You can find the ingredients for this soup year-round, but it seems to be custom-designed for each season. The bright green peas mark the emergence of spring, the mint symbolizes the heat of summer, carrots and onions are fall staples, and the split peas nourish on a cold winter day.

SERVES 4 TO 6

½ tablespoon	olive oil
4 cloves	garlic, minced (2 teaspoons)
2	medium yellow onions, chopped (2 cups)
3 ribs	celery, with leaves, chopped
3	carrots, peeled and chopped
4 cups	defatted chicken or vegetable stock or water

¼ cup	split peas, rinsed and picked through
1 10-ounce package	frozen peas
1 teaspoon	kosher salt
½ teaspoon	freshly ground pepper
2 tablespoons	minced fresh mint
	freshly grated Parmesan cheese for garnish (optional)

1. Heat the oil in a soup pot over low heat. Cook the garlic, onion, celery and carrots in the oil. Keep the pot covered between stirrings. The onion will turn golden, and the vegetables will sweat out liquid. Cook for about 15 minutes.

2. Add the stock and split peas. Bring to a boil, then reduce to a simmer. Cover and cook for 30 minutes until the peas are soft. Old split peas will take longer to cook. (They will be a duller color with an even duller flavor. Learn to recognize old split peas before cooking with them. They have a telltale olive tone.)

3. Add the frozen peas, salt, pepper and mint. Simmer for about 5 minutes until the peas are cooked.

4. Puree half the soup, then return it to the pot.

5. Serve with grated Parmesan cheese if desired.

214 CALORIES PER SERVING: 12 G PROTEIN, 3 G FAT, 37 G CARBOHYDRATE; 661 MG SODIUM, 0 MG CHOLESTEROL

Classic Lentil Soup

All the familiar ingredients are here, but this soup is never boring. The addition of balsamic vinegar and hot pepper sauce gives it pizzazz. Don't be put off by the long list of ingredients. This is an easy soup to make. It is wonderful left over and freezes well. After a day, it will thicken; eat it as a stew or thin it with stock.

SERVES 4 TO 6

2 teaspoons	vegetable oil
3	small carrots, peeled and chopped
1 rib	celery, chopped
1	small yellow onion, chopped (½ cup)
3 cloves	garlic, minced (1½ teaspoons)
1 cup	lentils, rinsed and picked through
4 cups	defatted chicken or vegetable stock
1 tablespoon	minced fresh parsley

1 14-ounce can	whole tomatoes, with juice, broken up with your hands
1 teaspoon	oregano
½ tablespoon	basil
¼ teaspoon	freshly ground pepper
1 teaspoon	balsamic vinegar
2	bay leaves
¹⁄₁₆ teaspoon	Tabasco or other hot pepper sauce
½ teaspoon	kosher salt

1. Heat the oil in a soup pot over low heat. Sauté the carrots, celery, onion and garlic in the oil. Keep the lid on between stirrings. Cook until the onion is soft and golden.
2. Add the remaining ingredients except the salt, to the pot.
3. Bring to a boil, then simmer, covered, for about 45 minutes until the lentils are soft. The older the lentils, the longer this will take.
4. Add the salt and adjust the other seasonings to taste.

266 CALORIES PER SERVING: 18 G PROTEIN, 4 G FAT, 43 G CARBOHYDRATE; 491 MG SODIUM, 0 MG CHOLESTEROL

Spinach & Lentil Soup

The nice thing about lentil soup is that lentils don't need to be soaked. Start to finish, this soup takes only about an hour to make—and most of that is just watching the pot simmer. Make a double batch, as this highly seasoned soup freezes well.

SERVES 7 TO 9

1 tablespoon	vegetable oil
1	medium yellow onion, chopped (1 cup)
2-3 cloves	garlic, minced (1½ teaspoons)
1 teaspoon	ground cumin
1 teaspoon	ground coriander
1 teaspoon	paprika
1 10-ounce package	fresh spinach, washed and trimmed of tough stems
⅛ teaspoon	Tabasco or hot pepper sauce
1 teaspoon	oregano
1 cup	lentils, rinsed and picked through
7 cups	defatted chicken or vegetable stock
1 teaspoon	kosher salt
¼ teaspoon	freshly ground pepper
1 tablespoon	lemon juice
2 tablespoons	tomato paste

1. Heat the oil in a soup pot over low heat. Sauté the onion and garlic in the oil until the onion is soft and golden. Add the cumin, coriander and paprika. Sir and cook until the aromas strengthen.
2. Roughly chop the spinach. Add it to the sauté and cook until it wilts.
3. Add the Tabasco, oregano, lentils and stock to the pot.
4. Bring the soup to a boil, then immediately reduce to a simmer. Cook, covered, for about 50 minutes until the lentils become very soft.
5. Add the salt and pepper, then add the lemon juice and tomato paste. Simmer for 10 minutes more. Add more salt and pepper to taste if desired.

159 CALORIES PER SERVING: 11 G PROTEIN, 3 G FAT, 23 G CARBOHYDRATE; 377 MG SODIUM, 0 MG CHOLESTEROL

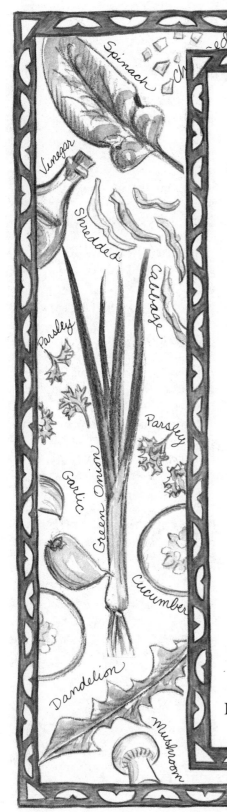

recipes

Strawberry Spinach Salad

Apple-Carrot Coleslaw

Snap Peas in Mint Vinaigrette

Beet & Orange Salad

Summer Beet Salad

Marinated Tomato Salad

Chinese Cucumber Salad

Greek Cucumber
Yogurt Salad

Black Bean & Corn Salad

Chickpea & Roasted
Red Pepper Salad

Pita Salad

Garlicky Garden
Potato Salad

Dilly Potato Salad

Sesame Soba Salad

Springtime Pasta Salad

Salmon Salad

Tuna Salad with Capers

Apple & Tuna Salad

Curried Chicken,
Fruit & Rice Salad

Chili Orange Vinaigrette

Tomato Tarragon Dressing

Honey-Poppy Seed Vinaigrette

Creamy Herb Dressing

Salads

Salads embody all that I desire from a recipe. They make use of fresh, colorful, aromatic ingredients. They showcase vegetables but can be as filling or as light as the weather or menu requires. They can be one-dish lunches, part of an eclectic dinner or carried to work in a container. Leftovers make late-morning or late-night snacks. Once put together, they don't demand any more attention. Most are best eaten at room temperature. For all these reasons, even if my refrigerator is filled with good food, it seems empty if there's not a bowl of salad in it.

Strawberry Spinach Salad

Versions of this salad are turning up at catered parties for several good reasons. The presentation of bright red berries set off by dark greens is dramatic and beautiful, and the combination of a sweet dressing with fruits and leafy greens pleases nearly everyone. All that for very little work!

SERVES 6 TO 8

10 cups	fresh spinach, loosely packed
1½ cups	strawberries
1 cup	mushrooms, sliced (¼ pound)
⅓	red onion, thinly sliced and cut into 1-inch or smaller pieces (⅓ cup)

⅓ cup   Honey-Poppy Seed Vinaigrette

1. Wash the spinach well, then spin it dry in a salad spinner. Trim off the thick stems. Tear the largest leaves into smaller pieces. Make sure the spinach leaves are manageable with a fork. You can prepare the spinach several hours ahead of time if you dry it well and store it in the refrigerator.

2. Remove the hulls and then slice the strawberries. Don't do this more than 1 hour before serving, or the strawberries will get mushy.

3. Toss 1 cup of the berries with the vegetables. Reserve the remaining berries for garnish.

4. Just prior to serving, toss with the dressing.

5. Arrange the reserved strawberries on top.

82 CALORIES PER SERVING: 3 G PROTEIN, 4 G FAT, 11 G CARBOHYDRATE; 92 MG SODIUM, 0 MG CHOLESTEROL

page 59

Apple-Carrot Coleslaw

There's no need for a thick dressing on slaw. This pretty mélange offers a nice balance between the cabbage and the sweeter carrots and apples. The tangy dressing is smoothed with a touch of honey.

SERVES 8

Dressing
2 tablespoons	lemon juice
2 tablespoons	apple cider vinegar
1 tablespoon	vegetable oil
1 tablespoon	honey
1 tablespoon	Dijon mustard
1 teaspoon	mild curry powder
¼ teaspoon	kosher salt
⅛ teaspoon	freshly ground pepper

2	firm apples, cored
⅓-½ pound	green cabbage (¼ of a medium cabbage)
2	medium carrots
½	medium red onion

1. Whisk together the dressing ingredients. Do this first so that you can toss the apples in the dressing immediately after grating so that they don't have a chance to turn brown.

2. Grate the apples and vegetables with a large-holed grater. This is easily accomplished with a food processor. I don't peel the apples unless they have been heavily waxed.

3. Toss the apples and vegetables with the dressing. You can make this several hours ahead of time.

63 CALORIES PER SERVING: 1 G PROTEIN, 2 G FAT, 12 G CARBOHYDRATE; 95 MG SODIUM, 0 MG CHOLESTEROL

Snap Peas in Mint Vinaigrette

Snap peas are one of my favorite vegetables. I grow them in my garden and eat them raw, as a snack. But out of season, or even in the summer, they can be hard to find and quite expensive. As an alternative, you can use snow peas, which will make a lovely salad but won't have the same crunch. I like to serve this cheerful dish at summer picnics and poolside parties. The vegetables and dressing can be prepared up to a day ahead of time, but shouldn't be tossed together until the last moment.

SERVES 6 TO 8

1 pound	snap peas (4 to 5 cups)
½	red bell pepper, cut julienne into 1½-inch strips (1 cup)
¼	red onion, thinly sliced and cut into ½-inch or smaller pieces (¼ cup)

Dressing

1 tablespoon	lemon juice
1 tablespoon	red wine vinegar
1 tablespoon	minced fresh mint
2 teaspoons	coarse-grained mustard
1 tablespoon	olive oil
1 tablespoon	honey

1. Snap the tip off each snap pea and peel off the string (unless it is a stringless hybrid). Leave the peas whole or cut them in half on the diagonal.
2. Bring a pot of water to a boil. Drop in the peas and cook them for about 1 minute until they turn bright green. Remove from water and immediately immerse them in cold water.

3. Mix all the vegetables together.
4. Whisk together the dressing ingredients. Pour the dressing over the vegetables and toss until the peas glisten with an even coating of dressing.

70 CALORIES PER SERVING: 2 G PROTEIN, 3 G FAT, 10 G CARBOHYDRATE; 27 MG SODIUM, 0 MG CHOLESTEROL

Beet & Orange Salad

Either you love beets or you hate them. I love them. They come in one of my favorite colors, have an earthy sweetness and a firm, but not chewy, texture.

SERVES 4

2	oranges
1 pound	fresh beets, cooked and sliced, or 2 cups canned sliced beets
⅓	red onion, thinly sliced and cut into 1-inch or smaller pieces (⅓ cup)

Dressing

2 tablespoons	orange juice
1 tablespoon	honey
2 tablespoons	apple cider vinegar
¼ teaspoon	kosher salt
⅛ teaspoon	freshly ground pepper

1. Cut the oranges in half. Cut out the segments as you would a grapefruit. Combine these with the beets. Squeeze the orange halves to extract any juice. You should be able to get the 2 tablespoons needed for the dressing. Strain or pick out the seeds. Put the juice in another bowl.

2. Add the onion to the beets and oranges.
3. Whisk together the dressing ingredients.
4. Pour the dressing over the beet mixture. Stir to combine.
5. Store the salad in a covered glass bowl in the refrigerator for up to a week.

82 CALORIES PER SERVING: 2 G PROTEIN, 0 G FAT, 20 G PROTEIN; 160 MG SODIUM, 0 MG CHOLESTEROL

Summer Beet Salad

Root vegetables are usually considered winter fare, and certainly beets are robust when served hot. But in the summer, when dressed with herbs and vinaigrettes, beets are cool and refreshing . Despite its sizzling magenta color, this salad is an ideal antidote to hot summer days.

SERVES 6

1½ pounds	fresh beets, cooked and sliced, or 3 cups canned sliced beets
2 tablespoons	chopped fresh mint, or cut into fine strips
¼	red onion, thinly sliced and cut into ½-inch or smaller pieces (¼ cup)

Dressing

1 tablespoon	balsamic vinegar
1 tablespoon	white wine vinegar
1 tablespoon	honey
1 tablespoon	olive oil

1. Toss the beets with the mint and onion.
2. Whisk together the dressing ingredients. Pour the dressing over the beets and toss until the beets are evenly coated.

3. Serve at room temperature.

63 CALORIES PER SERVING: 1 G PROTEIN, 2 G FAT, 10 G CARBOHYDRATE; 43 MG SODIUM, 0 MG CHOLESTEROL

Marinated Tomato Salad

This salad is wonderful as a side salad, but it is also a potential topping for bruschetta (grilled bread) and a refreshing filling for a pita pocket with chicken. It will keep for several days in the refrigerator.

SERVES 4 TO 6

4	medium tomatoes
2 cloves	garlic, peeled and crushed
½	red onion, thinly sliced and cut into thirds (½ cup)
2 tablespoons	minced fresh parsley

Dressing

1 tablespoon	olive oil
2 tablespoons	lemon juice
1 teaspoon	balsamic vinegar
½ teaspoon	yellow mustard seeds, slightly crushed
¼ teaspoon	ground coriander
¼ teaspoon	kosher salt
¼ teaspoon	freshly ground pepper

1. Core the tomatoes, then seed them by cutting them in half at their equators and gently pushing the seeds and watery juice out with your fingers. Slice the tomatoes.
2. Put a toothpick through the garlic so that it will be easier to find and remove later.
3. Combine the tomatoes, garlic, onion and parsley.

4. Whisk together the dressing ingredients. Pour the dressing over the tomatoes. Stir gently. Let the salad rest 1 hour before serving. The tomatoes will be most flavorful if served at room temperature. Remove and discard the garlic just prior to serving. If you want a strong garlic flavor, you can put the garlic back in any leftover salad. The garlic aroma will strengthen as time goes on.

73 CALORIES PER SERVING: 2 G PROTEIN, 4 G FAT, 9 G CARBOHYDRATE; 131 MG SODIUM, 0 MG CHOLESTEROL

Chinese Cucumber Salad

This simple cucumber salad—a cool mix of sweet and sour—goes especially well with spicy or hearty foods.

SERVES 4 TO 6

2   cucumbers, peeled

Dressing
1 tablespoon	soy sauce
1 tablespoon	honey
1 tablespoon	rice vinegar
1 teaspoon	toasted sesame oil

1. Seed the cucumbers by slicing them in half lengthwise, then scooping out the seeds with a teaspoon. Discard the seeds. The salad dressing will become too watery if they are left in.
2. Cut the cucumbers into thin slices.

3. Whisk together the dressing ingredients. Toss the cucumbers in the dressing, coating them well.
4. Refrigerate the salad before serving. This salad improves with a few hours rest and is still excellent the second day.

48 CALORIES PER SERVING: 1 G PROTEIN, 1 G FAT, 9 G CARBOHYDRATE; 261 MG SODIUM, 0 MG CHOLESTEROL

Greek Cucumber Yogurt Salad

Yogurt and cucumber salad is the perfect coolant for a spicy meal on a hot, humid day. Use it as a side dish, or serve it as a relish to balance fiery foods. Yogurt varies in flavor and texture. I like to use a thick tangy-tart yogurt. Add extra lemon juice if your yogurt is bland.

SERVES 6

2   cucumbers, peeled and seeded (see above)

Dressing
| 1 cup | low-fat or nonfat yogurt |
| 1 teaspoon | lemon juice |

1 clove	garlic, minced (½ teaspoon)
1 tablespoon	chopped fresh parsley
¾ teaspoon	oregano
¼ teaspoon	kosher salt
⅛ teaspoon	freshly ground pepper

1. To chop the cucumbers, slice each half into three long strips. Then, holding them all in a loglike pile, slice across the cucumbers in rhythmic strokes. This will give you just the right size tidily chopped pieces for little effort.

2. Stir the yogurt and seasonings together. Then stir in the cucumber. Serve immediately. The fresh garlic will get stronger and more aromatic as time goes on, so any leftovers are suitable only for true garlic aficionados.

39 CALORIES PER SERVING: 3 G PROTEIN, 1 G FAT, 6 G CARBOHYDRATE; 107 MG SODIUM, 2 MG CHOLESTEROL

Black Bean & Corn Salad

The ingredients for this salad can be found year-round. You can use fresh corn on the cob or frozen kernels. Beans cooked from scratch work fine, but in the summer I use frozen home-cooked beans or canned beans. I also buy canned chopped green chilies. They're easy to use, and their flavor is consistent.

SERVES 5

1½ cups	cooked black beans	**Dressing**		
2 cups	cooked corn kernels	1 tablespoon	olive oil
1	red bell pepper, fresh or roasted , chopped	2 tablespoons	red wine vinegar
3	scallions, sliced	1½ tablespoons	lemon juice
2 tablespoons	minced fresh parsley or cilantro	¼ teaspoon	kosher salt
2 tablespoons	chopped mild green chilies	⅛ teaspoon	red pepper flakes
		½ teaspoon	ground coriander
		½ teaspoon	ground cumin

1. Combine the salad ingredients.
2. Whisk together the dressing ingredients in a separate bowl.
3. Stir the dressing into the salad.

155 CALORIES PER SERVING: 7 G PROTEIN, 3 G FAT, 28 G CARBOHYDRATE; 149 MG SODIUM, 0 MG CHOLESTEROL

page 180

Chickpea & Roasted Red Pepper Salad

I like to place this dense, filling salad on a bed of lettuce leaves and have it for lunch.
Sometimes I splurge and have it with feta cheese.

SERVES 4

2 cups	cooked chickpeas, or 1 15-ounce can, drained and rinsed well	**Dressing**		
1	roasted red pepper, chopped (½ cup)	½ tablespoon	garlic oil
2 tablespoons	chopped fresh parsley	2 tablespoons	lemon juice
2 tablespoons	chopped red onion	1 teaspoon	red wine vinegar
		⅛ teaspoon	freshly ground pepper
		¼ teaspoon	kosher salt
		½ teaspoon	ground coriander
		⅛ teaspoon	Tabasco or other hot pepper sauce

1. Stir together the salad ingredients.
2. Whisk together the dressing ingredients. Pour the dressing over the chickpeas. Stir to coat.

129 CALORIES PER SERVING: 5 G PROTEIN, 4 G FAT, 20 G CARBOHYDRATE; 543 MG SODIUM, 0 MG CHOLESTEROL

page 180   page 138

Pita Salad

Salad is a great way to use up stale bread. The bread soaks up the dressing and provides
a crunchy contrast to light lettuce leaves.

SERVES 4

1	pita pocket, preferably whole wheat
4	large romaine lettuce leaves
½	medium red onion, chopped (½ cup)
3	scallions, chopped
1	cucumber, peeled, seeded and chopped
2	medium tomatoes, cored and chopped
2 tablespoons	minced fresh mint
3 tablespoons	chopped fresh parsley
1 small clove	garlic, minced (¼ teaspoon)

Dressing

¼ cup	lemon juice
1½ tablespoons	extra-virgin olive oil
½ teaspoon	kosher salt
½ teaspoon	freshly ground pepper

1. Toast the pita pocket until crispy. Break it into pieces the size of croutons.
2. Cut the lettuce leaves into pieces about 2 inches square. It's not necessary to tear the leaves; cutting them with a sharp knife is fine.
3. Combine the pita with the lettuce, onion, scallions, cucumber, tomatoes, herbs and garlic. If you don't like chopping, you can prepare the mint, parsley, onion and scallions in a food processor. I do think it is worth the extra couple of minutes to chop the cucumber and tomato by hand because the bigger and tidier squares you get with a knife are more appetizing in this salad.
4. Whisk together the dressing ingredients. Pour the dressing over the salad. Toss.

104 CALORIES PER SERVING: 3 G PROTEIN, 4 G FAT, 16 G CARBOHYDRATE; 302 MG SODIUM, 0 MG CHOLESTEROL

page 39

Garlicky Garden Potato Salad

Serious garlic lovers might want to add an extra clove to the dressing. Let the salad rest for a couple of hours before serving so that the flavors blend and permeate. The garlic aroma will increase with time. By the next day, it will be quite assertive.

SERVES 6

Dressing

1 or 2 cloves	garlic, peeled
1 tablespoon	extra-virgin olive oil
3 tablespoons	apple cider vinegar
¾ teaspoon	kosher salt
½ teaspoon	freshly ground pepper
¼ teaspoon	celery seed

8-10	small red potatoes (1 pound)
1 cup	vegetable of your choice (green beans, cucumber, broccoli, etc.)
½	red bell pepper, chopped (½ cup)
⅓	red onion, chopped (⅓ cup)
1 tablespoon	fresh parsley, chopped
½ cup	peas, lightly steamed

1. Puree the dressing ingredients until the garlic is smoothly incorporated into the liquid.
2. Scrub the potatoes well. Do not peel them, but trim off any bruises. Cut the potatoes into cubes. Steam or boil them until tender. Drain the potatoes, then immediately pour the dressing over them.
3. Cut your vegetable of choice into bite-size pieces. You might want to steam the vegetable lightly. For example, broccoli benefits from a quick cooking.
4. Once the potatoes are cool, toss in the remaining ingredients.

110 CALORIES PER SERVING: 3 G PROTEIN, 3 G FAT, 21 G CARBOHYDRATE; 241 MG SODIUM, 0 MG CHOLESTEROL

Pasta with Vegetables & Feta, page 93

Fish Baked with Mint, page 83

Sesame Soba Salad, page 52 and Asparagus in Gingerly Citrus Dressing, page 163

Oven-Baked Ratatouille, page 90

Grand Oranges, page 208 and Strawberry Sauce, page 210

Curried Chicken, Fruit & Rice Salad, page 56

48

Lemon Bread Pudding, page 217

Mandarin Soup, page 26 and Two-Pea Soup, page 29

Dilly Potato Salad

One way to achieve a full-flavored potato salad is to pour the vinaigrette over the potatoes while they are still hot. This allows the potatoes to soak up the flavors of the dressing. Obviously, this precludes using leftover potatoes, which is just as well, because freshly cooked potatoes taste better. Use very small new potatoes if you can find them. Otherwise, buy the waxy red-skinned variety and cut them into 1- to 2-inch cubes.

SERVES 8 TO 10

6	medium potatoes, scrubbed and cut into cubes (1½ pounds)
½	red onion, thinly sliced and cut into small pieces (½ cup)
2 ribs	celery, chopped
1	large dill pickle, chopped (⅔ cup)
1 tablespoon	chopped fresh parsley
1 tablespoon	minced fresh dill

Dressing

¼ cup	apple cider vinegar
2 tablespoons	vegetable oil
¼ teaspoon	dry mustard
½ teaspoon	sugar
⅛ teaspoon	paprika
½ teaspoon	kosher salt
¼ teaspoon	freshly ground pepper

1. Cook the potatoes until you can easily insert a fork, but not so long that they fall apart.
2. Meanwhile, combine the onion, celery, pickle, parsley and dill in a large bowl.
3. Whisk together the dressing ingredients.
4. When the potatoes are cooked, drain them and put them in the bowl with the other vegetables. Pour the dressing over them and toss well.
5. Serve this salad immediately while still hot, or chill it in the refrigerator and serve later at room temperature.

87 CALORIES PER SERVING: 1 G PROTEIN, 4 G FAT, 14 G CARBOHYDRATE; 234 MG SODIUM, 0 MG CHOLESTEROL

Sesame Soba Salad

Soba noodles have an earthy flavor just like buckwheat, the grain from which they are made. Unless you have a wheat allergy, I don't suggest buying 100 percent buckwheat soba because it falls apart when cooked and requires a very strong dressing to balance its flavor. Instead, get part-wheat, part-buckwheat soba. Soba noodles are available at most natural food stores and many gourmet shops.

SERVES 6 TO 8

1 8- to 9-ouncepackage soba noodles
6 scallions, sliced
1½ cups mung bean sprouts
6 radishes, sliced, or ½ cup grated daikon radish
1 teaspoon sesame seeds, toasted, for garnish (optional)

Dressing
2 tablespoons soy sauce
2 tablespoons mirin
½ tablespoon rice vinegar
1½ tablespoons toasted sesame oil
1 tablespoon tahini (also called sesame seed paste)
1/16 teaspoon cayenne pepper, preferably Chinese

1. Boil the soba noodles just as you would cook regular pasta. However, before dropping them in the boiling water, break the noodles in half. This will make the salad easier to toss later. When the noodles are cooked, drain them, then immediately immerse them in cold water and drain again. This rinses off any stickiness and keeps them from absorbing too much sauce later on.
2. Toss the noodles with the vegetables.

3. In a blender, liquefy the soy sauce, mirin, vinegar, oil, tahini and cayenne pepper until smooth. Tahini comes in different consistencies, from dense to oily. The oil usually separates out from the paste. Stir it back in before measuring, or the dressing will be too dense. If the blended dressing looks sticky and doesn't pour easily, add a tablespoon or two of water.
4. Pour the dressing over the salad. Toss to combine. Garnish with toasted sesame seeds if desired.

174 CALORIES PER SERVING: 7 G PROTEIN, 5 G FAT, 28 G CARBOHYDRATE; 417 MG SODIUM, 0 MG CHOLESTEROL

Mirin

mirin is a clear, shiny, sweet wine made from steamed and fermented rice. It is used for cooking, not drinking. It has a low alcohol content and a subtle flavor that blends well with other ingredients. You can find it at Asian markets, many gourmet shops and some supermarkets that have a wide selection of ethnic foods. Look for it next to the soy sauce. You may use sherry, although it has a different flavor, as an alternative to mirin in cooked dishes. The sherry's alcohol content is too high for use in uncooked recipes. Instead, substitute a touch of white sugar.

Springtime Pasta Salad

Although asparagus is now available year-round (for a price), I still think of it as a springtime delicacy. Certainly, when I buy asparagus freshly dug from a field only a few miles away, it is one of spring's finest pleasures. In this salad, I've also included peas, another vegetable that is no longer seasonal. In fact, frozen peas are often the sweetest ones you can get if you don't grow them yourself. For a special occasion, add 1 cup smoked salmon or trout.

SERVES 4 TO 6

10	asparagus spears, cut into 1-inch pieces
⅔ cup	peas
1½ cups	uncooked pasta, preferably a short, stubby type
½	red onion, cut into small slices (½ cup)
½	red bell pepper, cut julienne into 1-inch strips

Dressing

2	tablespoons red wine vinegar
½ tablespoon	balsamic vinegar
2 tablespoons	garlic oil
1 teaspoon	Dijon mustard
½ teaspoon	kosher salt
¼ teaspoon	freshly ground pepper
1 teaspoon	basil
½ teaspoon	marjoram
2 tablespoons	minced fresh parsley

1. Steam the asparagus until it turns a brighter shade of green and is tender but not soft. Cook the peas in the same manner, but not at the same time as the asparagus, as they take less time to cook. Once steamed, immerse the vegetables in cold water to prevent them from overcooking.
2. Cook the pasta. When it is done, rinse it under cold water to keep it from sticking and to bring it to room temperature.
3. Toss the asparagus, peas, pasta, onion and red pepper together.
4. Whisk together the dressing ingredients. Pour the dressing on the pasta and vegetables and stir until they are evenly coated.

205 CALORIES PER SERVING: 8 G PROTEIN, 8 G FAT, 28 G CARBOHYDRATE; 261 MG SODIUM, 0 MG CHOLESTEROL

 page 138

Salmon Salad

This pretty, elegant salad requires fresh salmon. Leftover salmon from the previous night's dinner is fine. Or you can poach the fish just for this recipe (page 79).

SERVES 6

1 pound	salmon, cooked
1 tablespoon	capers
½ teaspoon	green peppercorns, lightly crushed
2	scallions, sliced
1 cup	peas, lightly cooked
1 tablespoon	minced fresh dill
	lettuce (optional)
4	carrots, peeled and grated (optional)

Dressing

1 tablespoon	olive oil
2 tablespoons	lemon juice
½ tablespoon	white wine vinegar
¼ teaspoon	kosher salt

1. Break the salmon into large, bite-size flakes.
2. Gently combine the fish with the capers, peppercorns, scallions, peas and dill.
3. Whisk together the dressing ingredients. Pour the dressing over the salmon and toss.
4. For a formal presentation, arrange the lettuce on individual serving plates. Top with a small mound of carrots and a portion of the salmon salad.

112 CALORIES PER SERVING: 12 G PROTEIN, 5 G FAT, 4 G CARBOHYDRATE; 571 MG SODIUM, 14 MG CHOLESTEROL

Tuna Salad with Capers

I like to serve this salad on a bed of spinach or dark romaine lettuce leaves.

SERVES 4 TO 6

6	plum tomatoes, cut into large pieces	
1 6-ounce can	tuna packed in water, drained	
1 rib	celery, chopped	
3	scallions, sliced	
4	fresh or canned artichoke hearts, quartered	
2 tablespoons	capers	
1 tablespoon	minced fresh parsley	

Dressing

½ tablespoon	garlic oil
1 tablespoon	lemon juice
1 tablespoon	red wine vinegar
1 teaspoon	balsamic vinegar
¼ teaspoon	kosher salt
¼ teaspoon	freshly ground pepper

1. Stir together the tomatoes, tuna, celery, scallions, artichoke hearts, capers and parsley.

2. Whisk together the dressing ingredients. Pour the dressing over the salad. Stir to combine.

102 CALORIES PER SERVING: 14 G PROTEIN, 2 G FAT, 7 G CARBOHYDRATE; 387 MG SODIUM, 8 MG CHOLESTEROL

page 138

Apple & Tuna Salad

A young friend taught me this one. He learned it from his grandmother. We replaced the mayonnaise with nonfat yogurt, and he says it tastes just as good.

SERVES 2 TO 4

1 6-ounce can	tuna, packed in water, drained		1	medium apple, cored and chopped
2½ tablespoons	nonfat yogurt			
2 tablespoons	sweet relish		¼ teaspoon	kosher salt

1. Put all the ingredients in a bowl. Mix them together with a fork.

181 CALORIES PER SERVING: 26 G PROTEIN, 1 G FAT, 17 G CARBOHYDRATE; 676 MG SODIUM, 16 MG CHOLESTEROL

Curried Chicken, Fruit & Rice Salad

I use Major Grey's chutney for this salad. The color and flavor of this sweet, mango-based preserve complement the curry dressing and the fruit. Major Grey's is a standard and always available. Other chutneys can be wonderful but fleeting. A favorite of mine was a pineapple ginger chutney made in Maine that, much to my dismay, is no longer available.

SERVES 8 TO 10

1	apple, cored and cut into cubes
1 teaspoon	lemon juice
½	cantaloupe or other orange-fleshed melon
3 cups	cooked brown or white rice, preferably basmati
1 cup	seedless grapes
1	small whole chicken breast, cooked, skinned and cut into cubes (2 cups)
1 tablespoon	chopped nuts for garnish (optional)

Dressing

½ cup	nonfat yogurt
2 teaspoons	lemon juice
1 tablespoon	white wine vinegar
1 tablespoon	vegetable oil
½ tablespoon	curry powder
½ teaspoon	kosher salt
2 tablespoons	chutney

1. Coat the apple with the 1 teaspoon lemon juice to prevent it from browning.
2. Scoop out the melon's seeds, then make melon balls. Using a melon baller takes only a few minutes more than cutting the fruit into ungainly pieces.
3. Combine the apple, melon, rice (make sure it is room temperature or cooler), grapes and chicken.
4. Whisk together or puree the yogurt, 2 teaspoons lemon juice, vinegar, oil, curry powder and salt until the dressing is smooth. Stir in the chutney until it is evenly distributed throughout.
5. Stir the dressing into the rice mixture. Refrigerate the salad until you're ready to serve it.
6. Garnish with chopped nuts if desired.

183 CALORIES PER SERVING: 10 G PROTEIN, 3 G FAT, 29 G CARBOHYDRATE; 148 MG SODIUM, 19 MG CHOLESTEROL

Tossed Salad

Tossed green salads are mostly lettuce, so it pays to select the best greens and take care in preparing them. Crispness and true color are the criteria. A head of lettuce is OK if an outside leaf or two is wilted or crumpled, but the inner leaves must be free of dark, mushy spots, limp areas and dull colors. Not only do these blemishes affect the appearance, but they also determine how long the salad stays fresh and how good it tastes.

Once home, the lettuce will wilt, sometimes within a day, depending on how it was handled in the supermarket. This can be frustrating. Having your lettuce go bad before making it into salad is a deterrent to fresh salad-making. A solution is to wash and spin-dry all the leaves as soon as possible. Lettuce leaves that have been washed, dried and properly stored will stay fresh and edible for almost a week. This is very convenient. Store the lettuce in a partly open plastic bag or in the salad spinner in the refrigerator. Crisper drawers are designed especially for vegetables. Use them.

Ignore the debate over whether to cut or tear lettuce. The important thing is not to crush the leaves. Once bruised, the leaves will turn brown. If you have a sharp knife and don't crumple the leaves when you hold them, you can cut the leaves. Tearing them by hand requires gentle treatment too. Hold each leaf with great tenderness. Don't hold and twist, but tear cleanly and with as little creasing of the leaves as possible. You can tear or cut the leaves before you wash them for added convenience, although the edges will brown after two or three days. If the leaves discolor before that, or if the flat, uncut surfaces develop dark lines, the lettuce was handled too harshly.

As a rule of thumb, one head of lettuce makes six servings of a tossed dinner salad. Don't store other vegetables with the lettuce. Moisture from cucumbers and peppers, for example, will wilt the lettuce. You can prepare hard vegetables, such as cabbage, carrots and cauliflower, up to a day ahead of time. Keep them in a bag and toss them into the salad prior to dinner. If the vegetables dry out after a couple of days, you can steam them or use them in soups.

Dressing Salads

The dressing is essential to a salad. It unites the separate vegetables with a common seasoning and visually pulls the salad together with a glistening coating. In rare cases, salad dressings can be made without fat, but most dressings require oil to bind the ingredients together, balance the vinegar and enable the dressing to stick to the salad. Lettuce-based salads are composed of water-filled vegetables, so their dressings contribute most of the calories, which means that there will be a high percentage of fat. Salads with beans, pastas or other carbohydrates are higher in calories, and the percentage of calories that a dressing contributes will be smaller, although the overall fat content might be the same as that of a lettuce salad. Before avoiding a salad because the dressing contains oil, look at the total amount of fat. All the salads in this book have a moderate to low fat content. The dressings themselves are mostly fat, but they are not meant to be eaten alone. As long as dressings are used sparingly in conjunction with the other ingredients, they are worth including in a healthful diet.

Chili Orange Vinaigrette

This spicy salad dressing is wonderful on a tossed salad of romaine, carrots and scallions. Or try it with shredded lettuce and leftover chicken. I've yet to find a chili powder on the supermarket shelves that is worth using. They all taste flat and dull. Instead, I buy chili powder at a local natural food store or gourmet shop. The difference is astonishing.

MAKES ABOUT 1 CUP

⅓ cup	orange juice	1/16 teaspoon	Tabasco or other hot pepper sauce (or more to taste)
¼ cup	apple cider vinegar		
¼ cup	olive or peanut oil	1 clove	garlic, minced (½ teaspoon)
1 teaspoon	chili powder		
⅛ teaspoon	kosher salt (or more if chili powder is no-salt)		

1. Whisk all the ingredients together.
2. Store the dressing in a glass jar in the refrigerator for up to several months.

34 CALORIES PER TABLESPOON: 0 G PROTEIN, 4 G FAT, 1 G CARBOHYDRATE;17 MG SODIUM, 0 MG CHOLESTEROL

Tomato Tarragon Dressing

Using pureed tomatoes cuts the sharp flavor of the vinegar and reduces the amount of oil needed. It also gives the dressing a rosy glow. I use whole canned tomatoes that I blend until smooth. Tomato juice is another possibility, although it is a bit more assertive in flavor and thicker in texture. Don't use crushed canned tomatoes. They are too coarse and have seeds.

MAKES ABOUT 1⅔ CUPS

2	whole canned tomatoes, with juice, about ¾ cup	½ teaspoon	kosher salt
		1½ tablespoon	honey
½ cup	red wine vinegar	1 tablespoon	tarragon
1 tablespoon	Dijon mustard	½ cup	olive oil
⅛ teaspoon	freshly ground pepper		

1. You can make this recipe in the food processor. Start by pureeing the tomatoes and juice. Then pulse in all the remaining ingredients except the oil. Add the oil in a slow, steady stream as the machine is running.

2. Alternatively, you can puree the tomatoes in a blender, then whisk in the remaining ingredients by hand. Make sure the honey is well incorporated and doesn't stay as a lump at the bottom of the bowl.

41 CALORIES PER TABLESPOON: 0 G PROTEIN, 4 G FAT, 2 G CARBOHYDRATE; 52 MG SODIUM, 0 MG CHOLESTEROL

Honey-Poppy Seed Vinaigrette

An excellent dressing on all salads, but it is especially suited for salads with fruit in them, such as Strawberry Spinach Salad (page 34). This is partly because balsamic vinegar heightens the inherent sweetness of fruits and partly because the sharp flavors keep the salad from tasting like dessert. For the best results, use a high-quality red wine vinegar with a pronounced flavor. Cheaper versions won't provide enough balance for the balsamic vinegar and honey.

MAKES ABOUT 1 CUP

¼ cup	balsamic vinegar		⅛ teaspoon	kosher salt
¼ cup	red wine vinegar		¼ cup	olive oil
2 tablespoons	honey		1 tablespoon	poppy seeds
1 teaspoon	Dijon mustard			

1. Whisk together the vinegars, honey, mustard and salt.
2. While continuing to whisk, pour in the oil in a slow, steady stream. Continue whisking until the dressing is thoroughly mixed.
3. Stir in the poppy seeds.
4. Store the dressing in a glass jar in the refrigerator for up to several months.

46 CALORIES PER TABLESPOON: 0 G PROTEIN, 4 G FAT, 3 CARBOHYDRATE; 20 MG SODIUM, 0 MG CHOLESTEROL

Creamy Herb Dressing

I've smoothed this buttermilk dressing out with a little olive oil. The dressing adheres to the salad better and the flavors meld together more cohesively with the addition of the oil. If you have garlic oil in your pantry (see page 138), you can use it instead of olive oil and omit the minced garlic. This will not only reduce the prep work, but the dressing also won't smell so strongly of garlic the second day.

MAKES ABOUT ⅔ CUP

½ cup	buttermilk		¼ teaspoon	kosher salt
1 tablespoon	apple cider vinegar		⅛ teaspoon	celery seed
1 clove	garlic, minced (½ teaspoon)		⅛ teaspoon	freshly ground pepper
1 tablespoon	Dijon mustard		⅛ teaspoon	Tabasco or other hot pepper sauce
2 teaspoons	honey		1 teaspoon	dried fines herbes
1 tablespoon	olive oil			

1. Whisk together all the ingredients. "Fines herbes" is a medley of classic aromatic garden herbs. If you don't have a jar, combine parsley, tarragon and chives, or use other herbs of your choice.
2. Store the dressing in a glass jar in the refrigerator.

20 CALORIES PER TABLESPOON: 0 G PROTEIN, 1 G FAT, 2 G CARBOHYDRATE; 126 MG SODIUM, 0 MG CHOLESTEROL

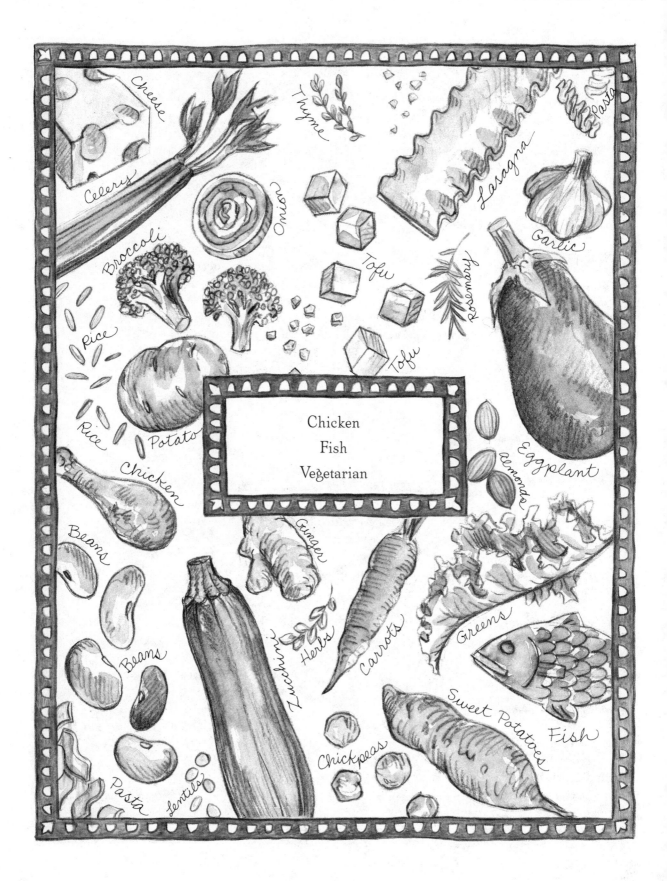

Main Courses

*D*ivisions between courses have become blurred. A soup can be the centerpiece of a meal. A variety of salads, without any being the focal point, can be served to both family and guests. And yet we remain more comfortable with a menu that features a main course. It no longer has to be a large slab of meat, but it does have to be the centerpiece. A bright tomato sauce served over pasta can be a main course, with a green salad and garlic bread to complete the picture. Or spicy beans and rice, complemented with salsa and corn on the cob, make a fine meal. Still, a roasted chicken served with mashed potatoes and steamed broccoli is a timeless classic. You'll find these selections and more in this chapter. Have fun putting your menus together.

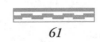

chicken

recipes

Papaya Baked Chicken
Breasts

Tandoori Chicken

Hoisin Chicken

Pecan Baked Chicken

Nutty Honey Chicken

Crusty Horseradish Chicken

Chicken & Rice

Chili Pumpkin Chicken

Lemon Roasted Chicken

Herb Roasted Chicken

Sweet Soy Roasted Chicken

Chicken Roasted with Red
Rubbing Spices

Garlic Chicken

*m*oderate quantities of lean meat fit well within the parameters of a healthy life-style. A person who eats small portions of meat as part of a carbohydrate-and-vegetable-centered diet will be getting plenty of easily assimilated protein and essential nutrients—not to mention the gustatory pleasure that comes from eating a slice of roast chicken. Although some lean red meats are as low in fat as poultry, in *Wholehearted Cooking* I cook only with chicken. This is a personal preference, but there are times when I do eat red meat. I can't pass it up when a nationally sanctioned barbecue cook-off comes to my town, or when a farmer friend offers some home-raised hamburger.

The recipes in this section are meant to be served along with a filling carbohydrate, such as potatoes or pasta, and bright, fresh vegetables or a salad. When the accompanying foods are pleasing to the eye and palate, they become equals on the plate with the meat, and the serving size for meat can be kept to a reasonable and healthy ¼ to ⅓ pound.

About Chicken

Some cuts of red meat are as low-fat as chicken, but with chicken, knowing what is lean is simple; you don't need a label. White breast meat is the lowest in fat (11 percent of calories). Dark meat is higher in fat (around 35 percent) but still within sensible bounds. Most of the fat is in the skin. Fifty percent of the calories in chicken breasts with the skin are from fat, whereas only 11 percent of the calories in skinless breasts come from fat. It's as simple as that. Strip off the skin, and you have low-fat meat.

Buying quality chicken is not so simple. Most supermarket chickens come from one of a handful of large chicken processors. These chickens are raised in crowded conditions, given feed that contains animal by-products (and is thought to carry disease) and fattened quickly, which yields bloated, bland birds. Under these stressful conditions, at least 30 percent of the chickens are given drugs to prevent disease. Seventy to 90 chickens are slaughtered and processed each minute. The U.S. Department of Agriculture (USDA) admits that one-third of the chickens sold are contaminated with salmonella (a bacteria that causes intestinal disruptions, flulike symptoms and other diseases in humans). Other groups claim that 50 to 90 percent are so contaminated. Proper cooking and handling can take care of the salmonella, but nothing can put the texture or flavor back into a bird that has lived a short and unnatural life.

Alternatives are available. Of the four supermarkets within 10 miles of my house, two carry chicken from smaller processors. These chickens have been raised in more spacious surroundings, have been fed whole grains and have been processed and handled with more care. This extra, conscientious effort is reflected in the flavor and price. The feed costs more. Letting the chickens grow at a slower pace costs more. Smaller farms don't have the economy of scale and buying power of the larger processors. Marketing is problematic. It is expensive and difficult for a small producer to get a USDA label that states anything about how the animals were raised or fed. For that rea-

son, the packages might say only "natural," which means nothing, because that label can be used by any processor that doesn't add anything to the meat. Sometimes the term "free-range" is used, meaning that the chickens weren't cramped in cages but were able to run and roost. However, there is no official definition. Some free-range birds are kept indoors; some have outside runs.

Generally, you can recognize good chicken because it costs 20 cents to a dollar more a pound. Yellow skin is not a sign of health, but is caused by a natural dye added to the feed. Ask the meat manager about a particular store's chicken. The manager at my local supermarket says that the free-range chicken tastes so much better that the butchers there cook it for themselves for lunch.

If you can't find this better chicken, use a national brand. You'll have to adjust to poorer texture and flavor. Don't simply roast it. A free-range chicken can taste superb when cooked with minimal treatment, but a national brand needs to be marinated, breaded or seasoned.

Whatever chicken you buy, keep it refrigerated, or freeze it if you won't be using it within two days. Wash it well before cooking. Never contaminate cooked chicken with raw chicken or with the utensils that you have used to handle raw chicken. For example, don't put cooked chicken on the same plate that held the raw bird. Don't leave the chicken unrefrigerated for any length of time. Marinate it in the refrigerator. Keep cooked dishes either hot or chilled.

Cooking chicken is simple, but without the protective and savory layer of skin, the chicken loses both moisture and flavor. Cook chicken with the skin on, then remove the skin prior to eating, or devise alternatives to the skin, such as breading or marinades. Following are a few basic techniques for cooking chicken.

Cooking Chicken

Poaching: Poaching is a gentle way of cooking chicken breasts that yields plump, moist, mild-tasting chicken useful for salads. Fill a pot with enough water, stock or both and a touch of wine to cover the chicken. Bring it to a gentle simmer (not a rolling boil), put in the poultry and cook for about 20 minutes until the meat is white all the way through and feels firm to the touch. Allow the chicken to cool for 10 minutes in the poaching liquid before serving or chilling it. You may boil the liquid down further to concentrate the flavors and make stock. Stews are a modified form of poaching in which the chicken is simmered at length with many ingredients and seasonings, which infuse the meat with flavor.

Baking and Roasting: Chicken can be baked plain, with the skin left on to keep the flesh moist. Once the skin is removed and discarded (or given to a grateful dog), however, the chicken tastes bland. Skinless chicken can be breaded to keep the meat moist and to add flavor. Or chicken with its skin can be prepared with marinades or spice rubs, which give the chicken flavor even when the skin is discarded. Bake chicken in a moderate oven, between 350 and 375 degrees F. Cook until the meat feels firm to the touch and is the same color throughout. Timing varies. Small pieces of boneless chicken breast will take 15 minutes, chicken thighs 40 minutes. Do not use clear glass dishes because the chicken will dry out.

Roasting is similar to baking, but the term is usually applied to whole birds or quarters, which take longer to bake than individual pieces. See "Roasting Chicken" on page 73.

Grilling and Broiling: Grilling and broiling are very hot and rapid methods in which the chicken cooks close to or on a direct heat source such as a flame or heating element. Both produce a flavorful, attractive exterior. Grill lines and brown skin are savory, but charred chicken is not. This works only with smaller cuts of meat that cook quickly, since a large piece will burn or dry out on the outside before it is done on the inside. Marinate the chicken before broiling or grilling, then baste it with liquid once or twice during cooking. Turn the meat over halfway through so that both sides get the benefits of being near the heat.

Chicken Terminology

A *broiler* weighs under 2½ pounds. A *fryer* weighs 2½ to 3½ pounds. Both are young and tender and can be cooked any way you like.

A *roaster* weighs up to 5 pounds and is ideal for roasting, but it also can be cut up and used for any of the recipes in this book.

A *stewing chicken* is an older, tougher bird that needs to be cooked at length in moist heat. It is a good choice for stock and old-fashioned, long-simmering chicken soup.

Serving Sizes

A moderate serving size is 4 to 6 ounces of cooked meat. Since each boneless, skinless chicken breast is about 1 to 1½ pounds, one whole breast will serve 3 to 4. Of an entire chicken, including bones and skin, slightly less than half is edible meat, so figure that a 4-pound roaster will feed 4. But that's without leftovers, and I can't imagine roasting a bird and not having leftovers the next day.

Papaya Baked Chicken Breasts

Papayas blend well with savory seasonings. In this case, the papaya forms a base for a thyme-in-fused marinade. Ripe papayas are slightly firm to the touch and mottled orange in color. They have much more flavor than the harder yellow ones. Papayas that have some orange color will ripen if left out on the counter.

SERVES 6 TO 8

1	ripe papaya
2 cloves	garlic
1	shallot, peeled
¼ cup	orange juice
¾ cup	defatted chicken stock
2 tablespoons	lemon juice
½ teaspoon	thyme

¼ teaspoon	dry mustard
¼ teaspoon	kosher salt
1 teaspoon	soy sauce
¼ teaspoon	freshly ground pepper
6 to 8	skinless chicken breast halves, with or without bones

1. Scoop out and discard the papaya's black seeds. Peel off the skin and cut the fruit into quarters.
2. In a processor, mince the garlic and shallot. Add the papaya and pulse until it is chopped. Add all the remaining ingredients except the chicken. Puree until smooth.
3. Transfer the marinade to a glass or stainless steel bowl. Add the chicken, turning the pieces until they are well coated. Marinate for 4 hours to 1 day. Turn the chicken occasionally. The marinade will solidify in the refrigerator.
4. Preheat the oven to 350 degrees F, or prepare your grill.
5. Take the chicken out of the marinade and shake off any excess papaya.
6. If baking, place the breasts in a heavy casserole. Brush the marinade onto the chicken so that it covers the chicken evenly with a ¼-inch-thick coating. Bake until done. Boneless pieces will take about 25 to 30 minutes; those with the bones will take 35 to 45 minutes, depending on the thickness.
7. If grilling, brush the chicken with the marinade, but do not coat it thickly. Turn the pieces once during cooking. The charred flavor and aroma from grilling bring out the best in this recipe.

165 CALORIES PER SERVING: 28 G PROTEIN, 3 G FAT, 5 G CARBOHYDRATE; 207 MG SODIUM, 73 MG CHOLESTEROL

Tandoori Chicken

Cooking chicken without the skin often results in dried-out, rubbery meat. But the chicken in this dish is moist, tender and flavorful because it is marinated in yogurt and then baked at a high temperature. In India, this is done in a large clay oven called a tandoor. This traditional oven adds a dimension to the chicken's flavor that can't be reproduced, but this recipe stands on its own merits.

SERVES 4 TO 6

2 pounds	skinless chicken parts, with bones		2 cloves	garlic, minced (1 teaspoon)
1 teaspoon	kosher salt		2 teaspoons	minced fresh gingerroot
2 tablespoons	lemon juice		2-3 teaspoons	mild curry powder
½ cup	low-fat yogurt		¼ teaspoon	ground chili pepper (optional)
1 tablespoon	apple cider vinegar			

1. Wash the chicken, then pat it dry.
2. Make ½-inch cuts in each chicken part.
3. Sprinkle the chicken with the salt, then 1 tablespoon of the lemon juice. Rub the salt and juice into the meat.
4. Combine the yogurt, remaining tablespoon of lemon juice and remaining ingredients in a glass or stainless-steel bowl.
5. Marinate the chicken in the yogurt mixture. Turn the pieces several times to make sure they are well coated. Leave the chicken in the marinade for at least several hours, preferably an entire day. Keep covered and refrigerated.

6. Preheat the broiler or grill. Remove the chicken from the marinade and shake off any excess, allowing some marinade to cling to the meat.
7. Place the chicken on the oven rack or grill. Cook for 7 to 10 minutes. Turn the chicken, then continue cooking for about 10 to 15 minutes more until done.

204 CALORIES PER SERVING: 35 G PROTEIN, 4 G FAT, 4 G CARBOHYDRATE; 570 MG SODIUM, 93 MG CHOLESTEROL

Hoisin Chicken

Hoisin sauce is a dark paste of fermented soybeans sweetened with sugar and flavored with chili, sesame oil and other seasonings. Used in marinades and dipping sauces, it adds a complex sweet-and-salty flavor to foods. Hoisin sauce is available in the specialty foods section of your supermarket (look near the soy sauce) and in most Asian markets. Once opened, it lasts indefinitely in the refrigerator.

SERVES 6

1 teaspoon	soy sauce	2 cloves	garlic, minced (1 teaspoon) (optional)
1 teaspoon	honey		
3 tablespoons	hoisin sauce	3 pounds	skinless chicken parts, preferably with bones
2 tablespoons	sherry		
1 teaspoon	grated fresh gingerroot (optional)		

1. Combine all the ingredients except the chicken in a bowl. The garlic and ginger are optional.
2. Generously coat the chicken with the hoisin mixture. Place the pieces in a stainless steel or glass bowl, cover and refrigerate. Reserve any extra marinade for basting later. Let the chicken marinate a few minutes to several hours. Obviously, the longer the chicken has to absorb in the sauce, the deeper the flavor penetrates. However, I find that soy marinades toughen chicken if left for more than a day.
3. Preheat the oven to 350 degrees F. Brush off excess sauce. Place the chicken pieces in a baking dish. Bake for 35 to 40 minutes, depending on the type of chicken part. Brush the chicken with the reserved marinade every 10 minutes or so. Basting heightens the flavor and keeps the chicken from drying out.

197 CALORIES PER SERVING: 34 G PROTEIN, 4 G FAT, 3 G CARBOHYDRATE; 481 MG SODIUM, 91 MG CHOLESTEROL

When is the Meat Done?

*P*rofessional chefs check to see whether meat is fully cooked by feeling it rather than cutting into it with a knife, which releases some of the juices and mars the appearance. As meat cooks, it gets firmer and more resilient, until it becomes overcooked and hard. These stages feel different to a light touch with a finger. Chicken cooked through but still moist feels just like the inside of your wrist. Medium-rare meat feels like the lower left padding on the inside of your right hand. Raw meat feels like that fleshy area right below your thumb. This technique really works. With a little practice, you can rely on this method too. While you're practicing, test the chicken both by making a slight cut and looking at the color and then by feeling it. Soon you will be able to rely solely on touch.

Pecan Baked Chicken

There are pecan trees on my husband's family's farm in Alabama. We picked, shelled and froze pounds and pounds of pecans one December, and I have been finding ways to use them in my recipes ever since. This one is so convenient that I make it several times a month. It works great with boneless breasts, but I often use the less expensive and more flavorful bone-in chicken pieces. You can make breadcrumbs from your favorite whole-wheat bread by grinding stale bread in the food processor. Homemade breadcrumbs usually come out thicker and softer than commercial breadcrumbs. Either type works nicely in this recipe.

SERVES 4

½ cup   ground or finely chopped pecans
½ cup   breadcrumbs, preferably whole
         wheat
¼ teaspoon   kosher salt

¼ teaspoon   freshly ground pepper
½ cup   buttermilk
2 pounds   skinless chicken parts, with or
            without bones

1. Preheat the oven to 350 degrees F.
2. On a plate, mix together the pecans, bread-crumbs, salt and pepper.
3. Pour the buttermilk into a bowl. Thoroughly coat the chicken with buttermilk.
4. Roll the chicken in the pecan mixture. Gently shake off excess. Place the chicken pieces in a casserole or baking pan. It does not have to be greased, although a light coating with a nonstick spray will prevent the minor sticking that might occur. Do not crowd the pieces together, or the coating will become soggy. The amount of breading needed for this recipe varies depending on the size of the chicken pieces. Small pieces of chicken have more surface area and will need more breading.
5. Bake, uncovered for 25 to 50 minutes, depending on the thickness of the chicken.

329 CALORIES PER SERVING: 37 G PROTEIN, 14 G FAT, 13 G CARBOHYDRATE; 321 MG SODIUM, 93 MG CHOLESTEROL

Nutty Honey Chicken

These chicken pieces are seasoned with the tang of mustard and the sweetness of honey and are wrapped in a crunchy coating. Nutty Honey Chicken can be part of a main-dish supper or served as an hors d'oeuvre. The amount of chicken you use depends on the cut you buy. This recipe makes enough to coat 12 chicken legs or 2 whole chicken breasts (cut into 24 strips for party food or 4 dinner servings).

SERVES 4

¼ cup	honey
2 tablespoons	Dijon mustard
1 tablespoon	soy sauce
½ cup	chopped pecans or other nuts

½ cup	breadcrumbs, preferably whole wheat
2 pounds	skinless chicken parts, cut according to your needs

1. Preheat the oven to 350 degrees F. Line a non-stick baking pan with parchment paper or use a nonstick spray.
2. Combine the honey, mustard and soy sauce in a bowl.
3. Toss the nuts and breadcrumbs together on a plate.
4. Brush each piece of chicken with the sauce, then roll it in the crumb mixture. Gently shake off the excess. Place the pieces on the baking pan. Do not bread the chicken ahead of time, or the breading will become soggy.
5. If you're using chicken strips for hors d'oeuvres, you might want to put them on skewers. Soak wooden skewers in water for about 30 minutes. Then, after breading the chicken, thread the skewer through the meat, using about three loops so that each piece is well secured.
6. Bake for 40 to 50 minutes for drumsticks and thighs, 25 to 30 minutes for large portions of boneless chicken or 12 minutes for boneless strips.

357 CALORIES PER SERVING: 36 G PROTEIN, 14 G FAT, 23 G CARBOHYDRATE; 468 MG SODIUM, 91 MG CHOLESTEROL

Crusty Horseradish Chicken

This recipe proves that a simply prepared entrée can have terrific flavor and texture. Homemade breadcrumbs will result in a softer, less crusty coating. I like this chicken with either homemade or store-bought crumbs, although I always use homemade if I have them in the cupboard.

SERVES 4

1 pound	boneless, skinless chicken breast
¾ cup	breadcrumbs, preferably whole wheat
¼ teaspoon	kosher salt
¼ teaspoon	freshly ground pepper

2 tablespoons	prepared white horseradish (usually found in the dairy case)
1 tablespoon	Dijon mustard
¼ cup	white wine

1. Preheat the oven to 350 degrees F.
2. Trim all the fat off the chicken. Cut the meat into 4 portions.
3. On a plate, mix together the bread crumbs, salt and pepper.
4. In a bowl, stir together the horseradish, mustard and wine.
5. Dip the chicken in the horseradish mixture until it is well coated. You can let it marinate for up to 1 hour.
6. Roll the chicken, piece by piece, in the breadcrumbs to form an even coating. Gently shake off any excess. Place the pieces in a casserole (any material except glass). Don't let the chicken pieces touch. I like to use metal salad bar tongs for these steps. They ease the preparation by keeping my fingers from getting sticky.
7. Bake, uncovered, for 25 to 30 minutes until the chicken feels firm to the touch.

227 CALORIES PER PERSON: 36 G PROTEIN, 5 G FAT, 5 G CARBOHYDRATE; 378 MG SODIUM, 96 MG CHOLESTEROL

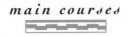

Chicken & Rice

There are as many versions of this dish as there are cultures that eat chicken and rice. Although my recipe has Spanish overtones, it is not a classic paella.

SERVES 6

2 teaspoons	olive oil
2½ pounds	skinless chicken pieces, with bones
1	green bell pepper, cut into 1-inch pieces
2 cloves	garlic, minced (1 teaspoon)
1	medium yellow onion, chopped (1 cup)
1 cup	uncooked brown rice
2 cups	defatted chicken stock

1½ cups	canned whole tomatoes, with juice
2 tablespoons	minced fresh parsley
1 teaspoon	paprika
½ teaspoon	kosher salt
¼ teaspoon	freshly ground pepper
1 teaspoon	thyme
2 teaspoons	basil
¼ teaspoon	Tabasco or other hot pepper sauce (optional)

1. This recipe starts on the stove top and ends up in the oven. If you have a large Dutch oven, you can use one pan for all the steps. Otherwise, use a separate saucepan for the first three steps, then transfer the mixture to a casserole. To start, heat 1 teaspoon of the oil in a large saucepan. Brown the chicken pieces in it. Remove the chicken to a plate.
2. Add the remaining teaspoon of oil. Sauté the pepper, garlic and onion in the oil until the onion is golden.
3. Put all the remaining ingredients, except the chicken, in this pan. Cover and simmer for 25 minutes, stirring occasionally. Break the tomatoes into pieces as you stir.
4. Preheat the oven to 350 degrees F.
5. Put the contents of the saucepan into a heavy casserole or large Dutch oven (clear glass will not work). Add the chicken. Stir once. Cover and bake for 40 minutes.

314 CALORIES PER SERVING: 32 G PROTEIN, 6 G FAT, 31 G CARBOHYDRATE; 343 MG SODIUM, 76 MG CHOLESTEROL

Chili Pumpkin Chicken

Serve this in a pumpkin tureen (page 25) for a harvest celebration. I use a mild chili powder and spice up the recipe with extra pure ground chili. Each brand of chili powder is different. If you are not familiar with your chili powder, add half, then taste and adjust the seasoning.

SERVES 6

1 2-pound	sugar pumpkin (or 4-5 cups cubed pumpkin or other winter squash)
1 tablespoon	vegetable oil
2	large yellow onions, chopped (about 2½ cups)
3 cloves	garlic, minced (1½ teaspoons)
½	green bell pepper, chopped (½ cup)
1 rib	celery, chopped
1 pound	boneless, skinless chicken breasts
2 cups	defatted chicken stock
1 14-ounce can	whole tomatoes
⅔ cup	pitted prunes
½ cup	dried apricots
⅛ teaspoon	ground chili pepper
1½ tablespoons	chili powder
½-1 teaspoon	kosher salt (depending on whether chili powder is salt free)
½ cup	roasted pumpkin seeds for garnish (optional)

1. Peel and cut the pumpkin into cubes. (See the suggestions for doing this on page 175.) Save the seeds to roast for garnish.
2. Heat the oil in a sauté pan. Sauté the onion, garlic, green pepper and celery in the oil for 7 to 10 minutes. Cover so that the steam from the vegetables helps them to cook.
3. Add the chicken to the vegetables. Stir and cook until the meat is white on all sides.
4. Add the pumpkin, stock, tomatoes, dried fruit and spices. Simmer, uncovered, for 20 minutes.
5. Garnish with roasted pumpkin seeds if desired.

280 CALORIES PER SERVING: 26 G PROTEIN, 6 G FAT, 34 G CARBOHYDRATE; 360 MG SODIUM, 58 MG CHOLESTEROL

Roasting Chicken

Roasted chicken suits most occasions, from casual dinners to buffet picnics to celebratory meals. Served hot, it reminds us of family gatherings around the Sunday table (even when carved for two on a Tuesday night). Served cold, it fits into any schedule and is especially convenient for families that don't all eat at the same time. Few leftovers are better than a chicken carcass in the refrigerator with enough meat to make a sandwich or salad. In the end, you can use the bones to make stock or soup.

Here is a foolproof method of roasting chicken. First, prepare the bird by removing whatever internal organs are wrapped and tucked inside. Then wash the chicken well and pat it dry. Cut off the fatty tail and other pieces of excess fat or skin that extend beyond the meat. Also cut off the last joint of the wing if it hasn't already been done by your butcher. Season the bird according to whichever recipe you choose. Trussing the bird (tying the legs together) is not necessary as long as there isn't any stuffing to hold in place. Besides, it brings the legs closer to the body, which means they will take even longer to cook. Too long, in fact, as the breast will dry out before the leg meat is done. Put the chicken in a roasting pan, breast side up. Use a roasting rack to support the meat above the bottom of the pan. It allows air to circulate, which decreases cooking time and keeps the bird from sitting in its own fat.

Start the chicken in a very hot (425 degree F) oven. This crisps the skin and reduces the overall cooking time. After 20 minutes, reduce the oven temperature to 350 degrees F. If the skin browns too quickly, tent a piece of foil over the bird.

Roasting time is easy to calculate. Figure on about 20 minutes per pound for birds under 3 pounds and 15 minutes per pound for larger birds. (This does not apply to stuffed chicken, which takes longer to cook and should be roasted at a lower temperature. Because I almost never stuff poultry, I haven't included directions for it in this book.)

Use of a meat thermometer is often recommended. When it reaches 165 degrees F, the chicken is fully cooked. However, I find that a thermometer is inaccurate in small birds and indicates a high temperature before the chicken is thoroughly cooked. I've also noticed that if the thermometer is not placed carefully in a thick part of the breast or thigh, it will give an inaccurate reading in a large bird. Pop-up thermometers also are not accurate. It is better to rely on visual clues. The chicken is cooked through when the leg joint moves easily and clear juices run out of a test cut near the thigh.

Baste the birds with pan juices, a marinade or oil to keep the meat moist and the skin shiny. A pastry brush is a good basting tool. It is necessary to baste poultry only a couple of times during roasting. If you remove the skin after roasting, basting will not add fat. It does not, however, impart as much flavor as marinating, rubbing spices under the skin or filling the cavity with herbs, vegetables or fruits.

After roasting, let the chicken rest in its pan for 15 minutes. Don't worry, it won't get cold. But the meat will be easier to carve.

Lemon Roasted Chicken

This is about as simple and delicious as it gets.

SERVES 4

1	whole chicken, preferably a free-range bird		kosher salt
1	lemon wedge or slice		freshly ground pepper
1 or 2 cloves	garlic, peeled and crushed		olive oil

1. Preheat the oven to 425 degree F.
2. Wash and prepare the bird as explained on page 73. Rub the chicken with the lemon and garlic cloves, then put the lemon and garlic in the cavity. Rub with salt and pepper. Use these seasonings sparingly.
3. Place the bird, breast side up, on a rack in a roasting pan.
4. Put the pan in the oven. If the chicken browns unevenly, rotate the pan a few times during roasting. Baste once with olive oil.
5. After 20 minutes, reduce the temperature to 350 degrees F. Continue to cook until the bird's joints are loose and its juices run clear. The average 3-pound fryer will take about 1 hour.
6. Remove the bird from the oven and let it rest for 15 minutes before carving.

333 CALORIES PER SERVING (WITHOUT SKIN): 50 G PROTEIN, 13 G FAT, 0 G CARBOHYDRATE; 383 MG SODIUM, 154 MG CHOLESTEROL

 page 63

Herb Roasted Chicken

When you fill the cavity of a chicken with aromatic and savory herbs, just the smell of the bird roasting is enough to call people to the kitchen in anticipation of dinner. The amount of herbs should suit all but the smallest broilers, which will have room for half the amount.

SERVES 4

1	whole chicken	1	small yellow onion, peeled and cut in half
½ cup	fresh parsley leaves		kosher salt
1 sprig	fresh thyme, or ½ tablespoon dried		freshly ground pepper
1 long sprig	fresh rosemary, or 1 tablespoon dried	½ teaspoon	paprika
			olive oil (optional)

Follow cooking instructions above.

336 CALORIES PER SERVING (WITHOUT SKIN): 50 G PROTEIN, 13 G FAT, 2 G CARBOHYDRATE; 270 MG SODIUM, 154 MG CHOLESTEROL

Sweet Soy Roasted Chicken

This marinade permeates the chicken before roasting. The result is a bird that is aromatic, moist and flavored to the bone. The chicken doesn't need to sit in the soy-based liquid for more than 1 hour, although 4 hours is ideal. Any longer than that, and the sauce will change the meat's texture.

SERVES 4

1	whole chicken		2 tablespoons	sherry
¼ cup	soy sauce		1 tablespoon	minced garlic
¼ cup	rice or white wine vinegar		1 tablespoon	minced gingerroot
2 tablespoons	honey		1 teaspoon	ground Sichuan peppercorns

1. Wash and prepare the bird as explained on page 73.
2. In a bowl large enough to hold the bird, combine the remaining ingredients.
3. Place the chicken in the bowl. Turn several times so that the color of the marinade darkens the entire bird. Cover the bowl and put it in the refrigerator.
4. Marinate the chicken for 1 to 4 hours. Turn the bird several times so that it evenly takes on the color of the marinade.
5. Preheat the oven to 425 degrees F.
6. Remove the chicken from the marinade. With a pastry brush, remove most of the bits of garlic and ginger sticking to the bird.
7. The marinade will stick to the roasting pan and burn, so either use a nonstick pan, line the pan with parchment paper or coat the pan with a nonstick spray. Place the bird, breast side up, on a rack in the pan.
8. Put the pan in the oven. If the chicken browns unevenly, rotate the pan a few times during roasting.
9. After 20 minutes, reduce the temperature to 350 degrees F. After the skin begins to crisp, tent with foil and brush with the marinade every 20 to 30 minutes to prevent the skin from cracking and scorching.
10. Remove the bird from the oven and let it rest for 15 minutes before carving.

382 CALORIES PER SERVING (WITHOUT SKIN): 51 G PROTEIN, 13 G FAT, 12 G CARBOHYDRATE; 1178 MG SODIUM, 154 MG CHOLESTEROL

Chicken Roasted with Red Rubbing Spices

This spice blend colors the chicken a warm brick red, with an equally warm flavor. Rub the spices on the skin, or under the skin or on chicken without the skin. I've tried it all three ways. Rubbing the spices on the meat itself has more of an impact on the flavor. These spices can be used for roasting chicken parts as well as whole birds. Save any extra spice blend in a glass jar in your cupboard. This recipe makes enough for several roasters.

SERVES 4

1 teaspoon	paprika
1 teaspoon	ground cumin
1 teaspoon	ground coriander
1 tablespoon	mild chili powder
¼ teaspoon	ground cinnamon
¹⁄₁₆ teaspoon	cayenne pepper
¼ teaspoon	kosher salt
1	whole chicken
	olive oil (optional)

1. Preheat the oven to 425 degrees F.
2. Stir all the spices together until the color is even throughout.
3. Wash and prepare the bird as explained on page 73.
4. Dust the chicken with the spice blend. Rub it in with your fingers. If desired, rub it on the meat under the skin.
5. Place the bird, breast side up, on a rack in a roasting pan
6. Put the pan in the oven. If the chicken browns unevenly, rotate the pan a few times during roasting.
7. After 20 minutes, reduce the temperature to 350 degrees F. After the chicken begins to crisp, tent with foil and baste with olive oil or pan juices every 20 minutes to prevent the spices from scorching. Continue to cook until the bird's joints are loose and its juices run clear. The average 3-pound fryer will take about 1 hour.
8. Remove the bird from the oven and let it rest for 15 minutes before carving.

333 CALORIES PER SERVING (WITHOUT SKIN): 50 G PROTEIN, 13 G FAT, 1 G CARBOHYDRATE; 218 MG SODIUM, 154 MG CHOLESTEROL

Garlic Chicken

The garlic cooked under the skin and in the pan juices loses its sharpness and becomes as spreadable as butter. The chicken skin keeps the moisture in, but as always, it's best to remove the skin to reduce your fat intake.

SERVES 4

1	whole chicken	½ cup	fresh parsley leaves
	kosher salt	1 teaspoon	thyme
	freshly ground pepper	2	bay leaves
2 bulbs	garlic	2 tablespoons	red wine vinegar
1	medium yellow onion, sliced (1 cup)	½ cup	white wine

1. Preheat the oven to 425 degrees F.
2. Wash and prepare the bird as explained on page 73. Rub it with salt and pepper.
3. Break the garlic bulbs into cloves. Peel one bulb.
4. Put the unpeeled garlic, one onion half and the parsley and thyme in the cavity.
5. Slice 4 large cloves of garlic. Cut small slits in the chicken skin and insert slide the sliced garlic under the skin.
6. Put the chicken in a roasting pan. Put the remaining onion half and peeled garlic around the bird. Add the bay leaves. Pour in the vinegar and wine.

7. Put the pan in the oven. If the chicken browns unevenly, rotate the pan a few times during roasting. Baste the bird once with the pan juices.
8. After 20 minutes, reduce the temperature to 350 degrees F. Continue to cook, basting the bird every 20 minutes, until the bird's joints are loose and its juices run clear. The average 3-pound fryer will take about 1 hour.
9. Remove the bird from the oven and let it rest for 15 minutes before carving.

378 CALORIES PER SERVING (WITHOUT SKIN): 51 G PROTEIN, 13 G FAT, 8 G CARBOHYDRATE; 391 MG SODIUM, 154 MG CHOLESTEROL

fish

recipes

Poached Fish with Herbs

Dill Poached Fish

Fish Baked with Mint

Orange Herb Fish

Golden Fish

Lime Thyme Fish

Pan-Cooked Fish Fillets

Fish in a Pot

*r*ecently much has been made of the health bene-fits of eating fish. Not only are most varieties low in fat, but the oilier fishes have essential nutri-ents that might fight disease. Even shellfish are con-sidered beneficial. All are so low-fat that despite the fact that some contain cholesterol, the overall picture is quite healthful. You won't find any shellfish in *Wholehearted Cooking,* though, because I'm allergic to them and couldn't test any recipes.

One-third pound of dressed (eviscerated and boned) fish will generously serve one person. But ⅓ pound still leaves a lot of room on the dinner plate. Fill it up with rice pilaf or oven-roasted potatoes, one or more vegetable side dishes and a basket of bread.

About Fish

Although fresh fish is now transported great dis-tances, it is still mainly regional and seasonal in sup-ply. Fish can be divided into two categories: white-fleshed fish and oily, darker fish. Within the two broad categories is a wide range of fish, each varying subtly from the other. Although we are most familiar with varieties such as flounder, bluefish, tuna and salmon, less widely known fish often are less expensive and fresher. To complicate matters further, the same fish might be called by different names in different parts of the country. When buying fish for dinner, don't just ask for the fish the recipe calls for; instead, ask your fishmonger which fish available that day is right for the dish you want to prepare.

Fish is highly perishable, and if it's not handled properly every step of the way, it will arrive in your home smelly, bruised and unfit for consumption. Buying from a fishmonger you trust assures you of quality fish, but it helps to be able to recognize fresh fish yourself.

Fish should smell faintly of the sea (if a saltwater variety) or of clean water (if a freshwater fish). It should never smell overtly fishy. Look for flesh that is shiny, moist and free of yellowed edges and bruises. Avoid fish that is sitting in melting ice water. Rather, buy fish that is displayed on ice or in a cooler. Ask the seller when the fish arrived in the store. Don't buy fish that is more than two days old, and use the fish within a day of purchasing it.

Cooking Fish

To cruise buoyantly through water and dart speedily ahead, a fish has short bundles of muscles (and very little fat) held together by thin connective tissue. This gives fish a delicate texture, but it also makes it susceptible to overcooking, as it falls apart easily and dries out quickly .

There are several ways to cook fish. With all of them, it is important to handle the fish as little as possible so as to keep the portion whole. Don't turn the fish over while it is cooking, or if you have to, flip it only once. If you can, serve the fish in the dish in which it was cooked, or transfer each portion directly to dinner plates. Another hint that works for all recipes is to slash the skin (if there is any) in a couple of places so that as the fish shrinks during cooking, it will stay flat.

Some people swear by the suggestion to cook fish 10 minutes per inch of thickness, but I find that awkward, as most fish is less than 1 inch thick, and figuring what to do with a ⅜-inch fillet is frustrating. Instead, I rely on color and feel, as I do with all my cooking, and it works fine. The inch rule does help, however, as a reminder of how fast fish cooks. The fish is done when the exterior and the interior take on the same opaque hue, when a knife can be inserted easily between the muscles and when the fish feels slightly firm to the touch (not rubbery as it does when raw).

If your fillet tapers to a thin end, tuck that piece under so that the end is as thick as the rest of the fish, and the fish will cook evenly. Fish will continue to cook away from the oven because the baking dish retains heat. If you're not sure whether the fish is done, remove it from the heat source and let it rest a few minutes before serving.

Note that all the recipes in this book call for already dressed (eviscerated and scaled) fillets or steaks. This is for convenience: You can get exactly the serving size you want with little waste and no fuss.

Following are several of the most common methods used to cook fish.

Poaching: Poaching is a technique in which the fish is partially submerged in gently simmering liquid (either water, lemon juice and wine, stock or a combination) and cooked until the translucent flesh turns opaque and begins to firm up. Cooking in a liquid ensures moist fish, but the fish can still overcook, especially if the water is boiling hard instead of simmering or if you're cooking a thin fillet.

When poaching fish, decide on the amount of liquid you need according to the size of the pan and the piece of fish. Bring it to a steady simmer (the type where a few bubbles rise to the surface), then gently ease the fish in. Cover the pan and continue to simmer until the fish changes to the same color throughout. As soon as the fish is done, or even a few minutes before, remove it from the poaching liquid, or it will continue to cook in the hot bath.

Poaching is suited for firm-fleshed fish, such as sole. It is not good for fish that falls apart easily, such as hake.

A modified form of poaching is used when making a fish stew. Even in stews, though, you should guard against overcooking by making the broth and vegetables, and then adding the fish at the last minute.

Baking: Baking often yields undercooked fish with dried-out edges. Because of this, I always bake fish on top of a moist bed of vegetables, liquid or both. The liquid keeps the exterior of the fish moist as the interior cooks. This gives you a margin for error in judging cooking time because an extra 2 minutes won't dry out the fish. It also imparts flavor. Bake in a preheated 350 degree F oven in a pan that is a good, even conductor of heat (don't use clear glass or thin metal). Baking is suitable for most types of fish.

Broiling and Grilling: These two methods cook fish near or on high, intense heat. Use the same size fillets, and make sure they are thin enough that they can cook evenly all the way through. Otherwise, the exterior will dry out well before the interior is done. Err on the side of underdone. Heat from the baking pan and from the exterior of the fish will finish the job in a few minutes. Restaurants are able to broil thick pieces of haddock because they melt copious amounts of butter on the fish as it quickly cooks under the flames of their commercial broilers, which can reach 800 to 1,000 degrees F. This is not possible or healthful for the home cook. However, an oil-based marinade and a preheated oven or grill will keep the fish moist and flavorful.

Panfrying: Panfrying is like sautéing, in that the food is cooked in a thin sheen of oil in a pan. This works only with very thin fillets dredged (lightly dusted) with flour and seasonings. Dredging is a way to apply seasonings, keep the fish from getting oily and create a nice, thin crust. Cooking takes only a minute or two. The fish is turned once.

Poached Fish with Herbs

Nothing is simpler than poaching fish on top of the stove. For those who like mild seasonings, the cooking technique and herbs in this recipe are just right. Fresh herbs are a necessity for poached fish.

SERVES 2

⅔-pound	white-fleshed fish fillets	2 tablespoons	lemon juice
⅛ teaspoon	kosher salt	2-inch sprig	fresh tarragon
⅛ teaspoon	pepper	1 tablespoon	minced fresh chives
¼ cup	white wine		

1. Rub the fish with the salt and pepper.
2. Combine the wine and lemon juice. Pour enough in a pan so that it will come halfway up the fish. The amount of liquid needed is determined by the size of the pan and the thickness of the fish. If your pan is large, you might need more than indicated.
3. Bring the wine and lemon juice to a simmer.
4. Add the fish, put the tarragon to one side and distribute the chives on top of the fish, with a bit in the poaching liquid.
5. Cover the pan and simmer very gently (a few slowly rising bubbles) until the fish is done. For a thin flounder fillet, this will take less than 4 minutes; for a thicker piece of haddock, it will take about 6 minutes. The fish is done when it "flakes" (but not to the point that it falls apart) and is opaque throughout.

151 CALORIES PER SERVING: 29 G PROTEIN, 2 G FAT, 1 G CARBOHYDRATE; 242 MG SODIUM, 81 MG CHOLESTEROL

Dill Poached Fish

The flavor of this fish is gentle but clear. Please use fresh dill. If it's not available, a few sprigs of parsley will work, but the dish will taste different.

SERVES 2 TO 4

⅔-1⅓ pounds	fish fillets
¼ teaspoon	kosher salt
⅛ teaspoon	freshly ground pepper
½ cup	white wine
¼ cup	lemon juice
4-inch sprig	fresh dill
1	shallot peeled and crushed
½ teaspoon	minced fresh dill for garnish

1. Rub the fish with the salt and pepper.
2. Combine the wine and lemon juice. Pour enough in a pan so that it will come two-thirds of the way up the fish. If you have some of the liquid left over, save it for another dinner.
3. Put the dill and shallot in the pan. Bring the liquid to a simmer and let it cook, covered, for 5 minutes before adding the fish. This is to infuse the cooking liquid with the herb and shallot flavors.
4. Before adding the fish, make sure the liquid is simmering very gently. Place the fish on top of the dill.
5. Cover the pan and simmer gently until the fish is done. This will vary with the thickness of the fish. A thin sole fillet will take about 3 minutes; a thicker fillet will take longer.
6. Transfer the fish directly from the saucepan to the dinner plates. Garnish with fresh dill.

133 CALORIES PER SERVING: 25 G PROTEIN, 2 G FAT, 0 G CARBOHYDRATE; 346 MG SODIUM, 71 MG CHOLESTEROL

Fish Baked with Mint

Baking fish on a bed of mint infuses the fish with a fresh and fragrant flavor. This recipe also calls for garlic, red onion (for color and sweetness), hot pepper (for a sharp contrast), balsamic vinegar (to heighten the flavors), and capers and lemon juice (because they have a natural place in fish dishes).

SERVES 2 TO 4

½ cup	fresh mint leaves	¹⁄₁₆ teaspoon	freshly ground pepper
½	red onion, peeled and sliced into rounds	¹⁄₁₆ teaspoon	red pepper flakes (optional)
2 cloves	garlic, minced (1 teaspoon)	1 tablespoon	balsamic vinegar
⅔-1⅓ pounds	thick fish fillet or steak, such as swordfish	2 tablespoons	lemon juice
		3 tablespoons	white wine
¹⁄₁₆ teaspoon	salt	1 tablespoon	capers

1. Preheat the oven to 425 degrees F.
2. Line the bottom of a baking dish with the mint leaves. For an attractive presentation, overlap the leaves so that they are layered like fish scales.
3. Place the onion rounds on top of the mint. Scatter the garlic over them.

4. Rinse the fish in water, then pat dry with a towel. Rub on the salt, pepper and red pepper flakes. Place the fish on top of the onion.
5. Combine the vinegar, lemon juice, wine and capers. Pour the mixture over the fish.
6. Bake for 10 to 20 minutes depending on the thickness of the fish and type of baking dish used.

237 CALORIES PER SERVING: 31 G PROTEIN, 6 G FAT, 9 G CARBOHYDRATE; 301 MG SODIUM, 60 MG CHOLESTEROL

Orange Herb Fish

Fish isn't tricky to cook if you bake it in a fragrant marinade. The liquid keeps it moist and imparts flavor, and a few minutes either way in the cooking time won't ruin the fish. I like to use a firm-fleshed white fish, such as ocean catfish or haddock. An oily fish, such as bluefish, will overpower the marinade. Also, fresh rosemary adds an aromatic piquancy, but if you can't find fresh rosemary, use 1 teaspoon of dried.

SERVES 6

½ cup	orange juice		¹⁄₁₆ teaspoon	cayenne pepper
⅓ cup	white wine		½ teaspoon	paprika
¼ cup	lemon juice		1 tablespoon	chopped fresh rosemary
1	large shallot, peeled and sliced		2 tablespoons	chopped fresh parsley
1 teaspoon	orange zest		2 pounds	fish fillets

1. Combine all the ingredients except the fish in a glass or metal bowl (plastic absorbs flavors).
2. Wash the fish, then put it in the marinade. Turn it once or twice so that all sides come in contact with the liquid, or you can submerge it. If you have time and the fillet is thicker than thin flounder, let the fish sit in the marinade for up to 30 minutes.
3. Preheat the oven to 350 degrees F.
4. Place the fish in a baking dish (I prefer white porcelain and avoid clear glass). Pour the marinade over the fish until the liquid comes about halfway up the sides of the fillet.
5. Bake until the fish feels firm to the touch, it is the same color all the way through and the muscles can be flaked apart. If the fish is very firm or tightly muscled, it might not flake. Many fillets take only 7 minutes to cook, although a thick piece of haddock might take 15 minutes.

125 CALORIES PER SERVING: 25 G PROTEIN, 1 G FAT, 2 G CARBOHYDRATE; 86 MG SODIUM, 60 MG CHOLESTEROL

page 127

Golden Fish

Saffron is costly, but you get a lot for your money.
It imparts a golden color and an exotic but smooth flavor to sauces.

SERVES 2 TO 4

5 threads	saffron
¼ cup	white wine
⅔-1⅓ pounds	mild white-fleshed fish fillets, such as haddock
⅛ teaspoon	kosher salt
⅛ teaspoon	freshly ground pepper
3	plum tomatoes, cored, cut in half lengthwise and sliced into half rounds
1 clove	garlic, peeled and crushed
1	shallot, minced (or 1 tablespoon minced red onion if shallots are not available)
1 teaspoon	capers
2 tablespoons	lemon juice

1. Crumble the saffron threads into the wine. Stir and let sit for 30 minutes so that the saffron colors the wine.
2. Preheat the oven to 375 degrees F.
3. Wash and dry the fish. Rub it with the salt and pepper. Put it into a casserole.
4. Arrange the tomatoes, garlic, shallot and capers around the fish.
5. Pour the saffron wine and lemon juice over the fish.
6. Cover the casserole and bake for 20 minutes. If it is an especially thick cut of fish, it might require 5 minutes more.

191 CALORIES PER SERVING: 27 G PROTEIN, 2 G FAT, 11 G CARBOHYDRATE; 276 MG SODIUM, 71 MG CHOLESTEROL

Shallots

i wish these small, purplish members of the onion family were more popular. Although I can find them in local markets, they are often old, shriveled and moldy. The standards for shallots are the same as for onions, and poor-quality shallots should be avoided. Fresh shallots are heavy for their size; have dry, papery skin and full, hard insides; and do not sprout green tops. Peel them as you would an onion, by slicing them in half and prying off the outside skin. Then slice or mince them with a chef's knife or a food processor. When sautéed, added to baked or roasted dishes or used raw in dressings, they add a sophisticated flavor that is distinct from other onions but fills the same role.

Lime Thyme Fish

Lime juice lends a surprising citrus flavor to this recipe. Use fresh lime juice if possible; bottled juice tastes old and artificial to me. You can prepare the cooking liquid several hours before baking, so this recipe is simple to make for guests.

SERVES 4

2 tablespoons	lime juice
2 tablespoons	white wine
1 tablespoon	water
1 teaspoon	capers
⅛ teaspoon	kosher salt
⅛ teaspoon	freshly ground pepper
¼ teaspoon	paprika

1/16 teaspoon	Tabasco or other hot pepper sauce
1 teaspoon	chopped fresh thyme, or ½ teaspoon dried
1⅓ pounds	fish fillets
1	lime cut into wedges, for garnish (optional)

1. Combine all the ingredients except the fish and lime wedges.
2. Preheat the oven to 375 degrees F.
3. Put the fish in a baking dish, preferably a heavy ceramic (not clear glass) casserole. Pour the baking liquid over the fish until it reaches halfway up the sides of the fillets. (Don't choose too large a baking dish, or there won't be enough liquid. Too small a dish will crowd the fish against the sides.)
4. Bake until the fish is the same texture and color throughout. Dense haddock will take about 15 minutes, perch only 5 to 7 minutes.
5. Garnish the fillets with lime wedges if desired.

130 CALORIES PER SERVING: 25 G PROTEIN, 2 G FAT, 1 G CARBOHYDRATE; 184 MG SODIUM, 71 MG CHOLESTEROL

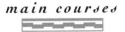
Pan-Cooked Fish Fillets

Thin, delicate white-fleshed fish fillets cook in a few minutes on the stove top. Dredge them in seasoned flour and place them in a nonstick pan with just a trace of olive or canola oil. I've given you three ideas on how to season your flour.

SERVES 3 TO 6

Blend 1

¼ cup	unbleached white flour
⅛ teaspoon	kosher salt
⅛ teaspoon	freshly ground pepper
¼ teaspoon	paprika

Blend 2

¼ cup	unbleached white flour
⅛ teaspoon	kosher salt
⅛ teaspoon	freshly ground pepper
½ teaspoon	mild curry powder

Blend 3

¼ cup	unbleached white flour
⅛ teaspoon	kosher salt
⅛ teaspoon	freshly ground pepper
¼ teaspoon	paprika
¼ teaspoon	ground allspice
¼ teaspoon	ground cumin

| ½ teaspoon to 1 tablespoon | olive or canola oil |
| 1-2 pounds | thin, boneless fish fillets, such as turbot or flounder |

1. Mix together the flour and spices until there are no spice streaks.
2. Wash the fish and pat it dry with a paper towel.
3. Heat a nonstick skillet over medium heat. Pour in the oil, spread it around and pour off any excess.
4. Dredge the fish in the seasoned flour by placing one side and then the other in the flour blend. Shake gently to remove any excess.
5. Place the fish in the skillet. Turn only once. Very thin fillets will require about 2 minutes per side, a thicker fish perhaps 3 minutes.

183 CALORIES PER SERVING: 29 G PROTEIN, 3 G FAT, 8 G CARBOHYDRATE; 202 MG SODIUM, 80 MG CHOLESTEROL

Fish in a Pot

This recipe has a lot of flavor for a little effort. Fresh herbs will make this stew all the better. Green peppercorns come either pickled in brine or freeze-dried. Unlike mature peppercorns, they can be eaten whole, but crushing them slightly is better. It is up to you whether to leave the skins on the potatoes. I like the color of red potato skins.

SERVES 4 TO 6

1 tablespoon	olive oil
2	medium yellow onions, chopped (2 cups)
3 cloves	garlic, minced (1½ teaspoons)
2	carrots, peeled and cut into rounds (cut the largest rounds in half)
2 ribs	celery, with leaves, chopped
¼ teaspoon	freshly ground pepper
1 teaspoon	kosher salt
1	bay leaf
3 tablespoons	lemon juice
1 cup	water
½ cup	white wine
2 tablespoons	chopped fresh parsley
1 teaspoon	minced fresh thyme, or ½ teaspoon dried
1½ teaspoons	chopped fresh rosemary, or ½ teaspoon dried
¾ teaspoon	green peppercorns, crushed
½ teaspoon	capers
¹⁄₁₆ teaspoon	Tabasco or other hot pepper sauce
¼ teaspoon	paprika
1 14-ounce can	whole tomatoes, drained
8	small new potatoes, cut into large cubes (1 pound)
1-pound	fish fillets, cut into 2-inch pieces

1. Heat the oil in a sauté pan. Sauté the onion, garlic, carrots and celery in the oil. Cook, covered, until the vegetables sweat out liquid and the onion is golden.
2. Add all the remaining ingredients except the fish. Cover and simmer for about 20 minutes until the potatoes are cooked through.
3. Reduce the temperature under the pot so that the liquid is simmering gently. Stir in the fish. Cook for 7 to 10 minutes until the fish is the same texture and color throughout.

206 CALORIES PER SERVING: 16 G PROTEIN, 4 G FAT, 26 G CARBOHYDRATE; 509 MG SODIUM, 35 MG CHOLESTEROL

vegetarian

*N*ot so long ago, having a meal without a big piece of meat on the plate was considered either adventurous or foolhardy. Times have changed. Meals with vegetables and carbohydrates as the focal point are appearing in fine restaurants and on home dinner tables. This doesn't mean a switch to a strictly vegetarian diet but it does mean that a meatless entrée is no longer considered lacking in nutrition or the ability to satisfy.

In the past, vegetarian entrées often relied too much on dairy products, or they looked like something you would eat in a monastery. Vegetarian meals have evolved toward lighter dishes with the vegetables showcased instead of smothered. This came about for many reasons. After years of being taught that protein is all-important, nutritionists are now convinced that in the United States, we eat far too much. Meat is no longer essential in providing protein, nor do vegetarians have to consume eggs or cheese in large amounts. Today, health concerns focus on fat, and people are starting to look for alternatives to greasy meats and fatty casseroles. Meanwhile, food writers have begun to extol the virtues of international cuisines, and many people have become more adventurous as ethnic foods have become part of the mainstream.

All of this has contributed to the acceptance of vegetarian main dishes. These entrées are inventive, low in fat, vibrant in color and flavor, and yet substantial, filling, and satisfying. The *Vegetables* chapter provides more ideas for vegetarian meals. Many of the sauces included there make full dinners when served over pasta or rice.

Oven-Baked Ratatouille

This recipe differs from other ratatouilles because instead of making it on the stove top, you bake it in the oven. The eggplant goes in first, with salt and oil. By the time you add the other ingredients, the excess moisture and bitterness of the eggplant has been roasted out. Ratatouille can be served hot as the centerpiece or as a vegetable accompaniment. It also can be served at room temperature with crackers as an hors d'oeuvre. If you do the latter, squeeze in a touch more lemon.

Serves 4 to 6

1	large eggplant (about 1 pound), cut into 1-inch or smaller cubes		4	very ripe plum tomatoes, or 4 canned plum tomatoes, coarsely chopped
1 tablespoon	vegetable or olive oil		2	bay leaves
2	small yellow onions, cut into medium-size pieces		½ cup	white wine
4 large cloves	garlic, minced (1 tablespoon)		2 tablespoons	chopped fresh parsley
1½ teaspoons	kosher salt		¼ cup	chopped fresh basil, or 1 tablespoon dried
1	green, red or yellow bell pepper, cut into large pieces		¼-½ teaspoon	freshly ground pepper
1	medium yellow summer squash (about ¼ pound), cubed		1 teaspoon	lemon juice
1	medium zucchini (about ½ pound), cubed			

1. Preheat the oven to 400 degrees F.
2. Put the eggplant, oil, onion, garlic and 1 teaspoon of the salt into a heavy casserole. Toss the ingredients so that the oil and salt evenly coat the eggplant. Bake, uncovered, for 30 minutes. Stir once or twice during cooking to keep the vegetables from sticking.
3. Reduce the oven temperature to 350 degrees F. Add the remaining ½ teaspoon salt and all the remaining ingredients, except the lemon juice, to the pot. Stir to combine. Cover the pot, leaving a small steam vent. Bake for 30 minutes.
4. Add the lemon juice. Add salt and pepper to taste. Remove the bay leaves before serving.

156 CALORIES PER SERVING: 4 G PROTEIN, 4 G FAT, 25 G CARBOHYDRATE; 728 MG SODIUM, 0 MG CHOLESTEROL

Moroccan Vegetables

Cinnamon is not just for desserts. This vegetable and chickpea mélange is seasoned with a cinnamon stick, as well as onion, garlic and hot pepper. The combination is spicy yet sweet and savory. For a traditional touch, serve it over couscous. It also is excellent with kasha or rice. Leave out the chickpeas, and it makes a lovely accompaniment to roast chicken.

SERVES 4

½ tablespoon	olive oil		1 teaspoon	paprika
1	medium yellow onion, chopped (1 cup)		1	cinnamon stick
2 cloves	garlic, minced (1 teaspoon)		1 teaspoon	turmeric
1 14-ounce can	whole tomatoes		½ teaspoon	kosher salt
1	green bell pepper, cut into ½-inch pieces		¼ teaspoon	freshly ground pepper
1 teaspoon	minced fresh gingerroot		1 tablespoon	lemon juice
3 tablespoons	minced fresh parsley		1/16 teaspoon	Tabasco or other hot pepper sauce (or to taste)
2	carrots, cut into small pieces or rounds		1 cup	defatted chicken or vegetable stock or water
1 cup	cooked chickpeas			
1 cup	vegetable(s) of choice, such as broccoli or green beans (If you use a leafy green, such as spinach, use 4 cups fresh, which will shrink down to 1 cup cooked.)			

1. Heat the oil in a heavy-bottomed pot. Sauté the onion and garlic in the oil.
2. Add the tomatoes. Break them up with a spoon or spatula once they are in the pot.
3. Add the remaining ingredients. Bring the mixture to a boil, then simmer until the carrots are fork tender (or softer, if you wish).

139 CALORIES PER SERVING: 6 G PROTEIN, 3 G FAT, 25 G CARBOHYDRATE; 624 MG SODIUM, 0 MG CHOLESTEROL

Greens & Pasta

If you are tempted by the kale or other dark leafy greens in the supermarket but pass them by because you don't know how to cook them, this recipe is for you. It is one of my favorite quick meals. The only preparation is the washing and chopping of the greens. You can use any leafy green in this dish. A nice combination is two-thirds kale and one-third white-ribbed Swiss chard. Any leftovers are good served cold with feta cheese.

SERVES 2

½ pound	greens, finely chopped (4 cups)
1¼ cups	defatted chicken or vegetable stock
3	whole canned tomatoes, with 1 tablespoon juice

1 teaspoon	garlic oil
4-6 ounces	dry pasta, cooked
⅛ teaspoon	red pepper flakes
¼ teaspoon	kosher salt (optional)
	Parmesan cheese (optional)

1. Please read the note on preparing greens on page 169. Simmer the greens in the stock for about 15 minutes. Kale from bigger leaves is a bit tougher and might need to be cooked an extra 5 minutes. I cook this in my wok because it is large enough to hold the greens, which take up a lot of space when raw. In the wok, they are easy to toss, and all the ingredients heat thoroughly and evenly. In a pinch, when I'm out of stock, I use water and make up the loss in flavor by adding more garlic oil.

2. Using your hands, crush the tomatoes directly into the pot. You may substitute fresh tomatoes, but they must be flavorful, and you'll have to peel them (page 110).
3. Stir in the garlic oil.
4. Toss in the pasta, red pepper flakes and salt (if using). Stir until everything is heated through.
5. Grate Parmesan cheese over the pasta just before serving if desired.

296 CALORIES PER SERVING: 13 G PROTEIN, 4 G FAT, 53 G CARBOHYDRATE; 528 MG SODIUM, 0 MG CHOLESTEROL

page 138

Pasta with Vegetables & Feta

This is one of those recipes that can be served as a one-dish supper or part of a larger meal. The method used here can serve as a basis for recipes of your invention. Start with sautéed garlic and onion, then add your favorite vegetable, herbs and pasta. At the end, toss in a small amount of feta cheese, which adds a creamy texture and sharp aroma. Or try other cheeses, such as smoked mozzarella or Gorgonzola. A few ounces of an assertive cheese makes a big impression for very little fat.

SERVES 2 TO 4

½ pound	pasta, preferably a short fat type like rigatoni (4 cups cooked)
1 small	carrot, peeled
1	small zucchini
1 tablespoon	olive oil
½	red onion, sliced (½ cup)
1 clove	garlic, minced (½ teaspoon)
¼ cup	defatted chicken or vegetable stock
½ cup	fresh or frozen peas (if frozen, defrost before using)
1 tablespoon	minced fresh parsley
1½ teaspoons	basil
½ teaspoon	oregano
1 teaspoon	kosher salt
¼ teaspoon	freshly ground pepper
2 ounces	feta cheese, cut into small cubes

1. Cook the pasta. If it is done at the same time as the sautéed vegetables, drain it and add it to the vegetables. If you cook the pasta earlier, cool it thoroughly in cold water, then drain it, so that it doesn't stick together.
2. Cut the carrot and the zucchini into matchsticks. If doing this is too much work, cut the vegetables in half lengthwise and then into thin half circles.
3. Heat the oil in a 10- or 12-inch nonstick sauté pan over low heat. Sauté the onion garlic and carrots in the oil. Cover between stirrings so that the steam helps to soften the carrots. Cook for about 5 minutes, until the carrots are tender.

4. Add the stock and zucchini. Continue to cook, covered, until the zucchini is tender but not mushy.
5. Stir in the pasta, peas, herbs, salt and pepper. Increase the heat to medium. If the pasta was at room temperature, keep stirring until everything is hot.
6. Stir in the feta. Serve as soon as its outside edges begin to melt.

583 CALORIES PER SERVING: 20 G PROTEIN, 15 G FAT, 92 G CARBOHYDRATE; 1543 MG SODIUM, 25 MG CHOLESTEROL

Basil & Broccoli Ziti

A basil and garlic puree sauces this recipe. The basil must be fresh. Select basil with large green leaves that are free of brown spots. Unfortunately, the fresh herbs you find at the market are often wilted. As long as the leaves are free of blemishes, this recipe will work fine with limp basil.

SERVES 2 TO 4

½ pound	ziti or other tubular or stubby pasta (4 cups cooked)
2 stalks	broccoli
1 cup	fresh basil, packed down
2 cloves	garlic, peeled
2 tablespoons	water

1 cup	roasted red peppers, cut julienne
½-1 teaspoon	kosher salt (or to taste)
¼ teaspoon	freshly ground pepper
	freshly grated Parmesan cheese for garnish

1. Cook the pasta. If you cook it ahead of time, stop the cooking by immersing it in cool water and then draining it well. This will prevent it from sticking together.
2. Cut the florets off the broccoli stems. You will have 2 to 3 cups of florets. Trim them so that they are all about the same size. Reserve the stems for another purpose. Steam the florets until they are brighter green and just tender. When they're done, remove them from the steamer and rinse them under cool water to stop them from cooking. You can do this up to a day ahead of time.
3. Wash the basil well, as it is often very gritty.
4. With the food processor running, drop in the garlic. Then pour in the oil and water. Scrape down the sides. Add the basil. Process until the basil is finely minced. If you don't have a processor, you can use a blender or a mortar and pestle.
5. Put the pasta, broccoli, roasted peppers, salt and pepper in a large sauté pan. Begin to warm it over medium heat.
6. Pour the basil puree over the pasta. Toss well. Heat until everything is warm. Serve immediately. Garnish each plate with Parmesan cheese if desired.

538 CALORIES PER SERVING: 16 G PROTEIN, 16 G FAT, 83 G CARBOHYDRATE; 506 MG SODIUM, 0 MG CHOLESTEROL

page 180

Asparagus & Spaghetti

For this dish, the asparagus is cooked separately from the rest of the ingredients because it turns whatever liquid it is cooked in bright green and slightly bitter. Nevertheless, this recipe meets the criteria for a simple one-dish meal. Cooking time and ingredients are minimal, but the end result is interesting in flavor, texture and color.

SERVES 2 TO 4

10 stalks	asparagus, tough ends snapped off
½ pound	spaghetti (4 cups cooked)
1 tablespoon	garlic oil, or 1 tablespoon oil plus ½ teaspoon minced garlic
1 8-ounce package	fancy mushrooms, such as cremini or oyster, thickly sliced (about 2 cups)
⅓ cup	defatted chicken stock
2 tablespoons	minced fresh parsley
1 teaspoon	lemon juice
½-1 teaspoon	kosher salt (or to taste)
⅛-¼ teaspoon	freshly ground pepper (or to taste)
	freshly grated Parmesan cheese for garnish

1. Cut the asparagus on the diagonal into 1- to 2-inch pieces. Steam or microwave the asparagus pieces about 3 minutes until they turn a brighter green and become slightly tender. Cool them under running water to stop the cooking. This can be done up to a day ahead of time.
2. Cook the pasta. This will take about 10 minutes. The rest of the recipe will take about 4 minutes. Try to time the pasta so that it is done at the same time as the mushrooms. That way, you can drain it and then immediately toss it in with the mushrooms and asparagus.
3. Heat the oil in a sauté pan. Sauté the mushrooms in the oil. When they begin to wilt, add the stock. Cook for another 2 minutes at a temperature high enough that the stock bubbles.
4. Add the asparagus, parsley, lemon juice, salt and pepper. Then add the pasta. Toss until everything is warmed through. It can be difficult to distribute vegetables evenly amount the spaghetti strands. I use my spring-loaded tongs to pick up and separate the pasta. When putting the pasta on individual dinner plated, I place a few asparagus nibs on top of each serving.
5. Garnish with Parmesan cheese. Serve immediately.

556 CALORIES PER SERVING: 23 G PROTEIN, 10 G FAT, 97 G CARBOHYDRATE; 498 MG SODIUM, 0 MG CHOLESTEROL

page 138

Peanut Butter Noodles

My take on this Asian dish is spicy enough to make it interesting, but not so spicy that your mouth will be on fire. (For those who like that sort of thing, increase the red pepper flakes to ¼ teaspoon or more.) Use my selection of vegetables, or make up your own. Bok choy and mung bean sprouts are good alternatives. The peanut butter should be freshly ground, no salt, oils or sugars added; it can often be found in the deli or cheese department.

SERVES 4

½ pound	spaghetti or Asian noodles	½ tablespoon	rice or white wine vinegar
1 cup	snow peas	¼ cup	all-natural peanut butter
1	carrot, peeled and diced or grated	¼ cup	water
3	scallions, sliced	1 clove	garlic, peeled
2 teaspoons	soy sauce	¹⁄₁₆ teaspoon	red pepper flakes (or to taste)
1 teaspoon	honey	2 tablespoons	chopped dry roasted peanuts for garnish (optional)

1. Cook and drain the pasta. Rinse it with cool water to stop the cooking and keep the strands from sticking together. Rinsing is essential; the dish will be too sticky and quickly dry out without it.
2. Blanch the snow peas and carrots. (Blanching is simply immersing the vegetables in boiling water for a short time until they turn a brighter color. Cooking the carrots for a couple of minutes in the microwave and the snowpeas for less than a minute also will do the trick.) Rinse them under cool water to stop the cooking. You want the vegetables to be crunchy and colorful, yet not taste or feel raw. Toss them with the pasta.
3. Add the scallions.
4. In a blender, puree the soy sauce, honey, vinegar, peanut butter, water, garlic and red pepper flakes. Pour the sauce over the pasta and vegetables. Toss to combine.
5. Serve at room temperature or warmed in the microwave. If desired, garnish with chopped peanuts.

352 CALORIES PER SERVING: 13 G PROTEIN, 9 G FAT, 55 G CARBOHYDRATE; 257 MG SODIUM, 0 MG CHOLESTEROL

Red Pepper Flakes

*t*hese are the flat, roundish pepper flakes found in shaker jars at pizzerias. Sometimes called crushed red pepper, it belongs to the genus *Capsicum* and is unrelated to the black pepper berries in your pepper mill. Red pepper has a long shelf life if kept away from light and heat, which is good, as it is usually sold in rather large containers.

Red pepper is hot, and a little goes a long way. Be wary if the dish looks as if it has red confetti in it! The flavor the flakes impart is complex enough to carry a simple recipe (such as Greens & Pasta, page 92). Red pepper also works well as part of a larger ensemble, such as in sauces and stews.

Lasagnas

Making lasagna is not a daunting task, despite the many ingredients and steps needed to put it together. Being organized and having all the ingredients on hand is the key to easy lasagna making.

All my recipes use a tomato-based red sauce. Which one you use depends on your preferences and what you have available. If you are using homemade sauce from the freezer, have it defrosted and measured. You can use sauce from a jar, but making a fresh-tasting red sauce from scratch takes less than half an hour. If you have the time and feel like cooking, it is well worth the minimal effort. (See the selection of tomato sauces in the *Sauces & Salsas* chapter.)

Pasta can be cooked up to 1 hour ahead of time. To cook lasagna noodles, bring a big pot of water to a boil. Place the noodles in the pot, arranged in X's, one on top of each other. Stacking the pasta in this way prevents the noodles from sticking together. Remove the noodles when they are flexible but not soft. They should bend when you take them out of the water. Have a clean kitchen towel spread out on the counter. Don't use paper towels. Take each noodle out of the water (preferably using long-handled salad bar tongs) and lay it flat on the towel. Don't let the noodles overlap, or they'll stick together. Avoid the instant lasagna noodles that don't require precooking; they don't taste as good. Have the filling mixtures ready to use.

Lasagna is held together with cheese, but the overall fat content can be kept low, especially when vegetables are added and very low-fat sauces used. I keep fat down by using low-fat mozzarella and ricotta, but do not try to reduce fat even more by using low-fat cottage cheese. I've tested lasagna with cottage cheese, and the results were not good. The cheese dried out as it exuded liquid into the casserole. Some low-fat ricottas and mozzarellas don't melt well and have little flavor. Taste them and add salt to adjust for blandness. If they melt like plastic, try a different brand the next time. For more about cheeses, see page 12.

Lasagna pans vary in size and material. My recipes call for a 9-by-11-inch pan. I have a ceramic glazed pan and basic stainless-steel pans at home. They bake about the same, although the heavier and darker pans distribute heat more evenly. You can use a clear glass casserole as long as you reduce the oven temperature by about 20 degrees F.

Lasagna is built in layers. Spread each layer of filling with a rubber spatula, making sure that it is not mounded in the center. Don't agonize over lumps and bumps. Part of the charm of lasagna is its rustic quality.

Bake lasagna in a preheated 350 degree F oven. If the cheese topping browns too quickly, tent foil over the casserole, taking care not to let the foil touch the lasagna, because the acid in the tomatoes will eat away at the foil, leaving bright flecks of aluminum in the lasagna.

Take the baked lasagna out of the oven and let it rest for about 10 minutes before cutting. My lasagna recipes are not fatty and heavy, so I have decided on a portion size according to what satisfies me. I figure that one 9-by-11-inch casserole will serve six generously, or nine if it's part of a larger meal. Leftovers are always welcome.

Spinach Lasagna

Using fresh spinach takes less time than defrosting a frozen package, and the quality and flavor are superior. Use whatever tomato sauce you like. Basic Basil Tomato Sauce (page 111) lends a light, fresh taste.

SERVES 6 TO 9

9	lasagna noodles
½ pound	spinach
1 pound	low-fat ricotta
½ teaspoon	kosher salt
½ teaspoon	freshly ground pepper
1 tablespoon	chives
1	egg white

3 cups	tomato sauce (see *Sauces & Salsas*)
4 ounces	part-skim or low-fat mozzarella, shredded (1½ cups)
2 tablespoons	freshly grated Parmesan cheese (optional)

1. Please read about lasagnas on page 97. Preheat the oven to 350 degrees F.
2. Cook the noodles in a big pot of boiling water. When they're pliable, lay each out flat on a clean cloth towel until you're ready to use them.
3. Wash the spinach (even if the package says that it's been washed). Break off and discard the tough stem ends. Microwave or briefly steam the leaves until they wilt. Chop the spinach, then squeeze out all the moisture. I do this by putting it in a wire mesh strainer set in the sink. Then I press against the spinach and squeeze it with my hands until most of the water comes out.
4. Combine the spinach, ricotta, salt, pepper, chives and egg white with a fork.
5. Spread half the tomato sauce in a 9-by-11-inch pan. Lay down 3 noodles, top with half the ricotta mixture, lay down 3 more noodles and top with the remaining ricotta. Lay down the last 3 noodles, top with the remaining tomato sauce and sprinkle the mozzarella and Parmesan (if using) on top.
6. Bake for 45 minutes.

344 CALORIES PER SERVING: 21 G PROTEIN, 10 G FAT, 44 G CARBOHYDRATE; 1110 MG SODIUM, 34 MG CHOLESTEROL

Broccoli & Carrot Lasagna

This colorful lasagna is constructed from a number of simple parts. Chopping the vegetables in the food processor saves a lot of time and trouble, as does having all the ingredients organized and at your work table before assembling it.

SERVES 6 TO 9

4	medium carrots, peeled and chopped (½ pound)
½	head broccoli, peeled and chopped (½ pound)
1 pound	low-fat ricotta
2 cloves	roasted garlic , or 2 cloves garlic, minced, sautéed in oil
1½ teaspoons	kosher salt (or more if ricotta is low salt)

¼ teaspoon	freshly ground pepper
1	egg
1 tablespoon	freshly grated Parmesan cheese
2½ cups	tomato sauce (see *Sauces & Salsas*)
9	lasagna noodles, cooked al dente
4 ounces	part-skim or low-fat mozzarella, shredded (1½ cups)

1. Please read about lasagnas on page 97. Preheat oven to 350 degrees F.
2. Cook the noodles in a big pot of boiling water. When they're pliable, lay each out flat on a clean cloth towel until you're ready to use them.
3. Steam or microwave the carrots and broccoli in separate containers. Drain the vegetables.
4. Combine the ricotta, garlic, salt, pepper, egg and Parmesan cheese.
5. Divide the cheese mixture in half. Combine one half with the broccoli and the other with the carrots.
6. Spread 1 cup of the tomato sauce in the bottom of a 9-by-11-inch pan. Lay down 3 of the noodles and spread the carrot mixture on top. Lay down another 3 noodles and spread the broccoli mixture on top. Lay down the last 3 noodles, cover with the remaining tomato sauce and sprinkle the mozzarella on top.
7. Bake for 45 minutes. Tent foil over the lasagna if the cheese browns within 30 minutes. Take care not to let the foil touch the tomato sauce, or the acid will eat into the metal.

399 CALORIES PER SERVING: 23 G PROTEIN, 11 G FAT, 50 G CARBOHYDRATE; 868 MG SODIUM, 70 MG CHOLESTEROL

page 179

Swiss Chard Lasagna

Spinach and broccoli aren't the only green vegetables that layer nicely in lasagna. White-ribbed Swiss chard contributes both garden-fresh flavor and crunch.

SERVES 6 TO 9

9	lasagna noodles
1 pound	low-fat ricotta
½ teaspoon	kosher salt
¼ teaspoon	freshly ground pepper
1	egg white
½ pound	white-ribbed Swiss chard

3 cups	tomato sauce (see *Sauces & Salsas*)
4 ounces	part-skim or low-fat mozzarella, shredded (1½ cups)
2 tablespoons	freshly grated Parmesan cheese

1. Please read about lasagnas on page 97. Preheat the oven to 350 degrees F.
2. Cook the noodles in a big pot of boiling water. When they're pliable, lay each out flat on a clean cloth towel until you're ready to use them.
3. Combine the ricotta, salt, pepper and egg white.
4. Cut the ribs away from the leafy green parts of the Swiss chard. Chop the stalks into small pieces. Cook these (either microwave or steam) for a few minutes until tender (they will always have a slight crunch). Slice the leafy parts into big pieces (remember, they'll shrink down just like spinach when cooked). Add the leaves to the stems. Cook until wilted. Drain the chard well, then stir it into the ricotta mixture.

5. In a 9-by-11-inch pan, layer half the tomato sauce, 3 noodles, half the ricotta mixture, 3 more noodles, the remaining ricotta mixture and the last 3 noodles. Top with the remaining tomato sauce, the mozzarella and the Parmesan.
6. Bake for 1 hour.

355 CALORIES PER SERVING: 22 G PROTEIN, 11 G FAT, 44 G CARBOHYDRATE; 1197 MG SODIUM, 36 MG CHOLESTEROL

No-Pasta Vegetable Lasagna

Pasta has become such a standard food at my house that there are times when I think I can't eat another plateful. But I never feel that way about vegetables with tomato sauce and melted cheese. That's why I created a lasagna without the noodles. Besides, an allergy to wheat runs in my family, so it's nice to serve something that everyone can eat.

SERVES 6 TO 9

2	large eggplants, an equivalent quantity of summer squash or a combination of the two		1 tablespoon	chives
1 teaspoon	kosher salt		2½ cups	tomato sauce (see *Sauces & Salsas*)
½ teaspoon	freshly ground pepper		3 ounces	part-skim mozzarella, shredded (1 cup)
1 pound	low-fat ricotta		2 ounces	freshly grated Parmesan cheese
1	egg white			

1. Preheat the oven to 425 degrees F.
2. Slice the eggplants lengthwise into long, ¼-inch strips. Use ½ teaspoon of the salt and ¼ teaspoon of the pepper to season both sides. Place the strips on a nonstick or greased baking sheet. Bake for 5 to 7 minutes on each side. You also may grill the vegetable strips. If you're using summer squash, you can steam or microwave it, but be sure to drain it well and dry it off, or it will make the lasagna watery. Reduce the oven temperature to 350 degrees F.
3. With a fork, mix together the ricotta, egg white, chives and remaining salt and pepper.

4. Spread 1½ cups of the tomato sauce on the bottom of a 9-by-11-inch pan. Then place a single layer of vegetables on top. Evenly spread half the ricotta mixture on top of the vegetables. Place another layer of vegetables on that, and the remaining ricotta and top with the remaining vegetables. Cover with the remaining tomato sauce, then evenly distribute the mozzarella and Parmesan on top.
5. Cover with foil and bake for 1 hour. Remove the foil for the last 5 to 10 minutes.

258 CALORIES PER SERVING: 19 G PROTEIN, 12 G FAT, 22 G CARBOHYDRATE; 1403 MG SODIUM, 39 MG CHOLESTEROL

Bean & Tortilla Lasagna

You can make this lasagna using ingredients from scratch or use prepared foods with almost the same results. I usually have some home-cooked beans in my freezer, but in a pinch I'll use canned beans (drained and washed well). I love fresh roasted peppers (page 180), but in this recipe a jar of roasted peppers (packed in water, not oil) won't compromise the flavor. The salsa can be homemade (page 120) or store-bought (try the fresh ones in the refrigerated section). You'll probably find the best tortillas in a natural food store.

SERVES 9

1 teaspoon	vegetable oil		⅛ teaspoon	Tabasco or other hot pepper sauce
1 small	yellow onion, chopped (½ cup)		2 cups	Red Chili Sauce
2 cloves	garlic, minced (1 teaspoon)		12	corn tortillas
1	green bell pepper, chopped (1 cup)		1 cup	sharp Cheddar cheese, shredded (2 ounces)
3 cups	cooked pinto beans		1½ cups	sliced roasted peppers (1 12-ounce jar or 2 to 3 peppers)
½ teaspoon	kosher salt			
¼ teaspoon	freshly ground pepper		1 cup	salsa

1. Preheat the oven to 350 degrees F.
2. Heat the oil in a large sauté pan. Sauté the onion, garlic and green pepper until the vegetables are soft. Remove the pan from the heat.
3. Stir in the pinto beans, salt, pepper and Tabasco. Mash the beans until about half are smooth but some are still whole. I do this with my hands.
4. Cover the bottom of a 9-by-11-inch pan with 1½ cups of the Red Chili Sauce. Place 4 tortillas on top. Spread on half the bean mixture, half the cheese and half the roasted peppers. Place 4 more tortillas on top. Repeat the layers of beans, cheese and peppers. Top again with tortillas. Then spread on the remaining sauce and the salsa. If the salsa is watery, drain it a bit first.
5. Cover with foil, taking care not to let the metal touch the tomatoes. You can make the casserole up to this point several hours ahead of time.
6. Bake for 45 minutes. Remove the foil for the last 5 minutes.
7. You might want to serve with extra salsa.

265 CALORIES PER SERVING: 12 G PROTEIN, 7 G FAT, 41 G CARBOHYDRATE; 517 MG SODIUM, 13 MG CHOLESTEROL

page 114

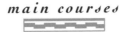
White Bean Stew

This stew can be served as a vegetarian entrée with a green salad and homemade bread, it can be one of many dishes served at a relaxing afternoon buffet, or it can be offered as a nosh with crackers. Serve it warm or at room temperature (if the latter, add a touch more lemon juice). Use dried cannellini or navy beans. Don't take a shortcut and use canned beans, because the garlic needs to cook along with the beans to become mild and sweet and to transfer its flavor to the beans.

SERVES 8 TO 10

1½ cups	dried cannellini or navy beans		2½	cups water
1 bulb	garlic		1 teaspoon	kosher salt
1 tablespoon	olive oil		¼ teaspoon	freshly ground pepper
2	medium yellow onions, chopped (2 cups)		1 cup	chopped fresh parsley
			1 tablespoon	lemon juice
4	carrots, peeled and chopped			
1 14-ounce can	whole tomatoes, drained and seeded			

1. Wash the beans, then soak them for 4 hours to 1 day in 3 cups water. When they are ready to use, drain and rinse them.
2. Break the garlic bulb into cloves. Peel the cloves. (See page 179 for an easy way to do this.)
3. Heat the oil in a heavy-bottomed stockpot over low heat. Cook the garlic, onion and carrots in the oil until the onion is soft and golden. Keep the lid on between stirrings.
4. Add the beans to the pot. Then add the tomatoes, crushing any large chunks into smaller

pieces. Add the water. Cover the pot and simmer for about 1½ hours, or until the beans are very soft. (Note: This time is variable and depends on the quality and freshness of the beans.

5. Stir in the salt and the pepper. If you're serving the stew right away, add all the parsley and the lemon juice. If you're serving it later or at room temperature, add half the parsley, then add the remaining parsley and the lemon juice right before serving.

182 CALORIES PER SERVING: 10 G PROTEIN, 2 G FAT, 32 G CARBOHYDRATE; 339 MG SODIUM, 0 MG CHOLESTEROL

Hoisin Tofu

Tofu is better when it has some texture, so I sauté these cubes in a small amount of sesame oil until they are dark and crispy outside but moist and soft inside. Although this recipe doesn't mention vegetables, the marinade makes a wonderful stir-fry sauce. If necessary, stretch it with stock or water. Cook some vegetables in the sauce, then toss in the cooked tofu. Serve it over brown rice or Asian noodles.

SERVES 4 TO 8

1 tablespoon	water		1 teaspoon	grated fresh gingerroot
1 tablespoon	soy sauce		2 cloves	garlic, minced (1 teaspoon)
2 tablespoons	hoisin sauce		¼ teaspoon	Tabasco or other hot pepper sauce
2 tablespoons	dry sherry		1 pound	firm tofu, cut into cubes
1 teaspoon	rice or white wine vinegar		½ tablespoon	toasted sesame oil

1. Whisk together everything except the tofu and sesame oil.
2. Stir in the tofu cubes, making sure they are well covered with sauce. Cover and refrigerate for at least 15 minutes and up to 1 day. The longer the tofu sits, the more flavors it will absorb.
3. Heat the sesame oil in a nonstick sauté pan. Use a slotted spoon to remove the tofu from the marinade. Put the tofu in the pan and cook for 7 to 10 minutes until the cubes are dark and crisp on the outside. Shake the pan frequently to keep the tofu from sticking and to cook the cubes on all sides.

202 CALORIES PER SERVING: 19 G PROTEIN, 12 G FAT, 8 G CARBOHYDRATE; 620 MG SODIUM; 0 MG CHOLESTEROL

Tandoori Tofu

This recipe is similar to Tandoori Chicken (page 66). You can serve both, side by side, and please both vegetarians and meat eaters with little extra work for yourself. I like this with curried pea pilaf and steamed vegetables. It is also wonderful, cold or hot, as a sandwich filling.

SERVES 4 TO 8

1-2 pounds	extra-firm or firm tofu, drained from its packing water		2 cloves	garlic, minced (1 teaspoon)
½ cup	low-fat yogurt		2 teaspoons	minced fresh ginger
2 tablespoons	lemon juice		1 teaspoon	kosher salt
1 tablespoon	apple cider vinegar		2-3 teaspoons	mild curry powder
			¼ teaspoon	ground chili pepper (optional)

1. Press the tofu in a cloth towel to squeeze out any excess water. Then cut it into cubes or slices.
2. Combine all the remaining ingredients.
3. Marinate the tofu in the yogurt mixture. Use a glass or stainless-steel bowl. Make sure that the tofu is evenly coated with the marinade. Marinate for 8 to 24 hours. Keep covered and refrigerated.

4. Preheat the broiler. As you place the tofu on a grill or broiler rack, shake off the excess marinade.

5. Broil the tofu about 20 to 30 minutes until the yogurt begins to bubble and brown. Turn the tofu every 5 to 7 minutes so that all sides are exposed to the heat.

177 CALORIES PER SERVING: 19 G PROTEIN, 10 G FAT, 7 G CARBOHYDRATE; 261 MG SODIUM, 1 MG CHOLESTEROL

Tofu

*t*ofu used to be considered an essential part of a vegetarian's diet. This soybean product is one of the best plant sources of protein. But nutritionists now feel that a person will get plenty of protein as long as he or she eats a small amount of animal-derived foods each day. A vegetarian who doesn't eat any animal products—no eggs or dairy products—might want to rely on tofu, although eating a combination of beans, rice and nuts also will do the trick.

So now that it isn't necessary to eat tofu for your health, why should you bother? Although a few people love to eat plain tofu, most people think that this chalky white block tastes as unappetizing as it looks. But it is exactly tofu's mild and neutral flavor that makes it so valuable in the kitchen. Like a sponge, it absorbs sauces and seasonings, while its firm texture gives an otherwise shapeless recipe body. Nutritionally, it provides protein while contributing very little saturated fat. Bear in mind that although about 52 percent of tofu's calories come from fat, tofu is almost always eaten with whole grains and vegetables, so the entire meal is usually low in fat.

Several types of tofu are widely available. Silken or soft tofu is high in moisture and has a custardlike consistency similar to flan. Cubes of it are stirred into miso soup and whole blocks are pureed into desserts. On the other end of the spectrum is firm tofu, which is what I've specified for the recipes in this book. It is a harder block of soybean curd that doesn't crumble easily or exude much liquid as it cooks.

Firm tofu is usually packaged in a plastic tub and requires refrigeration. A container of tofu will pick up odors and begin to go bad within a day or two of being opened. To extend its life, drain off the liquid, store it in a container filled with fresh water and change the water daily. With care, the tofu will last for several days.

Curried Pea Pilaf

This recipe is good when made with brown rice, but if you are able to find basmati rice or any of the other "aromatic" rices, use them. I love the combination of nuts and rice, so I've given you the option of including cashews. They'll add to the fat content, but their flavor complements the nutty taste of the rice, their texture is a welcome contrast to the soft grains, and they turn the dish into a nutritionally complete protein.

SERVES 4

2 teaspoons	vegetable oil
1 teaspoon	minced fresh gingerroot
2 cloves	garlic, minced (1 teaspoon)
1	small yellow onion, minced (½ cup)
1 teaspoon	curry powder
¼ teaspoon	ground cinnamon

½ teaspoon	kosher salt
¼ teaspoon	freshly ground pepper
2 cups	peas, fresh or frozen
½ cup	water
1½ cups	brown basmati or other rice, cooked
½ cup	cashews, toasted (optional)

1. Heat the oil in a 10-inch nonstick pan. Sauté the ginger, garlic and onion in the oil. Keep the pan covered between stirrings. Cook over low heat until the onion is soft and golden. Take care not to scorch the ginger.
2. Add the spices to the pan. Cook to release their aroma. You'll be able to smell the change as the spices get hot.
3. Add the peas and water. Gently cook until most of the liquid has evaporated.
4. Stir the rice into the curried peas. Heat through. Stir until the spices and peas are evenly distributed. Stir in the cashews if desired.

263 CALORIES PER SERVING: 8 G PROTEIN, 4 G FAT, 50 G CARBOHYDRATE; 246 MG SODIUM, 0 MG CHOLESTEROL

Toasting Nuts & Seeds

*t*oasting brings new and complex flavors out of nuts. Except for low-fat chestnuts, nuts are high in oils, and this allows them to be toasted as they are, without the addition of fats. Nuts can be toasted in the oven, in the toaster oven or in a sauté pan on top of the stove. Toast them over medium heat or in a moderate oven, in a single layer. Shake the pan occasionally so that they don't scorch and all sides get toasted. The nuts are ready when they darken slightly and their aroma becomes richer and fills the air. Seeds, such as sesame and mustard seeds, also can be toasted to enhance their flavor. They burn easily, so keep the heat low and keep an eye on them. As soon as the nuts or seeds are toasted, remove them from the hot pan, or they will continue to cook. Don't place the pan in the sink, where an unsuspecting person might touch it. Instead, let it cool in an out-of-the-way place.

Curried Yams & Greens

The individual ingredients never get lost in this curry. The colors remain vibrant, with the orange of the yams contrasting with the deep green of the kale. The slight bitterness of the greens is offset by the sweetness of the potato. Curry spices sharpen all the flavors. Increase the heat with more cayenne and cumin if you wish.

SERVES 4

½ tablespoon	peanut oil		1 cup	cooked chickpeas (if canned, rinse well)
2	medium leeks, including the light green tops, chopped (1½ cups)		4 cups	vegetable stock
			2 teaspoons	curry powder
3 cloves	garlic, minced (1½ teaspoon)		¼ teaspoon	ground coriander
¼ pound	dark leafy greens, such as kale or Swiss chard		¼ teaspoon	turmeric
			½ teaspoon	ground cumin
1	large yam or sweet potato, peeled and cubed (3 cups)		1/16 teaspoon	cayenne pepper
			1½ tablespoons	soy sauce

1. Heat the oil in a sauté pan over low heat. Sauté the leeks and garlic in the oil. Keep the pan covered between stirrings. Cook for about 5 to 7 minutes until the leeks are soft and turn a mellower color. Take care not to scorch the vegetables.

2. Meanwhile, wash the greens well. If you're using kale, cut out and discard the tough center rib. I prefer white-ribbed Swiss chard rather than red for this recipe because the red will turn the dish light purple. Chop the greens.

3. Add the remaining ingredients to the pot. Bring to a boil, then reduce to a simmer. Cover and cook for about 30 minutes, or until the yams are soft. The pot can stay on the stove longer. I took this dish to a potluck housewarming party, added a little extra water and kept the stew warm on the back burner of the stove. The curry kept its flavors and textures and warmed the guests throughout the evening.

195 CALORIES PER SERVING; 5 G PROTEIN, 3 G FAT, 39 G CARBOHYDRATE; 578 MG SODIUM, 0 MG CHOLESTEROL

recipes

Basic Basil Tomato Sauce

Freshly Minted Tomato Sauce

Roasted Tomato Sauce

Tomato Olivada

Red Chili Sauce

Mushroom,
Bean & Tomato Sauce

African Peanut Sauce

Red Pepper Sauce

Island Barbecue Sauce

Sweet & Sour Sauce

Gingered Marmalade Sauce

Red Salsa

Pineapple Salsa

Sauces & Salsas

auces used to be small, savory puddles that a cook put under or over food. Often they were rich highlights: hollandaise, butter sauces, cream sauces, tartar sauces. Now, thanks to the influence and mainstream acceptance of ethnic foods, meals can be based on sauces. These sauces were first popularized by Italian-American fare. Think of marinara and clam sauces. Then think farther afield, to Thai curries and Chinese garlic sauces. No longer just for decoration, these sauces may be the focal point of hearty main courses.

Despite their diversity, main course sauces have some common attributes that have led to their growing popularity. Sauces have the convenience of one-dish meals. They are usually cooked in one easy-to-clean pot. Some sauces take as little as 15 minutes to simmer, and none of those in this book is temperamental. Most freeze well, and all make welcome leftovers. They are versatile and can be served over any number of carbohydrates, from rice to pasta, or mixed in with a selection of vegetables. Some sauces are key ingredients in other recipes. A tomato sauce is needed for lasagna; red chili sauce is important in Mexican fare. Because of these sauces' flexibility, if you have a 2-cup container of sauce in the refrigerator or freezer, you'll be able to have a complete meal on the table in about 15 minutes. While the sauce is heating, cook up the starch and make a salad, and you'll be ready to sit down and eat.

~ ~ ~

Tomatoes

Every food writer has rhapsodized about the joys of eating ripe, homegrown tomatoes. It is worrisome that at least one entire generation of people does not know that tomatoes can taste better than the Styrofoam imitators in the supermarket. Food scientists claim that they are developing a tomato with flavor that can be handled as roughly as current mass-market tomatoes. I'll believe it when I see it.

None of the tomato recipes in this book is designed to be made with hard, unripe, bland tomatoes. Luckily, you can still find flavorful tomatoes. Some markets carry quite acceptable, deep red hothouse tomatoes, though usually at an unacceptably high price. Plum tomatoes and cherry tomatoes are flavorful throughout the year. During the summer, farm stands and your own garden are the best sources. Many seed catalogs now have bush varieties that grow well in containers so that even apartment dwellers can have fresh tomatoes.

Once you bring your precious ripe tomatoes home, proper storage is essential. Do not refrigerate tomatoes! Refrigeration harms tomatoes' texture and promotes decay. High temperatures do the same. Tomatoes store best between 55 and 68 degrees F. The refrigerator also destroys flavor. If you have to refrigerate tomatoes, such as cut tomatoes or those in a recipe, bring them back to room temperature before serving.

If ripe tomatoes are impossible to find, use canned. Canned tomatoes have remarkably good fla-

vor. They don't have the firmness you need for salads, but they are equal substitutes in most sauces. Tomato brands vary widely in quality, tomato size, flavor and thickness of the juice. Redpack and Hunt's are two excellent brands.

Peeling and Seeding Tomatoes

Some recipes call for peeled tomatoes. In addition, if you have a bonanza of tomatoes from your garden, you'll want to peel, simmer and freeze them. Peeling tomatoes with a knife or parer is a messy chore. It's better to blanch them. To do this, bring a large pot of water to a rolling boil. Reduce the heat so that it is simmering gently. Have another large pot or bowl filled with cool water. Cut out the core (not too deeply, only enough to remove the tough end) and score an X into the skin on the bottom of each tomato. Drop the tomatoes into the simmering water. I use a slotted spoon to slip them in gently. Within 30 seconds, the skin will start to peel up from the X. If this takes longer, it is probably because the tomatoes are not truly ripe. After 1 minute, remove the tomatoes regardless of how the skins look. Immediately immerse them in the cool water. This is an important step, as you must keep them from cooking. If you are peeling a lot of tomatoes, you might have to change the cold water once. In a few minutes, when the tomatoes are cool enough to handle, strip off their skins.

Although most of the vitamin C is in the gel that holds the tomato's seeds in place, there are times when a recipe asks for seeded tomatoes. Usually this is because the seeds would be unsightly or the juice would contribute too much liquid to the recipe. To seed a tomato, cut it in half across its equator. Set the tomato on a cutting board when you cut it. Don't hold it in your hand; it's easy to cut yourself. Cut in half, the inner pockets of seeds are exposed. The seeds can be removed easily by squeezing or poking them out with your finger.

Basic Basil Tomato Sauce

This simple sauce, though little more than fresh, ripe tomatoes warmed through with basil, sautéed onion and a touch of salt and pepper, is a most appreciated base for many summer meals. For variety, add red pepper flakes, chopped fresh oregano, fromage blanc, mozzarella, roasted garlic, freshly grated Parmesan cheese or all of the above.

If tomato season is over, you can still make this sauce. Don't use out-of-season plum tomatoes. Instead, use canned whole tomatoes. A good brand will provide plenty of flavor. Drain and discard the juice, and chop the tomatoes before putting them in the pot. The sauce will have a deeper flavor but still will taste wonderful over pasta.

MAKES ABOUT 2½ CUPS

½ tablespoon	olive oil
1	small yellow onion, minced (½ cup)
1 tablespoon	white wine
4	medium tomatoes, peeled and seeded, then chopped (2 pounds)

1 cup	fresh basil leaves, loosely packed, chopped
¼ teaspoon	kosher salt
¼ teaspoon	freshly ground pepper

1. Heat the oil in a saucepan over low heat. Sauté the onion in the oil for about 5 minutes. Keep the pan covered. This will bring out the sweetness of the onions. Add the wine and cook for 5 minutes more.

2. Stir in the tomatoes, basil, salt and pepper. Simmer for 15 minutes or longer.

117 CALORIES PER SERVING: 4 G PROTEIN, 4 G FAT, 20 G CARBOHYDRATE; 192 MG SODIUM, 0 MG CHOLESTEROL

 page 110

Freshly Minted Tomato Sauce

Mint in tomato sauce is not a new idea, but the outcome is always a bit surprising and revitalizing. This recipe takes little time to prepare. It's not one of those sauces that gets better after a long simmering, so make it up right before you want to eat. This recipe makes enough for two people, but if you are expecting a houseful, you can expand the recipe easily. You can use canned tomatoes, but the basil and mint must be fresh.

MAKES ABOUT 1¼ CUPS

4	medium tomatoes, peeled and seeded 🍴, then chopped (2 pounds)
2 cloves	garlic, minced (1 teaspoon)
1 teaspoon	minced fresh ginger
½ cup	fresh mint leaves (lightly packed), chopped

½ cup	fresh basil leaves (lightly packed), chopped
⅛ teaspoon	kosher salt
½ tablespoon	olive oil (optional)

1. You can chop the ingredients by hand or use a food processor equipped with a steel blade. If you're using a processor, quarter the tomatoes and keep the rest of the ingredients whole. With the machine running, drop in the garlic and a piece of ginger about the size of a teaspoon. Then pulse in the herbs and quartered tomatoes until the mixture is half smooth, half chunky. Add the salt, then pour the mixture into a saucepan. If you're chopping by hand, combine all the ingredients except the oil in a saucepan.

2. Gently simmer the mixture, uncovered, for 15 minutes.
3. Stir in the olive oil. You can leave out the oil, but the sauce won't be as smooth or rich.

166 CALORIES PER SERVING: 6 G PROTEIN, 6 G FAT, 29 G CARBOHYDRATE; 180 MG SODIUM, 0 MG CHOLESTEROL

🍴 page 110

Roasted Tomato Sauce

Roasting tomatoes gives them an outdoorsy flavor. The shallots and garlic mellow and sweeten with roasting. These flavors combine to create a perfect sauce that can be used as a bed for a grilled fish steak, a pasta topping or an alternative red sauce for lasagna. This sauce must be made with fresh tomatoes. In the winter, use plum tomatoes.

MAKES ABOUT 1½ CUPS

8	plum tomatoes, cored (1 pound)		¼ teaspoon	kosher salt
½ teaspoon	rosemary		¼ teaspoon	freshly ground pepper
2	shallots, peeled		1 teaspoon	extra-virgin olive oil
2 cloves	garlic, peeled			

1. Preheat the oven to 350 degrees F.
2. Place all the ingredients except the oil in a baking dish. Bake, uncovered, for about 40 minutes.
3. Puree the roasted vegetables, making sure to include all the liquid that has oozed out of the tomatoes.
4. Stir in the oil.

102 CALORIES PER SERVING: 3 G PROTEIN, 3 G FAT, 18 G CARBOHYDRATE; 263 MG SODIUM, 0 MG CHOLESTEROL

Tomato Olivada

This is a versatile robust sauce that doesn't require cooking. I like it tossed with hot pasta, as an appetizer on crostini (small servings of grilled bread) or as the topping for bruschetta (grilled, open-faced sandwiches). Pepperoncini are small, green hot peppers packed in a salty brine. You can find them in the Italian foods section of most supermarkets.

MAKES ABOUT 1¾ CUPS

2 cloves	garlic, peeled		1 tablespoon	capers
2	medium tomatoes, peeled and seeded (1 pound)		2 tablespoons	fresh parsley (packed in measurer)
2	pepperoncini		½ cup	pitted Calamata or other strongly flavored olives (don't use canned)

1. Pulse the garlic in the processor until it is finely chopped.
2. Add the remaining ingredients and puree. Leave grainy but not chunky.

80 CALORIES PER SERVING: 2 G PROTEIN, 7 G FAT, 8 G CARBOHYDRATE; 499 MG SODIUM, 0 MG CHOLESTEROL

Red Chili Sauce

This is one of those versatile tomato sauces that is convenient to have stored in two-cup containers in the freezer. Use it in Bean & Tortilla Lasagna (page 102) or to dress up some plain chicken. Or grab a can of beans and make some quick enchiladas with it. The amount of chili powder you use will vary with taste and how hot the chili powder is. When I tried this recipe with a commercial supermarket brand, ¼ cup wasn't enough. But when I used 1 tablespoon of a fiery chili powder that I'd bought in New Mexico, the sauce was resonant with flavor. I like to combine the New Mexico chili powder and a mild, deep red chili powder purchased from a local natural food store.

MAKES ABOUT 7 CUPS

1	medium yellow onion, minced (1 cup)	1 28-ounce can	crushed tomatoes
1	green bell pepper, minced (1 cup)	1 28-ounce can	tomato puree
2 cloves	garlic, minced (1 teaspoon)	1 teaspoon	kosher salt
1 cup	red wine (approximately)	2 tablespoons	chili powder

1. Put the onion, pepper and garlic in a pot. Pour in enough wine to cover the vegetables. Cover and simmer over low heat for about 10 minutes until the vegetables soften.

2. Add the tomato products, salt and chili powder. Simmer, covered, over low heat for at least 30 minutes, preferably longer if you have time.

113 CALORIES PER CUP: 4 G PROTEIN, 1 G FAT, 21 CARBOHYDRATE; 931 MG SODIUM, 0 MG CHOLESTEROL

Mushroom, Bean & Tomato Sauce

I've served this thick and hearty sauce for both lunch and dinner. It's good company fare for casual get-togethers because it remains delicious even if kept warm on top of the stove or if frozen and then reheated. When I have the time and don't mind heating up the kitchen, I cook the beans from scratch. You can use canned beans, but rinse them very well before putting them in the pot. Serve this sauce with pasta or rice.

MAKES ABOUT 5 CUPS

2 teaspoons	olive oil	1 teaspoon	sage
1	medium yellow onion, chopped (1 cup)	½-1 teaspoon	kosher salt (depending on how salty the beans are)
4 cloves	garlic, minced (2 teaspoons)	¼-½ teaspoon	freshly ground pepper (or to taste)
8 ounces	mushrooms (about 2 cups), sliced	¼ cup	fresh parsley, minced
2 cups	cooked navy or cannellini beans		
1 28-ounce can	whole tomatoes, with juice		

1. Heat the oil in a heavy-bottomed pot. Sauté the onion and garlic in the oil.
2. Add the mushrooms and sauté until they wilt.
3. Break up the tomatoes with your hands as you add them to the pot. Stir in all the remaining ingredients except the parsley. Simmer over medium heat (it should be boiling, but not spattering out of the pot) for 15 minutes.
4. Add the parsley. Cook for 5 minutes more.

148 CALORIES PER SERVING: 8 G PROTEIN, 2 G FAT, 26 G CARBOHYDRATE; 379 MG SODIUM, 0 MG CHOLESTEROL

African Peanut Sauce

This has become one of the standards in my kitchen. All the ingredients are always in my cupboard, and making the sauce takes little effort. Use it with pasta, polenta or rice. When paired with a salad or green vegetable, it makes a colorful, spicy and nutritious meal. Leftovers are great.

MAKES ABOUT 4 CUPS

1½ teaspoons	peanut oil
1	medium yellow onion, minced (1 cup)
2 cloves	garlic, minced (1 teaspoon)
2 teaspoons	curry powder
½ teaspoon	ground coriander
1 28-ounce can	crushed tomatoes
½ teaspoon	kosher salt
⅛ teaspoon	crushed red pepper flakes
⅛ teaspoon	Tabasco or other hot pepper sauce
2 tablespoons	peanut butter
¼ cup	unsalted roasted peanuts, coarsely chopped

1. Heat the oil in a heavy-bottomed pot. Sauté the onion and garlic in the oil until the onion is soft and golden.
2. Add the curry powder and coriander, then cook for 1 minute more.
3. Pour in the tomatoes, then stir in the salt, crushed pepper flakes and Tabasco. Cover and simmer over low heat for 15 minutes.
4. Stir in the peanut butter and peanuts. Cook for about 5 minutes more. Stir frequently so that the sauce at the bottom of the pot doesn't overcook. The sauce is done when it thickens.

117 CALORIES PER SERVING: 4 G PROTEIN, 7 G FAT, 11 G CARBOHYDRATE; 400 MG SODIUM, 0 MG CHOLESTEROL

Red Pepper Sauce

This velvety smooth, cheerfully colored sauce is mild yet has an interesting flavor. Pour it over baked or broiled fish, toss it with pasta and vegetables, or pour a pool of it on a dinner plate and arrange sliced chicken breast on top.

MAKES ABOUT 1¼ CUPS

2	large red bell peppers
1 teaspoon	olive oil
2 cloves	garlic, peeled

½ teaspoon	kosher salt
¼ teaspoon	freshly ground pepper
⅓-½ cup	defatted chicken or vegetable stock

1. Preheat the oven to 400 degrees F.
2. Cut the peppers in half. Remove and discard the cores and seeds. Trim off the whitish membranes.
3. In a heavy casserole dish, toss together the peppers, oil, garlic, salt and pepper.
4. Bake the peppers for about 30 minutes until their skins begin to blister and the peppers wilt.
5. Put the contents of the casserole (including the juice) in a blender or food mill and puree. Add at least ⅓ cup stock to thin the sauce to the desired consistency. If the peppers were very large, you might want to use ½ cup stock.
6. Use the sauce immediately or reheat it later.

25 CALORIES PER SERVING: 1 G PROTEIN, 1 G FAT, 3 G CARBOHYDRATE; 240 MG SODIUM, 0 MG CHOLESTEROL

Island Barbecue Sauce

The molasses in this sauce gives it a Caribbean flair. Brush it on chicken or marinate the meat in it. For a shortcut, put a skinless piece of chicken in a glass casserole, pour a generous amount of sauce over it, cover and microwave on high until done. The sauce keeps for several weeks in a glass jar in the refrigerator.

MAKES ABOUT 2⅓ CUPS

½ cup	honey
½ cup	molasses
½ cup	apple cider vinegar
¼ cup	catsup
3 tablespoons	soy sauce

2 tablespoons	Dijon mustard
½ teaspoon	Tabasco or other hot pepper sauce
¼ cup	orange juice concentrate
2 tablespoons	tomato paste

1. Blend all the ingredients until smooth, but don't liquefy.
2. Taste and adjust the seasonings. You might want to increase the soy and Tabasco sauce or give it more of a citrus punch with some added orange juice.

80 CALORIES PER TABLESPOON: .5 G PROTEIN, 0 G FAT, 21 G CARBOHYDRATE; 305 MG SODIUM, 0 MG CHOLESTEROL

Sweet & Sour Sauce

This sauce is sweet enough for kids but complex enough for adults.
It can be reheated, but it will be a bit thinner.

MAKES ABOUT 1¼ CUPS

2 tablespoons	honey
2 tablespoons	catsup
2 tablespoons	rice or white wine vinegar
2 tablespoons	dry sherry
2 tablespoons	soy sauce

1 8-ounce can	pineapple chunks packed in their own juice
2 teaspoons	arrowroot
1 tablespoon	water

1. In a small saucepan, stir together the honey, catsup, vinegar, sherry and soy sauce. Drain the pineapple juice into the pan. Simmer for 5 minutes.
2. Mix together the arrowroot and water to form a paste. Pour it slowly (to prevent lumping) into the gently simmering liquid. It will turn the liquid cloudy. Stir until the sauce thickens and clears.
3. Add the pineapple chunks. You might want to cut them into smaller pieces first, although I've found that children like the big chunks. Heat through.

63 CALORIES PER SERVING: .5 G PROTEIN, 0 G FAT, 15 G CARBOHYDRATE; 396 MG SODIUM, 0 MG CHOLESTEROL

Gingered Marmalade Sauce

I love good marmalade, the type made with the peels of Seville oranges. Purchase marmalade that lists these bitter oranges as the first ingredient on its label. Also, check to make sure that the marmalade is sweetened with sugar, not corn syrup. Brush this sauce on skinless chicken pieces or even a whole bird. Baste the poultry every 15 minutes to keep it moist.

MAKES ABOUT 1 CUP

½ cup	orange marmalade
½ cup	orange juice
½ teaspoon	minced or grated fresh ginger
1 tablespoon	Dijon mustard

⅛ teaspoon	Tabasco or other hot pepper sauce
½ teaspoon	kosher salt
¼ teaspoon	freshly ground pepper

1. Blend all the ingredients together.

80 CALORIES PER TABLESPOON: .5 G PROTEIN, 0 G FAT, 21 G CARBOHYDRATE; 305 MG SODIUM, 0 MG CHOLESTEROL

Arrowroot

Without thickeners, pies would be more like fruit soups and sauces wouldn't adhere to foods. All three of the most frequently used thickeners are starches. Cornstarch, flour and arrowroot swell and form a viscous matrix when mixed with hot liquids. They'll also all clump if added directly to hot water, which is why they are first mixed with cold water to form a paste, then gradually stirred into the hot sauce. (A roux works the same way, but because it is butter based, it is not discussed here.)

Sauces become thickest between 175 and 200 degrees F (212 degrees F is a full boil). But they are not stable. If they are heated for a long time or heated to the boiling point, or if an overzealous cook vigorously stirs the pot, the starch granules will swell and shatter, and the sauce will thin.

My thickener of choice is arrowroot for many reasons. Flour is not a powerful thickener. It has about half the strength of cornstarch and arrowroot. Also, it contains proteins, which prevent the sauce from clearing. Some people like cloudy sauces for some recipes, such as apple pie. But cornstarch and arrowroot create translucent sauces, which look much nicer for poached fruit glazes, such as Sweet-and-Sour Sauce (opposite).

Cornstarch and flour are derived from grains. Unless they are cooked first, they may give the sauce a pasty, raw taste. Arrowroot has virtually no flavor. For this reason alone, I prefer it. Additionally, cornstarch takes longer to thicken and requires higher temperatures than arrowroot. Thus, when you're working with delicate foods, arrowroot is preferable.

Arrowroot is not always available in the supermarket. When it is, sometimes it is sold in small, overpriced jars. Natural food stores and Asian markets usually offer arrowroot at a better price. If you can't find it, cornstarch is an acceptable alternative.

Red Salsa

No longer just a chip dip, salsa is just right for adding spark to bean dishes, as a relish for chicken and as the spread in a turkey sandwich. This version (and there are as many as there are cooks) is very easy to make. All the ingredients are chopped in the food processor. I use canned sliced jalapeños, which eases preparation even more.

Ripe, juicy homegrown tomatoes will make the salsa soupy unless they are seeded first. Just cut the tomatoes in half around the equator and squeeze out the juice and seeds. In most cases, this won't be necessary, because most supermarket tomatoes, even when ripe, are not very juicy.

MAKES ABOUT 2 CUPS

2	large tomatoes, cored and quartered		1	lime, peeled and quartered
2 cloves	garlic		½ teaspoon	kosher salt
2 tablespoons	canned sliced jalapeños		¼ teaspoon	freshly ground pepper
6	scallions, cut into fourths		2 teaspoons	oregano
1 tablespoon	fresh parsley		¼ teaspoon	ground cumin

1. Put all the ingredients in the food processor. Pulse until coarsely chopped. This will take only a few whirs of the machine. If you want the salsa chunky, start with the ingredients that need to be minced—the garlic, scallions and lime. The rest can be pulsed once or twice. The fineness of the texture is up to you. Be aware that if the machine is left running (instead of using the pulse switch), the salsa will become soupy.

55 CALORIES PER CUP: 2 G PROTEIN, 1 G FAT, 13 G CARBOHYDRATE; 485 MG SODIUM, 0 MG CHOLESTEROL

page 208

Pineapple Salsa

Unusual and festive, this salsa goes with chips but also makes a terrific relish for fish or chicken. I use commonly available jalapeños, but if you have access to hotter peppers or smoky chipotles or habañeros, feel free to experiment. Cilantro can overwhelm the subtle sweet flavors in this recipe, so if you're adding this herb, use only 1 tablespoon.

MAKES ABOUT 5 CUPS

2½ cups	fresh pineapple, or 1 20-ounce can chunks
2 tablespoons	canned jalapeño pepper, or 1 to 2 fresh jalapeños
2 tablespoons	fresh parsley
1 clove	garlic, peeled
½	green or red bell pepper, seeded
2	large tomatoes, cored, seeded and quartered
1	medium red onion, peeled and quartered
¼ cup	lime juice
1 teaspoon	kosher salt

1. This is a food processor recipe. If you don't own a processor, just mince everything.
2. If you're using canned pineapple, drain and discard the juice.
3. Start the processor (fitted with a steel blade) then drop in the jalapeño, parsley and garlic. Mince.
4. Add the rest of the ingredients. Pulse to chop to the desired chunkiness. This will take only a few whirs of the processor. Too many pulses and the salsa will become watery.
5. Store for up to 1 week in a glass jar in the refrigerator.

4 CALORIES PER TABLESPOON: 0 G PROTEIN, 0 G FAT, 1 G CARBOHYDRATE; 27 MG SODIUM, 0 MG CHOLESTEROL

page 110

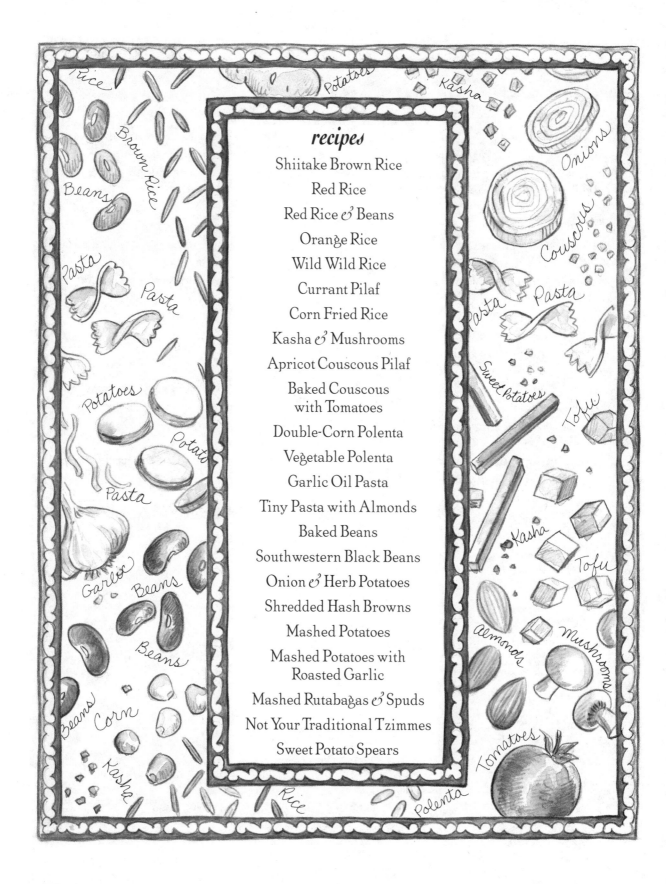

recipes

Shiitake Brown Rice

Red Rice

Red Rice & Beans

Orange Rice

Wild Wild Rice

Currant Pilaf

Corn Fried Rice

Kasha & Mushrooms

Apricot Couscous Pilaf

Baked Couscous
with Tomatoes

Double-Corn Polenta

Vegetable Polenta

Garlic Oil Pasta

Tiny Pasta with Almonds

Baked Beans

Southwestern Black Beans

Onion & Herb Potatoes

Shredded Hash Browns

Mashed Potatoes

Mashed Potatoes with
Roasted Garlic

Mashed Rutabagas & Spuds

Not Your Traditional Tzimmes

Sweet Potato Spears

Grains, Pastas, Beans & Potatoes

*t*hank goodness the lowly "starch" is finally getting the good PR it deserves. Once thought of as only a minor side dish—the potato next to the steak or the slice of bread to be buttered—carbohydrates have proven themselves to be as enticing, wholesome and varied as the rest of the meal. Once they were wrongly seen as fattening, but now it is agreed that when cooked with little fat, they are fibrous and nutrient-dense foods—an important part of a healthy weight-maintenance program.

With the growing interest in world cuisines, the selection of carbohydrates and the way they are prepared have expanded. There are a dozen types of rice, new golden potatoes, crusty peasant breads, grains from Eastern Europe and North Africa, and pastas in a panoply of shapes and sizes. These can be cooked simply or made into complex meals. And, of course, the basics, such as baked potatoes and boiled long-grain rice, never go out of style.

In this chapter, I provide background and shopping information for carbohydrates and easy cooking directions so that each starch can become a familiar part of your repertoire. The recipes that follow build on those basics.

Grains

Rice

North America is one of the few places in the world where people prefer fluffy, slightly dry rice. The Italians use a creamy arborio rice. Across Asia, there are many varieties of gelatinous and sticky sweet rice to form into balls. All rice-eating nations have one thing in common, though: the preference for white rice. Like hearty bread, brown rice is seen as a food for peasants. White and light is a sign of status. Of great importance, too, is that when rice is polished and the bran, germ and husk are removed, the grains can be kept indefinitely. Brown rice goes rancid by the sixth month. Long-term storage is of critical importance when the product being held and distributed is the main source of energy and nutrients for a population, as rice is for much of the world.

But polished rice also has problems. Protein, B-vitamin complexes, other nutrients and fiber are greatly reduced in refined rice. Compared to nutty brown rice, the flavor is bland and the texture soft. For these reasons, all my recipes call for brown rice. If you would rather use white rice you can adjust most recipes by reducing the liquid by ½ cup per cup of rice and reducing the cooking time by one-half.

Brown rice is sold in four general types. Long-grain rice cooks up the lightest and fluffiest and is most like the regular white rice sold in North Amer-ica. Medium-grain rice is a tad stickier. Short-grain rice is the sweetest and most gelatinous rice. Aromatic rices, such as basmati, Texmati or Wehani, are generally long grain and perfume the kitchen with popcornlike smells as they simmer. Some supermarkets sell long-grain brown rice in small boxes. All natural food stores sell brown rice. Purchase rice from a store that has a high turnover of product. Select it from a bin where the grains are clean, not dusty, and the kernels are whole and tan, not green.

Brown rice is easy to cook. All you need is a pot of boiling water with a lid. Rice can be boiled like pasta. When it tests done, drain it in a fine-mesh colander. Or measure out 2 cups of water for every 1 cup of rice. Bring the water to a boil, add the rice, reduce the heat to a simmer, cover and cook until the water is absorbed. In both cases, the texture of the rice is improved if it rests for 10 minutes before serving. Keep it covered to keep the steam and heat in. I can't give an accurate cooking time because it varies with the type of rice used and how recently it was harvested. Generally, brown rice takes 40 to 50 minutes to cook.

As a rule of thumb, remember that 1 cup of rice expands to three times its volume when cooked. Cooked rice can be refrigerated for 5 days or frozen for 4 months to be used later in soups and casseroles.

Shiitake Brown Rice

Shiitake mushrooms are now widely, though sporadically, available in many supermarkets. If your store doesn't stock them, ask; the produce manager can often purchase a small amount by special order. If your market has other "exotic" mushrooms on your shopping day, try one of those when you want a gutsier flavor than what the standard white button mushrooms provide.

SERVES 3 TO 4

6	medium shiitake mushrooms, sliced (1 cup)	2 teaspoons	soy sauce
1 teaspoon	vegetable oil	2 tablespoons	defatted chicken or vegetable stock
1 clove	garlic, minced (½ teaspoon)	2 cups	cooked brown rice
½	small leek, cut into half rounds (½ cup)		

1. Snap the stems off the mushrooms and discard. Quickly wash the shiitakes under cool running water. Pat them dry. Cut extra-large mushrooms in half before slicing. Slice into strips.
2. Heat the oil in a nonstick pan. Sauté the garlic and leeks in the oil until the leeks are golden. Be careful not to scorch the garlic.

3. Add the mushrooms to the pan along with 1 teaspoon of the soy sauce and 1 tablespoon of the stock. Cook until the mushrooms soften and wilt a bit.
4. Stir in the rice and the remaining 1 teaspoon soy sauce and 1 tablespoon stock. Heat through and serve.

198 CALORIES PER SERVING: 4 G PROTEIN, 3 G FAT, 40 G CARBOHYDRATE; 237 MG SODIUM, 0 MG CHOLESTEROL

Red Rice

This robustly flavored rice mélange is tinged a light red. Brown rice is used for its chewy texture and nutty flavor. You can use white rice, but decrease the water by ½ cup and simmer for 20 to 30 minutes. These red rice recipes may be served as main courses or side dishes.

SERVES 4 TO 8

1 teaspoon	vegetable oil		2	bay leaves
2 cloves	garlic, minced (1 teaspoon)		1 cup	brown rice, rinsed
1	small yellow onion, chopped (½ cup)		1¾ cups	water
1 rib	celery, chopped		½ teaspoon	kosher salt
½	green bell pepper, chopped (½ cup)		¼ teaspoon	freshly ground pepper
2	medium tomatoes, peeled and seeded, then chopped		⅛ teaspoon	cayenne pepper (or to taste)

1. Heat the oil in a 2 quart saucepan. Sauté the garlic, onion, celery and green pepper in the oil. Keep the pan covered between stirrings. Cook for at least 5 minutes until the vegetables are thoroughly softened and the onion is golden.
2. Add the tomatoes, bay leaves and rice. Sauté for 2 minutes more.
3. Add the water and the remaining seasonings.
4. Bring to a boil, then reduce to a simmer. Cook, covered, for about 50 minutes until all the liquid is absorbed.

210 CALORIES PER SERVING: 5 G PROTEIN, 3 G FAT, 43 G CARBOHYDRATE; 260 MG SODIUM, 0 MG CHOLESTEROL

page 110

Red Rice & Beans

The combination of beans and rice is important for vegetarians because each food's amino acids complement the other to form a complete protein.

SERVES 4 TO 8

Red Rice (see above)

2 cups cooked kidney, pinto or black beans

1. Either heat the beans and then stir them into the hot rice or heat the two together in the microwave.

322 CALORIES PER SERVING: 12 G PROTEIN, 3 G FAT, 63 G CARBOHYDRATE; 262 MG SODIUM, 0 MG CHOLESTEROL

Orange Rice

Plain rice is fine for a simple dinner, but when you've put a lot of effort into the rest of the meal, it's nice to have the side dish live up to the other components. This recipe helps you to dress up rice so that it looks and tastes as special as everything else on the table.

SERVES 4 TO 6

1	orange	¼ teaspoon	kosher salt
1½ cups	water	1 cup	long-grain brown rice

1. Zest the orange. Reserve ½ tablespoon of zest.
2. Juice the orange. Measure out ½ cup of juice. One orange should yield enough juice, but if it doesn't (sometimes navels are rather dry), squeeze another orange or add some commercial juice.
3. Bring the orange juice, water and salt to a boil. Rinse the rice, then stir it in.
4. Reduce the heat to a simmer. Cover and cook for about 45 minutes until all the liquid is absorbed.
5. Remove the pan from the stove. Stir in the zest. Cover again and let the rice rest for 10 minutes (this will fluff it a bit). Rice cooked in a heavy pot that retains heat will remain hot.

185 CALORIES PER SERVING: 4 G PROTEIN, 1 G FAT, 39 G CARBOHYDRATE; 124 MG SODIUM, 0 MG CHOLESTEROL

Zest

Citrus adds a fresh, clean taste and aroma to recipes. But citrus juice is not the only part of the fruit that can be used to liven up foods. The peel, too, is edible. The part of the citrus skin that is used for cooking is called the zest. It is the colorful outer layer, with none of the bitter white pith of the underside.

You can carefully peel the skin using a sharp paring knife or vegetable peeler and achieve moderate success, or you can invest in an inexpensive and simple tool that makes short work of this chore. This tool is called a zester. It is a small, hand-held utensil that has several sharp holes in its blade. These holes pull fine strips of zest off the peel. An average lemon yields 1 to 2 tablespoons of zest.

You also can use a hand-held grater (the type used for Parmesan cheese and ginger) to zest a fruit. Grating gives you the texture of minced zest, but it won't yield pretty strips like the zester.

When a recipe calls for zest, the tendency is to strip the skin and then put the fruit back in the refrigerator, where it will soon dry out and become inedible. This is a waste of a perfectly good orange or fresh juice. Try to counter this by eating the fruit or juicing it right away. Lemon juice will last a week in the refrigerator and up to 6 months in the freezer. Always zest before peeling because it is difficult to zest a hollowed-out rind.

Wild Wild Rice

Wild rice is expensive, but a little goes a long way. The long, dark brown grains contribute an earthy flavor, an enticing aroma and a lovely color to rice dishes. Porcini mushrooms are expensive, too, but they add a lot of value for their cost. If you can't find these dried Italian mushrooms, any wild dried mushrooms will do. Dried mushrooms are essential to this dish because they release their flavor into the rice broth.

SERVES 4 TO 6

½ cup	porcini or similar dried mushrooms
2½ cups	water
¼ teaspoon	kosher salt
¾ cup	long-grain brown rice
½ cup	wild rice

¼ teaspoon	thyme
¼ teaspoon	sage
⅛ teaspoon	freshly ground pepper
½ cup	nuts, toasted and chopped (optional)
1 tablespoon	minced fresh parsley for garnish

1. Rinse the mushrooms thoroughly under cold running water. Then soak them in hot water for about 5 minutes until they become soft enough to slice. Cut them into thin strips.
2. Bring the 2½ cups water and salt to a boil. Stir in the rices and the sliced mushrooms. Reduce to a simmer, cover and cook for 1 hour until the rice is done.
3. Remove the pan from the stove. Stir in the herbs and pepper. Use a fork to stir and fluff. Cover the rice and let it rest for 10 minutes before serving.
4. Just prior to putting the rice in a serving bowl, stir in the toasted nuts if desired.
5. Garnish with parsley.

203 CALORIES PER SERVING: 6 G PROTEIN, 1 G FAT, 42 G CARBOHYDRATE; 127 MG SODIUM, 0 MG CHOLESTEROL

Currant Pilaf

Cooking rice in chicken stock gives it a rich flavor and color. Canned stocks are convenient, but they sometimes taste too strong or bitter. Also, some brands contain MSG, too much salt or sugar, so read the labels and shop wisely. If I do have to use canned stock, I dilute it with an equal amount of water to get a more homemade flavor.

SERVES 6 TO 8

2 teaspoons	olive oil		3 cups	defatted chicken stock
2	carrots, grated or diced (1 cup)		½ teaspoon	kosher salt
¼ teaspoon	turmeric		¼ teaspoon	freshly ground pepper
1½ cups	long-grain brown rice, rinsed		⅓ cup	currants

1. Heat the oil in a sauté pan over medium heat. Sauté the carrots in the oil for about 5 minutes.
2. Add the turmeric and rice, and continue to sauté until all the grains are golden.
3. Add the stock, salt and pepper. Bring the stock to a boil, then reduce to a simmer. Cover and cook for 30 minutes.

4. Stir in the currants. Cover again and continue to cook for 10 to 15 minutes until all the liquid is absorbed.
5. Turn off the heat. Fluff the rice with a fork, then let it rest, covered, for about 10 minutes.

226 CALORIES PER SERVING: 6 G PROTEIN, 3 G FAT, 44 G CARBOHYDRATE; 194 MG SODIUM, 0 MG CHOLESTEROL

Corn Fried Rice

Lots of ginger and the sweet zing of Sichuan peppercorns define this dish. It is especially good during corn season, when I use corn picked in the morning, still cool from the fields.

SERVES 4 TO 6

2 cups	corn kernels		1 tablespoon	soy sauce
1 teaspoon	peanut oil		¼ teaspoon	freshly ground pepper
1 tablespoon	minced fresh gingerroot		¼ teaspoon	crushed Sichuan peppercorns
1 clove	garlic, minced (½ teaspoon)		2 tablespoons	sherry
3	scallions, sliced		1 teaspoon	toasted sesame oil
1 cup	cooked brown rice			

1. If the corn is frozen, defrost and partially cook it.
2. Heat the peanut oil in a sauté pan over low heat. Sauté the ginger and garlic in the oil until they are golden. Keep the heat low because ginger tends to scorch.
3. Stir in the scallions. Cook for about 2 minutes until the scallions wilt.
4. Add the corn, rice, soy sauce, pepper, peppercorns, sherry and sesame oil. Increase the heat, cover and cook about 5 minutes. Stir the rice a couple of times while it is cooking.

157 CALORIES PER SERVING: 4 G PROTEIN, 3 G FAT, 30 G CARBOHYDRATE; 265 MG SODIUM, 0 MG CHOLESTEROL

Sichuan Peppercorns

*S*ichuan peppercorns are tiny, dark berries held in the center of a reddish, partially open husk. Like other peppercorns, they'll last indefinitely if stored in an airtight container in a dark place. Also like other peppercorns, they need to be ground to be used. This can be accomplished with a mortar and pestle or a small processor. Sichuan peppercorns contribute a unique, warm, spicy flavor to foods.

Kasha

Kasha, also called buckwheat, is not a member of the wheat family. Botanically, it isn't even a grain, but it is considered and used as such by cooks throughout the world, especially in Eastern Europe. Nutritionally, there are good reasons to cook with it, as it is high in protein and potassium. But I use it because it has such a unique flavor and, compared to other grains, it takes only a few minutes to cook.

Basic Kasha

SERVES 4

| 2 cups | water |
| 1 cup | kasha |

| 1 | egg white, lightly beaten |

1. Bring the water to a boil.
2. Meanwhile, mix together the kasha and egg white. Heat them in a small pan over medium heat until the egg white cooks and dries out. Stir constantly and break apart any clumps.
3. Add the kasha to the boiling water. Cover and reduce to a simmer. Cook gently for about 10 minutes until the kasha has absorbed all the liquid.
4. Remove the pot from the stove and allow the kasha to steam, with the lid on, for another couple of minutes.

146 CALORIES PER SERVING: 6 G PROTEIN, 1 G FAT, 31 G CARBOHYDRATE; 22 MG SODIUM, 0 MG CHOLESTEROL

Kasha & Mushrooms

Instead of trying to subdue kasha's dark, earthy, roasted flavor, I celebrate it here with mushrooms. Still, I don't like kasha that is heavy and mushy, so I cook it a day in advance. Time in the refrigerator separates the kernels and dries them out.

SERVES 4

½ pound	mushrooms
1 teaspoon	olive oil
1 small	carrot, peeled and chopped
2 cups	cooked kasha (see preceding recipe)

¼ teaspoon	kosher salt
¼ teaspoon	freshly ground pepper
2 tablespoons	minced fresh parsley

1. Put the mushrooms in a colander and wash them quickly under cool running water. Shake the colander as you do this. Wipe off any stubborn spots of dirt with a paper towel. Cut the dried-out ends off the mushroom stems, then cut the mushrooms into quarters.
2. Heat the oil in a 10-inch nonstick pan. Sauté the mushrooms and carrots in the oil until the mushrooms exude liquid.
3. Add the kasha, salt, pepper and parsley. Break up any clumps of kasha as it is being heated.

131 CALORIES PER SERVING: 5 G PROTEIN, 2 G FAT, 25 G CARBOHYDRATE; 141 MG SODIUM; 0 MG CHOLESTEROL

Couscous

The tiny rounds of couscous are made from semolina, a hybrid of wheat that also is used for pasta. Couscous is a staple in Morocco, where a traditional version of couscous is carefully steamed in a special pot. It is possible to get this type of couscous in specialty shops in this country, but you can find instant couscous in your supermarket. It is no match for the original, but it stands on its own merits, and I use it frequently.

Instant couscous is the fastest cooking carbohydrate. Drop it into boiling water, cover the pan and remove it from the burner. Then allow it to sit for a couple of minutes, and it will swell and fluff up. Like the best pasta, it is a golden color. Couscous is soft yet chewy enough and tasty yet bland enough to suit picky young eaters. It is the perfect backdrop for other flavors and holds sauces well.

The directions on the box suggest adding butter. Ignore this unnecessary advice. Add salt only if you want the added flavor. Figure that ¼ cup couscous added to ½ cup boiling water will yield a ⅔-cup serving.

Apricot Couscous Pilaf

Most commercially available couscous takes only minutes to cook, so it is perfect for hot days when you don't want to be near a stove and for camping because it requires very little fuel. If couscous is unavailable, you can substitute fine bulgur wheat.

SERVES 4 TO 6

1 teaspoon	vegetable oil
½	carrot, peeled and cut into small cubes (½ cup)
3 tablespoons	sliced pecans or almonds
1½ cups	water
¾ cup	uncooked couscous
½ teaspoon	curry powder
¼ teaspoon	kosher salt
¼ cup	dried apricots, sliced

1. Heat the oil in a nonstick pan. Cook the carrots in the oil for about 3 minutes until they begin to soften. Keep the pan covered. Add the nuts, increase the heat to high and cook for 1 minute until the nuts begin to brown. You'll be able to smell the change in their flavor.

2. In another pot, bring the water to a boil. Stir in the couscous, curry powder, salt, apricots and carrot mixture. Cover, remove from heat and let rest for 5 minutes.

200 CALORIES PER SERVING: 5 G PROTEIN, 5 G FAT, 34 G CARBOHYDRATE; 129 MG SODIUM, 0 MG CHOLESTEROL

Baked Couscous with Tomatoes

This is a pretty dish; tiny golden grains of couscous are decorated with the rich red color of diced tomatoes. I've kept the seasonings simple so that this casserole can complement many other recipes. It makes a nice bed for Oven-Baked Ratatouille (page 90) or Turkish Tomatoes & Zucchini (page 166) and is a lovely side dish for Fish Baked with Mint (page 83).

SERVES 6

1 tablespoon	olive oil
1	small yellow onion, minced (½ cup)
3	tomatoes, peeled and seeded then diced, or 1 14-ounce can whole tomatoes, diced

2 cups	uncooked couscous
3 cups	defatted chicken or vegetable stock or water
1 teaspoon	kosher salt
¼ teaspoon	freshly ground pepper
½ teaspoon	ground coriander

1. Preheat the oven to 375 degrees F. The temperature is not critical. If you are using the oven for another recipe that requires a temperature anywhere from 350 to 400 degrees F, you can bake the couscous at the same time.
2. Heat the oil in a sauté pan. Sauté the onion in the oil about 5 minutes until it is soft and golden.
3. Combine the sautéed onion and all the remaining ingredients in a bowl. Transfer the mixture to a 2-quart casserole. Don't try to mix the ingredients in the casserole because it won't be big enough and some will spill over the sides.
4. Bake for 20 minutes.

270 CALORIES PER SERVING: 9 G PROTEIN, 3 G FAT, 51 G CARBOHYDRATE; 329 MG SODIUM, 0 MG CHOLESTEROL

page 110

Polenta

If you are looking for a carbohydrate but are tired of pasta and potatoes, try polenta. Polenta is cooked cornmeal. To make polenta, you have to start with quality cornmeal that has not been degerminated. This is not available in supermarkets, since the germ contains oils that go rancid quickly and supermarkets stock only shelf-stable grains. To me, the trade-off for a long shelf life isn't worth it, since supermarket cornmeal tastes like yellow grit. Cornmeal that still contains the germ has flavor and many more vitamins, so it is worth a trip to an Italian grocer or natural food store to purchase it. Buy cornmeal from a store that keeps it in the refrigerator case. Store it in a glass container in your refrigerator, where it will keep for months.

Boiled in water, like oatmeal, polenta turns into mush. Some people like to eat it right out of the pot, but I like it firmed up into chewy squares. To do this, spread the polenta about ½ inch thick on a tray. The tray does not have to be greased. Surprisingly, the polenta won't stick to it. I don't cover polenta with plastic wrap because the water in it will condense as it cools, collect under the plastic and make the cornmeal soggy.

Once the polenta has firmed up, cover and refrigerate it. It will stay fresh for several days. When you want to eat a piece of polenta, cut a square out of the tray. Use polenta squares as you would pasta—as a base for sautéed vegetables or sauce or as a side starch. The polenta will need to be reheated. It can be toasted like bread, browned in a 400 degree F oven or panfried in a small amount of oil in a nonstick pan until the edges are crispy.

Basic Polenta

SERVES 12

1 cup	cornmeal
½ teaspoon	kosher salt
4 cups	water

1. Combine the cornmeal and salt with 1 cup of the water to form a smooth, loose paste.
2. Bring the remaining 3 cups water to a simmer.
3. Slowly pour in the cornmeal slurry, stirring constantly with a wooden spoon until the cornmeal is spread evenly throughout the water and there aren't any lumps.
4. Coarse cornmeal, which is the only type commonly available in natural food stores, will take up to 20 minutes to cook. Heat over a medium-low heat so that the surface of the cornmeal bubbles gently. Polenta requires frequent stirring to prevent lumps and sticking and to develop the right texture. Spoon down the cornmeal that sticks to the sides of the pot. Cook until the cornmeal absorbs the water and the polenta becomes thick like oatmeal and hard to stir.
5. Serve immediately, or pour onto an ungreased baking sheet to let the polenta solidify. Follow the serving ideas above.

37 CALORIES PER SERVING: 1 G PROTEIN, 0 G FAT, 8 G CARBOHYDRATE; 84 MG SODIUM, 0 MG CHOLESTEROL

Double-Corn Polenta

In this version of polenta, corn kernels are added for double-corn flavor and extra texture.

SERVES 12

4½ cups	water
1 teaspoon	kosher salt

1½ cups	cornmeal
1 cup	cooked corn kernels

1. Bring 3½ cups of the water and the salt to a boil. Reduce to a simmer.
2. In a bowl, stir together the cornmeal and the remaining 1 cup water until smooth.
3. Pour the cornmeal mixture slowly into the simmering water. Stir constantly to prevent lumps.
4. Simmer, uncovered, for 20 minutes, stirring frequently. Keep the heat very low to prevent scorching.
5. Stir in the corn kernels, then simmer for another 15 minutes, again stirring frequently.
6. Pour into an ungreased baking sheet. Spread it out so that the polenta is about ½ inch thick. It might not fill up the entire sheet.
7. Allow the polenta to cool. Store it for up to 3 days in the refrigerator.

66 CALORIES PER SERVING: 2 G PROTEIN, 0.5 G FAT, 15 G CARBOHYDRATE; 164 MG SODIUM, 0 MG CHOLESTEROL

Vegetable Polenta

For this recipe, I've stirred vegetables and a small amount of Parmesan cheese into the polenta to add texture, color and flavor. These are only guidelines; the specific flavors and textures are up to you. As long as you follow the proportions set down, the recipe will work fine.

SERVES 12

	Basic Polenta ▥, still warm and in the pot
1 teaspoon	vegetable oil
1	medium yellow onion, chopped (1 cup)
4 cups	dark, leafy greens, such as spinach or white-ribbed Swiss chard, or 1 cup harder vegetables, such as green beans, asparagus or broccoli, cut into bite-size pieces

¼ teaspoon	kosher salt
⅛ teaspoon	freshly ground pepper
2 tablespoons	freshly grated Parmesan cheese (optional)

1. Heat the oil in a sauté pan over low heat. Sauté the onion in the oil for about 10 minutes until it is golden.
2. Meanwhile, cook the vegetables. Most types will need a light steaming or microwaving until they become softer but still have texture. If you're using leafy greens, wilt them in a pan or the microwave, then squeeze out any excess moisture. Don't use red-ribbed Swiss chard, or the polenta will have streaks of purple.
3. Stir the onion, vegetables, salt, pepper and Parmesan (if using) into the polenta.

4. Spread the polenta in an ungreased 9-by-12-inch pan. I like my polenta firm, so give it time to set. If you're going to refrigerate it, let it cool on the counter, or condensation will drip off the pan's cover and into the polenta.
5. There are a couple of ways to handle the polenta once it is firm. See page 134 for some ideas. A favorite of mine is to bake the entire pan at 400 degrees F until the top begins to brown and bubble. I do not think that brushing oil on top (as is often suggested) improves the taste.

49 CALORIES PER SERVING: 1 G PROTEIN, 1 G FAT, 10 G CARBOHYDRATE; 134 MG SODIUM, 0 MG CHOLESTEROL

▥ page 134

Pasta

Widely available, affordable, convenient to store, quick to cook and easy to make into a meal, this low-fat complex carbohydrate is deservedly popular. The "fresh" pastas in the refrigerator case at the supermarket have a long shelf life, a high price tag and poor texture and flavor. Good-quality dried pastas are better. Brands vary widely. The well-known commercial names, such as Prince and Ronzoni are adequate. Cheaper versions taste like pasty white bread. The best pastas are made from hard semolina wheat, which gives the pasta a warm yellow cast, nutty flavor and toothsome texture. They are slightly rough, which indicates that they were produced with more care and that they hold sauces better. Most often the best brands are imported, although I've found a few made in North America. They are a bit more expensive, but even the best pastas are relatively cheap. (Prohibitively priced pastas aren't worth the money and are usually just trading on snob appeal.) Try several brands before you settle on a favorite.

Pasta comes in a multitude of shapes. Traditionalists insist on certain shapes with certain sauces. Generally, nubby and twisted pastas hold thick and chunky sauces well. Spaghetti-type shapes work well with thinner, olive oil-based sauces.

To cook pasta, bring a large pot of water to a rolling boil. If desired, you can add salt. Don't pour in oil. It doesn't prevent the pasta from sticking. All it does is keep the pot from foaming. It also can be dangerous. Oil rises to the surface, and if the pot boils over, the fat could spill onto the flame and ignite. Stir the pasta a couple of times as it cooks to prevent it from sticking together or settling to the bottom of the pot. Keep an eye on the clock and test the pasta every minute or so as it nears the recommended cooking time. As soon as it feels done (this varies from person to person and pasta to pasta), pour it into a colander set in the sink. Pick up the colander and shake it a couple of times to remove excess water. *Do not rinse.* Eat immediately!

For some, eating leftover pasta is a travesty, but I do it. I eat leftover pasta salad, I reheat leftover pasta with garlic oil on top of the stove, and I eat the previous night's red sauce and pasta for lunch with the help of the microwave. Many restaurant kitchens reheat cooked pasta in a pot of boiling water or toss it in a hot pan with sauce just before serving. Boiling pasta fresh for each use is better, but not so much that most people would notice. If you are going to cook pasta ahead of time, do not overcook it. Also, to prevent it from sticking together later, cool it quickly. Pour out as much of the water as possible while keeping the pasta in the pot. Then fill the pot with cold water. Pour off the water again. Add cold water a second time. At this point, the pasta will be at room temperature or cooler. Drain the pasta in a colander and shake the colander to remove excess water. Store the pasta in a covered bowl in the refrigerator. Tossing the pasta with a touch of oil will make it easier to work with later, but this is not necessary. Cheap pastas made from soft flour will be too gummy to use the next day.

The following pasta recipes are intended as side dishes. You will find a number of other pasta recipes in the Vegetarian section of the *Main Courses* chapter, pages 92-101.

Garlic Oil Pasta

This is the type of recipe that I rely on frequently. It takes only a few minutes to make (especially if you have yesterday's leftover pasta). And although it is wonderful in this form, the best thing about it is its flexibility. If you don't have roasted peppers, try steamed broccoli or canned artichoke hearts. Do you have fresh basil? Put it in. Did you forget to replenish your jar of garlic oil? Use fresh garlic. Do you want to expand this recipe into a full dinner? Toss in pieces of roast chicken and a few cherry tomatoes.

SERVES 2 TO 4

½ tablespoon	garlic oil		⅛ teaspoon	kosher salt
3 cups	cooked pasta		⅛ teaspoon	freshly ground pepper
½ cup	roasted peppers, cut julienne			
1 tablespoon	chopped fresh parsley			

1. Heat the oil in a wok or large sauté pan over medium-high heat.
2. Toss in the rest of the ingredients. Shake the pan and stir constantly. A wooden spatula is the best tool for this job.

3. Heat through. This should take 3 to 4 minutes.

264 CALORIES PER SERVING: 8 G PROTEIN, 5 G FAT, 47 G CARBOHYDRATE; 121 MG SODIUM, 0 MG CHOLESTEROL

page 180

Garlic Oil

*S*ometimes it is too much of a bother to peel and mince fresh garlic. Other times I don't want the texture of little bits of garlic in the recipe. That is when I use garlic oil. Although it is no more than oil infused with the flavor of garlic, it imparts a clear, smooth garlic flavor to foods. Once made, it lasts in the refrigerator for up to 6 months.

To make garlic oil, put 1 cup of olive oil and 2 peeled cloves of garlic in an airtight glass jar. Store it in the refrigerator. As time passes, the garlic aroma and flavor will become stronger. Remove the garlic when the oil gets to the strength you desire. Then again, if you are a garlic fanatic, you can leave the garlic in until you've used all of the oil. Olive oil solidifies in the refrigerator. You can use a spoon to scoop out the amount you need, or you can bring the jar to room temperature and pour out the oil.

Broccoli & Carrot Lasagna, page 99

Moroccan Vegetables, page 91 and Double-Corn Polenta, page 135

Blueberry Lemon Muffins, page 199 and Ginger Carrot Muffins, page 200

141

Red Salsa, page 120, and Pineapple Salsa, page 121

Spicy Shredded Chicken in Flour Tortillas, page 185

Papaya Baked Chicken Breasts, page 65, Sweet Potato Spears, page 157 and Black Bean & Corn Salad, page 40

Blueberry-Peach Cobbler, page 216

Tiny Pasta with Almonds

Orzo is a classic tiny pasta in the shape of rice that can be turned into lovely salads and side dishes. This recipe is meant to accompany a main dish. It goes especially well with poached salmon or roast chicken. Just for fun, you might want to substitute miniature bow ties, wagon wheels or alphabets.

SERVES 4

½ tablespoon	olive oil
1	shallot, minced (1 tablespoon)
2 tablespoons	orange juice
1 teaspoon	lemon juice
½ teaspoon	kosher salt
¼ teaspoon	freshly ground pepper
2 tablespoons	minced fresh parsley
2 tablespoons	sliced almonds
3 cups	cooked tiny pasta

1. Heat the oil in a sauté pan. Sauté the shallot in the oil.
2. In a bowl, whisk together the orange juice, lemon juice, salt and pepper. Using a rubber spatula, scrape the shallots and oil from the pan into the bowl. Add the parsley. Stir to combine. You can do this several hours ahead of time.
3. Toast the almonds in a sauté pan over medium heat until they become aromatic and start to darken.
4. Add the pasta to the almonds. Pour the sauce on top. Stir and heat thoroughly in the pan or later in the microwave.

154 CALORIES PER SERVING: 5 G PROTEIN, 4 G FAT, 25 G CARBOHYDRATE; 237 MG SODIUM, 0 MG CHOLESTEROL

Beans

Dried beans are not a glamorous food. They look like colorful pebbles—something to collect on a vacation but not to cook. People raised during hard times remember beans as being poor people's food. Others see them as being consumed only by "crunchy granola" types. Beans have a reputation for taking a lot of time to cook into a heavy mass. There's a grain of truth in all these views of beans, but the reality is much more savory, sophisticated and timely.

Beans have pleasant, mild flavors that provide an excellent base for other foods and seasonings. If not overcooked, they have a pleasing texture—a chewy exterior with a soft middle. Beans are versatile and can be used in soups, salads, main courses and side dishes. They are inexpensive, healthy, low in fat, high in fiber and a good source of protein.

Cooking dried beans takes some forethought but no skills or fancy equipment. Except for split peas and lentils, most beans take a long time to soften. To shorten their cooking time, soak them in water for at least 4 hours. Beans are dirty, and sometimes little rocks are hiding in them, so sort through them and wash them under running water before soaking. Soak them in a glass or metal bowl and cover them with several inches of water. Make sure there is plenty of water, because you don't want to leave any beans stranded as they expand. Discard beans that float to the surface. You can let them soak, unrefrigerated, overnight or during the day while you're at work. To decide how much you'll need to soak, figure that ½ pound dried beans = 1 cup dried beans = about 2 to 3 cups cooked.

After soaking, rinse them one more time. They are now ready to cook. Some recipes call for beans to be cooked with other ingredients. Others require plain-cooked beans. Plenty of charts give cooking times for different varieties of beans, but none of them is accurate. The only guidelines are that old beans take longer to cook than younger ones and bigger beans take longer to cook than smaller ones. It can be hard to tell old beans from this year's crop. Usually the color of older beans is duller, and often the bags have been sitting on the shelf for so long that they're dusty. Shop at a store that sells a lot of beans. Old beans will eventually soften, but they'll always be a touch gritty. Organic beans taste better.

To cook beans, just put them in a pot with a lot of water and get them simmering. A full boil bangs them around too much, so use medium heat. Most beans will take 50 minutes to 1½ hours to cook. Beans used in salads can be firmer than those used in stews. Don't add acidic or salty ingredients until the beans are soft, as these will lengthen or prevent cooking.

Once the beans are cooked, drain the cooking liquid off (unless otherwise directed by the recipe). Cooked beans stay fresh for only a few days in the refrigerator. Use them quickly, or their flavor will turn. Cooked beans freeze very well for up to 9 months. Whenever you go to the trouble of cooking beans, make a double batch and freeze half. Having frozen beans is a great convenience. Also, if you've soaked beans for a day, but your schedule changes and you don't have time to cook them, don't leave them soaking (they'll sprout). Instead, drain and freeze them. Next time you need beans, prepare them from where you left off.

Beans cooked from scratch have a lighter, clearer flavor and a firmer, more distinct texture than canned beans. With that said, I confess to keeping canned beans in the cupboard and relying on them time and again. Some beans are packed with lard and sugar. Avoid them. Buy beans that are processed only with salt or citric acid. Rinse the beans thoroughly before using. For spicy dishes, such as Southwestern Black Beans (page 150), canned beans are fine.

Baked Beans

Baked beans don't have to take six hours in a slow oven. This recipe takes less than 1½ hours to make. And it works fine with canned beans, so you don't have to cook the beans from scratch. Eat baked beans in the winter as part of a hearty meal, or serve them in the summer as part of a traditional picnic.

SERVES 6

½ teaspoon	vegetable oil		2 tablespoons	catsup
1	small yellow onion, chopped (½ cup)		1 tablespoon	soy sauce
4 cups	cooked pinto or white beans		½-¾ cup	water
1 teaspoon	dry mustard		½ cup	molasses (or to taste)

1. Preheat the oven to 350 degrees F.
2. Heat the oil in a nonstick pan. Sauté the onion in the oil.
3. If you're using canned beans, put them in a colander and rinse them under cool running water.
4. Put the onion, beans and remaining ingredients in a casserole, preferably ceramic, and stir until well combined. Or you can mix them in a large bowl and then transfer them to the casserole. The water content of cooked beans varies a great deal, which is why I am not more specific with the amount of water to add. The mixture should be loose but not soupy. You can add water during cooking or extend the baking time until excess water evaporates.

5. Cover the casserole and put it in the oven. Bake for 1 hour. Stir once and check to see if there is enough liquid in the casserole. The desired final consistency is moist with a "gravy" around the beans. After an hour, if the beans are too watery, take off the cover and cook until the liquid evaporates.

241 CALORIES PER SERVING: 10 G PROTEIN, 1 G FAT, 50 G CARBOHYDRATE; 231 MG SODIUM, 0 MG CHOLESTEROL

Southwestern Black Beans

Few preparations are more versatile and satisfying than a dish of spicy mashed beans. This dish can be an accompaniment to Spicy Shredded Chicken (page 185) , or you can make a meal of it with Red Rice (page 126) and steamed vegetables. I also like to roll these black beans in tortillas and top them off with salsa and yogurt.

SERVES 4

1 teaspoon	vegetable oil		½ teaspoon	ground coriander
1	small yellow onion, chopped (½ cup)		½ teaspoon	kosher salt
2 cloves	garlic, minced (1 teaspoon)		¼ teaspoon	Tabasco or other hot pepper sauce (or to taste)
½ tablespoon	ground cumin		1 tablespoon	sherry

1. Heat the oil in a sauté pan. Sauté the onion and garlic in the oil.
2. Add the cumin, coriander and salt to the pan. Heat and stir until the aroma intensifies.
3. Add the Tabasco, sherry and beans. If you're using canned beans, first drain them and rinse them well. Cook, covered, until heated through.
4. Mash the beans. I like to do this quickly in the food processor so that there are still definable pieces of beans left. If the beans are too dry to mash, you might have to add water or cooking liquid (but never the liquid from canned beans). You can leave the beans whole or only half-mash them by hand. Leftovers freeze well.

199 CALORIES PER SERVING: 12 G PROTEIN, 2 G FAT, 34 G CARBOHYDRATE; 240 MG SODIUM, 0 MG CHOLESTEROL

Catsup

most likely the brand of catsup that you buy is the same brand that you grew up with. Catsup is one of those nostalgic foods, but that doesn't mean its time has passed. As a condiment, it has wide-ranging uses. Personally, I like catsup on leftover chicken, combined with relish on a bun with Tofu Burgers (page 184) and with oven-fried potatoes or Shredded Hash Browns (page 153). As committed to healthy eating as I am, I couldn't resist introducing a young friend to potato chip and catsup sandwiches. Catsup will do that to you.

Sweeteners make up about 20 percent of catsup's weight. As much as I try to avoid refined sweeteners and foods that unnecessarily rely on sugar for much of their flavoring, in the case of catsup and other sweet-and-sour condiments, the sugar is essential to balancing the vinegar and sharp seasonings. I use catsup in recipes for its piquant sweetness. Without that convenient bottle, I'd have to add several more ingredients to the recipe's list. This is one case where a commercial product is a boon to the cook and doesn't make the recipe taste any less fresh.

Potatoes

There are only a few types of commercially available potatoes. These are the Russet or baking potato, the round whites and reds, and the all-purpose potato. Within these groupings, farmers grow a wide variety. Each agricultural region, from Washington to Maine, claims to produce the most delicious and nutritious potato. Soil type and weather are considered crucial in determining quality and flavor. Nonetheless, when the spuds reach the supermarket, the labels won't tell you much beyond what general category they fall into, and the produce manager rarely knows more. This is unfortunate, because the differences between potatoes are noticeable. Fortunately, the main categories do make sense, and you can select and cook potatoes without knowing much about them.

The most popular potato is the Russet. This is sometimes called the Russet Burbank or the Idaho potato, although it is grown in many states. It is oblong and burlap-colored with pale flesh. Because of its high starch and low moisture content, it is ideal for baking. The starch expands and fluffs when heated, and the low moisture keeps the potato from getting soggy. The Russet is, however, a bad choice for salads, as it disintegrates when boiled.

A similar potato is the all-purpose or chef's potato. This potato also is dark-skinned, but it's rounder and not as uniform in appearance. Usually moister, it is best when used for mashed potatoes or in soups.

There are two types of thin-skinned, waxy potatoes—the red and the white. These round spuds have smaller starch grains than the Russet, so the grains don't swell and fluff as much, resulting in baked potatoes that are too firm. They do, however, hold together well when steamed and are perfect for potato salads. They also are excellent roasted.

A potato similar in shape to the round red has recently become more widely available. The Yukon Gold (also called Yellow Finn) is a beige-colored,

golden-fleshed potato that tastes as if grown with butter inside. It cooks up soft and flavorful, makes superb mashed potatoes and is good steamed or roasted.

There is no consensus on the definition of "new" potatoes. Some say that they are simply small, immature potatoes. Others say that they are recently harvested young potatoes that have never been in storage. I have tasted potatoes that would fit both definitions. Small potatoes that have been around a while are still tasty and I find their size delightful. But they are not the same cause for celebration as truly "new" potatoes that have only recently been harvested. Tiny, freshly dug potatoes are a treat. A gentle steaming, a glint of olive oil and a dusting of minced parsley are all that they need. I have eaten entire meals of these fine morsels. The best new potatoes are found at farm stands with some dirt still clinging to their tender skins. We recently went to a "farm days" celebration where we were able to dig our own spuds. The work (being an outing and not true, hard farm labor) was like a treasure hunt. I have never seen children so excited about potatoes. And the nice thing was that when we brought the potatoes home, cooked them and served them for dinner, the children were still excited about them.

Despite their sturdy appearance, potatoes require the same gentle care as other vegetables and fruits. They'll bruise as easily as an apple. However, you won't see the damage until you cut into the potato and find a dark spot. This can be cut out, but it is wasteful.

Also damaging to potatoes is storage at the wrong temperature. Potatoes are perfectly suited to old-fashioned root cellars, which are dark, cool, humid and well-ventilated. Most homes no longer have these useful rooms. Instead, we rely on refrigerators. However, potatoes stored at a temperature at or below 40 degrees F, which is the average refrigerator setting, will become unpleasantly sweet and darken when cooked. It is best to store spuds at 50 degrees. Warmer than that, at room temperature, they will keep for about a week, after which they sprout and shrivel. Try to find a place away from a heat source like your stove. Also, keep them in the dark or loosely covered. Potatoes exposed to light will develop chlorophyll and an associated chemical called solanin. Solanin tastes bitter. Green potatoes are salvageable if you trim off all the green spots, which are usually only on the surface.

Onion & Herb Potatoes

Few recipes are easier to make or more satisfying to eat than potatoes roasted in the oven with a touch of olive oil. This version adds onion, which tastes sweet and rich when baked, and a seasoning of herbs. If you have fresh herbs, use them instead of the dried. Rosemary and thyme are a savory combination, but if you have other fresh herbs or a yearning for dill and chives, go ahead and make substitutions.

SERVES 4 TO 6

1	medium yellow onion, sliced (1 cup)
6	medium potatoes, peeled and cut into 1-inch chunks (2 pounds)
1 tablespoon	olive oil
2 tablespoons	water
½ teaspoon	kosher salt
¼ teaspoon	dried thyme, or 1 teaspoon minced fresh
¼ teaspoon	dried rosemary, or 1 teaspoon minced fresh

1. Preheat the oven to 375 degrees F. The temperature isn't critical, so if you are baking something else at the same time, you can set the dial for anywhere from 350 to 450 degrees F.
2. Coat a casserole with a nonstick cooking spray.
3. Combine all the ingredients in a bowl, then transfer them to the casserole. The water will evaporate, which will soften and moisten the potatoes.
4. Place the casserole in the oven. Bake for 45 minutes to 1 hour. The timing will depend on the oven setting and the variety of potatoes. Stir the potatoes every 20 minutes to promote even cooking and browning.

271 CALORIES PER SERVING: 5 G PROTEIN, 4 G FAT, 56 G CARBOHYDRATE; 252 MG SODIUM, 0 MG CHOLESTEROL

Shredded Hash Browns

Good hash browns must be crispy, which is possible even when the recipe is low-fat. To cook the potatoes through without quantities of oil, you'll have to keep the pan covered. And you'll need a non-stick pan to keep them from burning. Hash browns are not just for breakfast. They're wonderful with roast chicken, and dressier versions are served at trendy restaurants. Still, I always eat mine with catsup.

SERVES 2

1	**Russet potato, peeled (½ pound)**
1 teaspoon	**vegetable oil**

kosher salt (optional)
freshly ground pepper (optional)

1. Trim off any green areas, blemishes and eyes on the potato. Grate it (easily accomplished in a food processor), then wrap the grated potato in a cloth towel and squeeze out any excess moisture.
2. Heat the oil in a 10-inch nonstick pan. Add the potato, distributing it evenly and patting it down with a spatula.
3. Cover and cook over medium-low heat for 10 minutes. Shake the pan occasionally to keep the hash browns from sticking.
4. Flip the patty. Cook for 5 minutes, covered. Then remove the lid and cook for a few minutes more.
5. Slip the potatoes out of the pan and onto a serving dish. Cut the patty in half or into wedges. Season with salt and pepper at the table if desired.

116 CALORIES PER SERVING: 2 G PROTEIN, 2 G FAT, 22 G CARBOHYDRATE; 6 MG SODIUM, 0 MG CHOLESTEROL

Mashed Potatoes

Surprisingly, there are no set rules for such a standard dish. Different potatoes will contribute their own attributes. Yukon Gold potatoes taste buttery, whereas Russets make a fluffy bowlful. Leave the skin on or peel the potatoes. Mash them quickly and leave lumps, or use a ricer to press the potato through small holes to get a perfectly smooth texture. My only admonition is never to use a food processor. It makes the potatoes elastic like glue.

SERVES 6

5	medium potatoes (1½ pounds)	¼ teaspoon	kosher salt (or to taste)
1½ cups	low-fat milk	⅛ teaspoon	freshly ground pepper (or to taste)
	water		

1. Scrub the potatoes well. If you're leaving the skins on, cut off any green areas, eyes and bruises. Cut the potatoes into quarters.
2. Put the potatoes in a pot. Pour in the milk. Add enough water to just cover the potatoes. Bring to a boil, then reduce the heat and simmer until the potatoes are soft and a dull knife can be inserted easily.
3. Using a slotted spoon, remove the potatoes and put them in a mixing bowl. Mash them, adding some cooking liquid if moisture is needed. Depending on the type and age of the potatoes, I've had to use 1 cup or more of liquid. Mash in the salt and pepper. Taste and adjust the seasonings if desired.

170 CALORIES PER SERVING, 5 G PROTEIN, 1 G FAT, 37 G CARBOHYDRATE; 157 MG SODIUM, 3 MG CHOLESTEROL

Mashed Potatoes with Roasted Garlic

Few things are more satisfying than basic mashed potatoes, but I think this dish is one of them. Roasted garlic is so smooth and buttery that although it disappears into the potatoes, its mellow flavor permeates the dish.

SERVES 6

5	medium potatoes (1½ pounds)	⅛ teaspoon	freshly ground pepper (or to taste)
1½ cups	low-fat milk	4 large cloves	roasted garlic, peeled
	water		
¼ teaspoon	kosher salt (or to taste)		

Follow the instructions for mashed potatoes above. Add the roasted garlic after the salt and pepper.

175 CALORIES PER SERVING: 5 G PROTEIN, 1 G FAT, 38 G CARBOHYDRATE; 157 MG SODIUM, 3 MG CHOLESTEROL

page 179

Mashed Rutabagas & Spuds

The rutabagas are simmered in milk to mellow their bite without removing their earthy essence.

SERVES 6 TO 8

1	rutabaga (about 1 pound)	1-1½ cups	water
3	medium potatoes, preferably	½ teaspoon	kosher salt
	Yukon Gold (about 1 pound)	½ teaspoon	freshly ground pepper
1¼ cups	low-fat milk		

1. To peel the rutabaga, cut off a slice so that you have a safe, flat surface to work from. Cut off the peel and the wax by following the shape of the vegetable with your knife, cutting in the direction of the cutting board. If you have to cut into the flesh, don't worry. Rutabagas are inexpensive. Cut the rutabaga into chunks.
2. Peel and cube the potatoes.
3. Put the vegetables in a saucepan. Pour in 1 cup of the milk. Add enough water to cover the vegetables.

4. Bring to a simmer. Cover the pot and cook for 20 to 30 minutes until the rutabagas are soft all the way through.
5. Using a slotted spoon, remove the vegetables to a bowl. Pour the remaining ¼ cup milk over them. Mash in the salt and pepper. Leave the mixture a little lumpy.

101 CALORIES PER SERVING: 3 G PROTEIN, 1 G FAT, 22 G CARBOHYDRATE; 189 MG SODIUM, 1 MG CHOLESTEROL

Yams and Sweet Potatoes

*t*he words *yam* and *sweet potato* have caused a lot of confusion. Even the growers aren't consistent. A southern Sweet Potato Board changed its name to the Yam Commission and then back again to sweet potato. One state called its potatoes yams to distinguish them from its neighbors' sweet potatoes.

The truth is you are unlikely ever to see a botanically true yam. If you do, you'll know for sure that it is nothing like the sweet potato you are used to. In the United States, yams and sweet potatoes are simply two versions of the same vegetable. Generally, the "yam" is a darker, redder version, and the "sweet potato" is more yellow-orange. The many varieties that appear at your grocer's under one name or the other vary widely in flavor, texture and moisture. All are excellent. Purchase sweet potatoes that look fresh and full (avoid withered potatoes) and that have dry, firm skin. Whatever the variety, they are nutritional powerhouses and are one of the few truly sweet vegetables—which is a real plus if you are trying to get your kids to eat those beta carotenes.

Like other potatoes, sweets store best at around 50 degrees F. Their flavor and quality deteriorate below 40 degrees F, so they should not be refrigerated. You can store them in a cool, dark corner of your kitchen for a few days, but make sure that you don't leave them in the plastic produce bag. Plastic retains moisture, which causes soft patches to appear quickly on the potatoes.

Not Your Traditional Tzimmes

Tzimmes are part of the legacy of Eastern European Jewish cooking. These vegetable and fruit stews often feature carrots, chunks of meat and chicken fat. I remember the delight at being fed vegetables that were sweet and that had surprises of dried fruits mixed in with them. I've left out the fat and added my own surprise to this recipe in the form of sweet yet tart chutney and a trace of curry powder. Curry powder lends just the right touch of spice to balance the sweet vegetables and fruits.

SERVES 4

1	large sweet potato, peeled and cut into small cubes (1 pound)	½ cup	pitted prunes, each cut in half
		½ cup	water
4	carrots, peeled and cut into small cubes (½ pound)	¼ teaspoon	kosher salt
		½ teaspoon	curry powder
2 tablespoons	chutney		

1. Preheat the oven to 400 degrees F.
2. Combine all the ingredients in a bowl. Stir well.
3. Transfer the tzimmes to a 2-quart casserole. Cover and bake for 40 minutes. Uncover and bake for 20 minutes more.
4. You can make this dish ahead of time and then reheat it.

183 CALORIES PER SERVING: 3 G PROTEIN, 0 G FAT, 45 G CARBOHYDRATE; 164 MG SODIUM, 0 MG CHOLESTEROL

Sweet Potato Spears

Sweet potatoes have the benefit of being one of the few truly sugary tasting vegetables. This makes them pleasing to anyone with a sweet tooth, especially children. Try this as an alternative to French fries.

SERVES 4 TO 6

4	medium sweet potatoes (about 2 pounds)
1½ tablespoons	vegetable oil
¼ teaspoon	kosher salt
⅛ teaspoon	freshly ground pepper

1. Preheat the oven to 425 degrees F. A hot oven will crisp the potatoes. If you need the oven to be at a lower temperature because you are also baking something else, don't worry. The potatoes will still bake, but they won't be as firm. At the last minute, you can turn up the heat to crisp them.

2. If the potatoes are free of blemishes, just scrub them. Otherwise, you'll need to peel them. Then cut them into pickle-sized spears. If the potatoes are especially round, you might have to cut the thickest part of the spears off so that they look like fat French fries. Make the spears about ½ inch thick, the same as steak fries.

3. Toss the spears with the oil, salt and pepper until they are well coated with oil.

4. Place the spears in one layer on a baking sheet. Bake for 40 minutes. Turn them over with a metal spatula several times to prevent them from sticking to the pan and so that they'll brown on all sides.

227 CALORIES PER SERVING: 3 G PROTEIN, 5 G FAT, 43 G CARBOHYDRATE; 135 SODIUM, 0 MG CHOLESTEROL

recipes

Asparagus in a Gingerly
Citrus Dressing

Asian Green Beans

Broccoli & Peanuts

Turkish Tomatoes & Zucchini

Sage Tomatoes

Orange Ginger Carrots

Roasted Garlic & Greens

Dressed Cauliflower Florets

Thyme Mushrooms

Oven-Roasted
Brussels Sprouts & Carrots

Brussels Sprouts
with Chestnuts

Parsnips & Pineapple

Layered Apples & Turnip

Lemony Squash & Carrots

Spiced Maple Pumpkin Mash

Winter Squash Gratin

Black Beans & Pumpkin

Roasted Garlic

Roasted Peppers

Caramelized Onions

Vegetables

During the summer, I rarely use recipes when cooking vegetables. Green beans, eaten while standing in the garden and followed by a ripe cherry tomato warm from the sun, cannot be improved upon. Once picked and brought inside, the vegetables benefit from nothing more than a light steaming or a hint of salad dressing.

But because I have a small garden and the growing season is only a few months, I feel fortunate that I am able to purchase fresh vegetables year-round and do not have to resort only to hubbard squash and rutabagas toward the end of winter. However, out-of-season vegetables, or those trucked great distances, lack what the green beans from my garden have. Vegetables in supermarkets need to be selected with care. Bring home only the freshest and crispest. These vegetables need special attention. Cooking is an essential step in making many vegetables digestible, improving their flavor, emphasizing their fine qualities and masking the wear from their travels. It is important to mention that although overcooking vegetables is, thankfully, no longer fashionable, you should not undercook them either. Raw vegetables are wonderful, but if you are going to cook them, make sure that they are thoroughly cooked. This doesn't mean boiling them to a mush, but it does mean cooking them until they are tender throughout. For example, members of the cabbage family, such as broccoli and cauliflower, can actually turn bitter if only lightly steamed. And parboiling can wash out a summer squash's flavor.

Vegetable Cooking Guide

At one point, I thought about writing a vegetable cookbook. I was going to discuss individual vegetables and give the best cooking methods and recipes for each. After some work on this project, I realized that I would be continually repeating myself because vegetables can be divided into three categories, and within those divisions, you can handle them all about the same. As I see it, there are hard vegetables, which include root vegetables, such as carrots and beets, and winter squash, such as butternut; firm to soft vegetables such as cauliflower, summer squash and tomatoes; and leafy green vegetables, such as chard, spinach and kale. Understanding these vegetables' commonalities and differences allows you to shop for the best ingredients. If the spinach doesn't look fresh, you'll know that you can substitute chard. If the broccoli looks gray, you'll feel secure purchasing green beans instead.

What follows is my vegetable cookbook, in a much abbreviated form. First I describe the categories of vegetables. Then I explain various cooking techniques.

Types of Vegetables

Hard Vegetables: Dense and often starchy hard vegetables take longer to cook, require more cooking liquid and are more filling than other vegetables. The technique best suited to these vegetables is roasting or baking. Slow oven cooking intensifies their flavors and often makes them sweeter as they soften. Long-simmering stews also bring out the flavors and make their textures more palatable. Another option is dicing or grating them into small pieces that can be sautéed or steamed in less than 15 minutes.

Firm to Soft Vegetables: Firm to soft vegetables take well to any number of cooking methods. They can be roasted (although timing will vary between a ripe tomato and an eggplant), steamed, chopped and then sautéed, stewed in a broth, or sometimes eaten raw. These vegetables cook fairly quickly and are not as filling as the hard vegetables.

Leafy Green Vegetables: The leafy green vegetables cook very fast. They can usually be sautéed using the water clinging to their leaves for liquid. Leafy greens cook down to one-third or less of their raw volume. This depends on whether you are using the tougher stems, which are more like celery and don't shrink, or only using the tender leaves.

Cooking Methods

Roasting: This is an easy, carefree way to cook vegetables. You can roast one type at a time or several together. Cut them into pieces and toss them with a small amount of olive oil (just enough to make them glisten; usually around 1 tablespoon is enough for vegetables serving 8 to 10 people). Add salt, pepper and perhaps some herbs, cumin or coriander. Place them in a casserole and bake at 350 to 400 degrees F. If the vegetables were dense, old or dry, you might need to add a few tablespoons of water and cover them for a while so that they can steam as they roast. Use a metal spatula to toss the vegetables so that they don't stick to the pan and all sides get nicely browned. When the hardest vegetables are soft, the casserole is done.

Steaming: All vegetables can be steamed. Steaming is simply cooking vegetables over boiling water. Usually this is accomplished with a steamer basket, which is a perforated stainless-steel container on legs. The steamer is set in a covered saucepan. It adjusts to any size pot and keeps the vegetables out of the water while allowing the steam to reach them.

Steamed vegetables are done when they turn a brighter shade of color than they were originally and the firmest part of the vegetable can be easily penetrated with a sharp knife. The tenderest vegetables will take a few minutes. Harder vegetables might take 30 minutes and require that you add more water to the pot as the water evaporates.

When the steaming is complete, it is essential that you remove the vegetables from the pot immediately, or they will keep cooking in the steam (even if the water is no longer boiling). Most steamer baskets have a ring in the center that you are supposed to use to pull the basket out of the water. This is not safe, however, as the steam can burn you when you reach into the pot. I suggest that you use stainless-steel salad bar tongs to grasp the ring instead of your fingers.

Steamed vegetables should be eaten right away or chilled so that they don't cook any further. I like plain steamed vegetables, but my favorite way to eat them is to pour a touch of Honey-Poppy Seed Dressing (page 59) on them while they are hot. A seven-year-old friend of mine asks for second helpings of broccoli when it is served in this way. Red Pepper Sauce (page 117) and Sweet & Sour Sauce (page 118) also are wonderful when tossed with steamed vegetables

When vegetables are to be served chilled or held for another day, immerse them in cool water immediately after steaming to remove all traces of heat. This prevents them from overcooking. Then drain them and either add them to salads, or reserve them for soup, or perhaps chop them for pita pocket sandwiches.

Microwaving: This is essentially another form of steaming. Microwaving is a good method when you are making only enough for one to four people. Put the vegetables in a glass bowl, add a little water, cover, and put the bowl into the microwave. Cook the vegetables on high for as long as it takes for them to soften. This will vary with the microwave and the vegetable. When the vegetables are done, handle them the same way you would if they had been steamed.

The benefits of microwaving larger quantities are questionable, because it takes almost as long to microwave a large amount as it does to steam it. Besides, the microwave cooks unevenly, and unless you stir and turn the vegetables, some will be overcooked and others remain nearly raw.

One problem with microwaving vegetables occurs when not enough liquid is included in the cooking dish. Moisture is needed to steam the vegetables. Without it, the vegetables toughen instead of cooking.

Sautéing and Stir-frying: These two methods are essentially the same. In both cases, chopped vegetables are cooked in a hot pan that has been coated lightly with oil. Sautéing differs from steaming because the oil not only softens but also browns the ingredients. Usually onion, garlic and sometimes ginger are sautéed first in a pan or wok. Not much oil is used, and when other vegetables like zucchini and peppers are tossed in, additional liquid is needed to cook the vegetables. Instead of more oil, water or stock is often added, and the pan is covered. In this way, the onion contributes a rich browned flavor while the other vegetables soften in a nonfat or low-fat liquid. That nonfat liquid can be intensely seasoned. Hoisin Tofu (page 104), or Hoisin Chicken (page 67) are two excellent bases for stir-fries. Sweet & Sour Sauce (page 118) is another good choice.

Stews: A stew is a long-simmered mélange of ingredients cooked in a flavorful broth. Stews disprove the notion that vegetables should be cooked only lightly. A stew gives seasonings a chance to mature and sharp flavors time to mellow. The soft texture can be offset with firmer ingredients, such as chickpeas or raw vegetables, added in the final moments. Stews are like sauces in consistency and can be used to dress pastas, rice, or other carbohydrates. Or, they can be served as a vegetable side dish.

A Note on Serving Size: I believe in large servings of vegetables and have written my recipes accordingly.

However, this varies from person to person and depends on whether the vegetable is a minor side dish, or takes center stage with the main course. Also, vegetables vary greatly in size, and one head of broccoli might feed four to six. I have tried to give volumes and weights where appropriate to give you a better indication of vegetable size, but you'll still have to decide for yourself how much to cook up and whether my serving sizes are right for you.

Asparagus in a Gingerly Citrus Dressing

When the first of the local asparagus appears in the market, I get carried away. I buy a few pounds and eat asparagus all week long. I don't dress the stalks with heavy sauces because I don't want to hide their fresh flavor. Instead, after a light steaming, I accent their flavor with a vinaigrette. This dressing has a mild citrus flavor. Freshly squeezed juice imparts a subtler flavor than the store-bought brands.

Serves 3 to 4

½-inch piece	fresh gingerroot
1	orange, preferably organic
1 tablespoon	extra-virgin olive oil
2 teaspoons	balsamic vinegar

¼ teaspoon	kosher salt
¼ teaspoon	freshly ground pepper
¼ teaspoon	soy sauce
¾ pound	asparagus (about 20 stalks)

1. Peel the ginger. Cut it into thin rounds, then slice those pieces so that you have very narrow strips of ginger.
2. Wash the orange well. Zest the orange (see page 127).
3. Boil the ginger and orange strips for 5 minutes, then remove them from the water. It is easiest to drain it all through a wire mesh sieve.
4. Juice the orange. You'll need ¼ cup juice for this recipe.
5. Whisk the olive oil, vinegar, salt, pepper and soy sauce into the juice. Stir in the orange peel and ginger. You can make this dressing well ahead of time; it actually benefits from a few hours' rest.
6. Snap off the tough ends of the asparagus. Steam or microwave the stalks until they turn bright green and are pliable but not soft (about 6 minutes, but this varies).
7. Put the asparagus on a platter and pour the dressing over the asparagus while it is still hot. Store any leftover dressing in a jar in the refrigerator. Serve the asparagus hot, warm or cold.

82 CALORIES PER SERVING: 3 G PROTEIN, 5 G FAT, 8 G CARBOHYDRATE; 191 MG SODIUM, 0 MG CHOLESTEROL

Asian Green Beans

I love the taste of green beans cooked at Chinese restaurants, but unfortunately, they are usually sautéed with pork and pork fat. This vegetarian recipe has a lot of flavor, uses ingredients and cooking methods readily available to the home cook, and is good either hot or cold.

SERVES 4 TO 6

1 pound	green beans		1/16 teaspoon	red pepper flakes (or to taste)
1 teaspoon	toasted sesame oil		1/2 tablespoon	soy sauce
1 teaspoon	peanut oil		2 tablespoons	water
2 cloves	garlic, minced (1 teaspoon)		1 teaspoon	sesame seeds, toasted, for
1 teaspoon	minced fresh gingerroot			garnish (optional)

1. Trim the ends off the green beans. If the beans are fresh and thin, you can leave on the tapering end, but you still need to snap off the end that had been attached to the plant.
2. Lightly steam the beans. You can do this up to a day ahead of time.
3. Heat the oils in a sauté pan over low heat. Sauté the garlic and ginger in the oils until the garlic is golden and you can smell its sweetening aroma.
4. Add the beans, red pepper flakes, soy sauce and water. Stir to combine. Cook, covered, over high heat for a few minutes until the water evaporates and the oil coats the beans and makes them shiny. Shake the pan and stir occasionally while the mixture is cooking.
5. Garnish with toasted sesame seeds if desired.

63 CALORIES PER SERVING: 3 G PROTEIN, 3 G FAT, 10 G CARBOHYDRATE; 133 MG SODIUM, 0 MG CHOLESTEROL

Broccoli & Peanuts

It doesn't take a lot of oil or nuts to distinguish this recipe from plain steamed broccoli. This serves at least four people, but don't hesitate to try it if you are cooking for one. Or, if cooked lightly the first time, leftovers will be just as good reheated the following day. Tossed with mushrooms, roasted peppers and pasta, it makes a fine dinner.

SERVES 4 TO 6

1 head	broccoli
1 teaspoon	toasted sesame oil
2 cloves	garlic, minced (1 teaspoon)
1 tablespoon	soy sauce
1 tablespoon	dry roasted peanuts, coarsely chopped
1/16 teaspoon	red pepper flakes (optional)
1 tablespoon	defatted chicken or vegetable stock or water

1. Trim the dry ends off the broccoli. Peel the stems using a vegetable peeler or a paring knife. A knife is better if the stems are long and tough. Peel from the bottom up. Broccoli's outer skin pulls off easily once you get a handle on it. Slice the stems, and cut the head into florets.
2. Lightly steam the broccoli until it turns a brighter shade of green, then immediately stop the cooking by rinsing it under cold running water.
3. Heat the oil in a large pan or wok. Sauté the garlic in the oil until it is golden.
4. Toss in the broccoli. Add the remaining ingredients. Use the red pepper flakes if you want a spicy dish. Cover the pan. Toss the vegetables by shaking the pan or lift the lid and stir. Cook until the broccoli reaches the desired tenderness.

72 CALORIES PER SERVING: 6 G PROTEIN, 3 G FAT, 10 G CARBOHYDRATE; 323 MG SODIUM, 0 MG CHOLESTEROL

Turkish Tomatoes & Zucchini

Flavorful, but not spicy hot, this vegetable mélange goes nicely with rice. Unlike many vegetable dishes, this one makes great leftovers because the soft texture loses nothing when reheated. As with all other tomato-based recipes, this one will be juicy and bursting with flavor when you use ripe summer tomatoes.

SERVES 4 TO 6

½ tablespoon	vegetable oil
1	medium yellow onion, chopped (1 cup)
4	beefsteak-type tomatoes (about 2 pounds), cored, seeded and chopped
1 or 2	zucchini (¾ to 1 pound), cut into ¼-inch-thick rounds
⅓ cup	fresh basil, chopped
⅛ teaspoon	ground allspice
¼ teaspoon	ground cumin
¼ teaspoon	kosher salt
⅛ teaspoon	freshly ground pepper

1. Heat the oil in a sauté pan. Sauté the onion in the oil until it is soft and golden. Add the remaining ingredients. Cook, covered, over low heat until the vegetables exude moisture and the mixture looks soupy. Timing will vary with the ripeness of the tomatoes. Fresh beefsteaks will take less than 10 minutes, whereas plum tomatoes will require at least 15 minutes.

2. Uncover and cook for 10 minutes more, which will dry the dish out slightly and intensify the flavors.

70 CALORIES PER SERVING: 2 G PROTEIN, 2 G FAT, 12 G CARBOHYDRATE; 134 MG SODIUM, 0 MG CHOLESTEROL

page 110

Sage Tomatoes

This is one of my favorite ways of eating tomatoes. The only thing better is standing in a garden and eating tomatoes straight off the vine. Eat these with grilled fish or chicken, over pasta or on grilled bread.

SERVES 4

½	medium leek
1 teaspoon	olive oil
2 cloves	garlic, minced (1 teaspoon)
2	large beefsteak-style tomatoes (about 1 pound), or 8 plum tomatoes, cored, and cut into large cubes or wedges

½ teaspoon	sage
⅛ teaspoon	kosher salt
⅛ teaspoon	freshly ground pepper

1. Cut the root end off the leek, leaving as much of the white part as possible. Cut off and discard the dark green top at the point where it looks tough. The light green stem and younger leaves are good to eat. Slice the leek in half lengthwise. Rinse it under cool running water. Expose each layer to the water and rinse thoroughly. Most leeks have sand in them, and it is worth taking a minute to get them clean. Slice the leek into half rounds.

2. Heat the oil in a sauté pan over medium heat. Sauté the garlic and leek in the oil until the leek is golden.

3. Add the tomatoes and seasonings. Cook 4 minutes more until the tomatoes soften, but not so long that they lose their shape and turn to mush. Taste and add more salt if desired.

35 CALORIES PER SERVING: 1 G PROTEIN, 1 G FAT, 6 G CARBOHYDRATE; 135 MG SODIUM, 0 MG CHOLESTEROL

Orange Ginger Carrots

This recipe is a favorite in my house because even when I fear that I don't have any vegetables at hand for dinner, I remember that I have a bag of carrots and can make this zesty pretty side dish.

SERVES 4

| 8 | carrots (1 pound) | ¼ teaspoon | grated fresh gingerroot |
| ¼ cup | orange juice | 1-2 teaspoons | honey |

1. Peel the carrots, then slice them Chinese-style on an angle.
2. Combine the carrots with the orange juice, ginger and 1 teaspoon of the honey.
3. Microwave on high for 4 minutes. Stir, then microwave for a few minutes more until the carrots are cooked through (timing will depend on your microwave.) Or cook in a covered nonstick pan until the carrots soften.
4. You can serve the carrots like this or glaze them by putting them and the liquids into a pan, adding the remaining teaspoon of honey and cooking them over medium-high heat until the orange juice evaporates and the carrots are shiny.

59 CALORIES PER SERVING: 1 G PROTEIN, 0 G FAT, 14 G CARBOHYDRATE; 69 MG SODIUM, 0 MG CHOLESTEROL

Roasted Garlic & Greens

When dark green leafy vegetables like spinach, chard and watercress are combined with strong flavors, their own inherent flavors are enhanced, not overwhelmed—which makes a simple preparation like this one better than the sum of its parts.

SERVES 4

1   10- to 12-ounce package fresh spinach, or 10-12 cups other dark leafy greens

1 teaspoon oil of choice (sesame for Asian, olive for Mediterranean, etc.)
4 cloves roasted garlic , or more to taste
¼ teaspoon kosher salt (optional)

1. Prepare the spinach by tearing off the tough, dried-out stems. Wash the spinach well, then drain it in a colander. Do not dry it in a salad spinner; the clean water that clings to the leaves will provide the cooking liquid. Tear the very large leaves into smaller pieces.
2. Heat the oil in a large saucepan or wok.
3. Slice the garlic and toss it into the wok. Sauté gently until its aroma reaches you. Take care not to burn the garlic.
4. Add the greens and salt. Cook, covered, over high heat for 3 to 5 minutes until the greens wilt. Shake the pan and stir frequently.

27 CALORIES PER SERVING, 2 G PROTEIN, 1 G FAT, 3 G CARBOHYDRATE; 39 MG SODIUM, 0 MG CHOLESTEROL

page 179

A Greens Primer

*D*ark leafy greens are packed with nutrients, including essential beta carotenes, antioxidants, B vitamins and even some calcium. Luckily, they are as delicious as they are good for you.

All greens need a thorough washing. Fill a large bowl with cool water, put in the greens, swish them around and let them soak for a few minutes. Remove the greens, empty, rinse and refill the bowl, and wash the greens again. Repeat these steps until the water is free of grit. If preparing an hour or more ahead of time, dry the leaves in a salad spinner before refrigerating them. Water left on the greens will cause them to wilt and bruise.

All leafy greens have ribs. Some are edible; some are not. Kale has tough, tubular ribs that must be removed. Do this by gently folding the leaf in half along the rib and cutting out the rib with a knife. Spinach also has a center rib, but only the last portion of the stem needs to be torn off. Swiss chard looks like spinach with flattened stalks of celery for ribs. These ribs taste sweet and crunchy, but because they take longer to cook than the leafy parts, they need to be removed, sliced, and put in the pan before the greens.

Leafy greens cook down to one-third their raw volume, so it is a good idea to slice them into smaller pieces with a chef's knife. Handle greens carefully. If scrunched up, the leaves will bruise and darken.

Dressed Cauliflower Florets

Cauliflower can be a difficult vegetable to work with. On its own, it assertively reminds you of its familial relationship with cabbage—which is why many recipes try to hide this vegetable under thick, fatty cheese sauces. My solution is to dress cauliflower with a mild, herb-laced dressing. The dish can be served at room temperature or slightly warmer, which makes it ideal for a buffet. Toss leftovers in a green salad.

SERVES 6

1 small head	cauliflower florets (1 cup)		¼ teaspoon	kosher salt
½ tablespoon	olive oil		⅛ teaspoon	freshly ground pepper
½ tablespoon	honey		½ teaspoon	tarragon
½ teaspoon	Dijon mustard		½ teaspoon	chives
1 tablespoon	lemon juice			

1. Steam or microwave the cauliflower until tender. Do not undercook.
2. Whisk together the remaining ingredients. Be sure to rub and crush the herbs between your fingers before adding them to the dressing. This releases their flavors. Better yet, use fresh herbs (1½ teaspoons of fresh chopped tarragon and ½ teaspoon fresh minced chives.)
3. Pour the dressing over the cauliflower while the florets are still warm.

50 CALORIES PER SERVING: 3 G PROTEIN, 1 G FAT, 8 G CARBOHYDRATE; 93 MG SODIUM, 0 MG CHOLESTEROL

Thyme Mushrooms

Mushrooms have a hearty image despite the light, delicate flavors of the ones commonly available in the supermarket. This recipe browns and seasons the mushrooms to make a vegetable accompaniment that you want to eat with a knife and fork.

SERVES 2 TO 4

1 8-ounce package	mushrooms		1 tablespoon	minced fresh parsley
½ teaspoon	olive oil		⅛ teaspoon	kosher salt
½ teaspoon	thyme		1/16 teaspoon	freshly ground pepper

1. Clean the mushrooms quickly under cool running water. I put all the mushrooms in a colander and shake gently as the water washes them. You also can brush off the dirt with a paper towel. Don't soak them, or they will discolor and turn mushy. Trim off the dry stem ends, but leave as much of the stems as possible. If the mushrooms are very large, cut them in half or quarters. Otherwise, leave them whole.

2. Heat the oil in a 10-inch nonstick sauté pan. Add the mushrooms. Cook, tossing frequently, until the caps brown.

3. Reduce the heat to medium low, add the seasonings and continue to cook until the mushrooms exude liquid. Then increase the heat and cook most of the liquid off. Some very dry mushrooms won't give off any liquid. In that case, simply cook until they begin to soften. The entire cooking time is no more than 7 minutes or so.

42 CALORIES PER SERVING: 2 G PROTEIN, 2 G FAT, 6 G CARBOHYDRATE; 121 MG SODIUM, 0 MG CHOLESTEROL

Oven-Roasted Brussels Sprouts & Carrots

It might not be a popular thing to admit, but I love Brussels sprouts. I like them straightforward and whole, like the bold little cabbages they are. This preparation keeps their integrity while mellowing them enough so that they won't overwhelm the rest of the meal. I precook them, which cuts the roasting time by more than half and makes the Brussels sprouts tender without being too soft.

SERVES 3 TO 4

4	carrots, peeled (½ pound)	¼ teaspoon	kosher salt
½ pound	Brussels sprouts (about 12 to 16)	¼ teaspoon	freshly ground pepper
2 teaspoons	olive oil		

1. Cut the carrots into rounds or cubes.
2. Trim the Brussels sprouts by cutting off their tough ends and peeling off the dark, discolored outer leaves.
3. Preheat the oven to 400 degrees F.
4. Steam or microwave the carrots and Brussels sprouts together until they begin to soften. This will take about 6 minutes on high in the microwave. Remember to put water in the dish, or the vegetables will harden instead of soften.
5. Put the vegetables in a casserole. Toss them with the oil, salt and pepper. Bake for 20 minutes. Shake and stir once while roasting.

91 CALORIES PER SERVING: 3 G PROTEIN, 4 G FAT, 15 G CARBOHYDRATE; 220 MG SODIUM, 0 MG CHOLESTEROL

Brussels Sprouts with Chestnuts

Here's a traditional way to serve Brussels sprouts that actually makes this vegetable elegant.

SERVES 4 TO 6

1 pound	Brussels sprouts, trimmed	⅛ teaspoon	kosher salt
1 teaspoon	vegetable oil	⅛ teaspoon	freshly ground pepper
1 cup	chestnuts, roasted, peeled and coarsely chopped		

1. Cook the Brussels sprouts by steaming or microwaving them until you can easily insert a fork.
2. Heat the oil in a nonstick pan. Add the Brussels sprouts, chestnuts, salt and pepper. Toss until the Brussels sprouts are heated through and are coated with oil.

160 CALORIES PER SERVING: 5 G PROTEIN, 2 G FAT, 33 G CARBOHYDRATE; 86 MG SODIUM, 0 MG CHOLESTEROL

 opposite

Chestnuts

*b*y early winter markets have chestnuts for sale by the pound. The objects of songs ("Chestnuts roasting on an open fire...") and childhood memories (of street vendors selling small paper bags filled with hot nuts), chestnuts are different from other nuts in that they are low-fat. Only about 6 percent of chestnuts' calories come from fat, which contrasts dramatically with other nuts, such as pecans and walnuts, which are 75 to 85 percent fat. Chestnuts taste rich and sweet, but one chestnut contains less than 1 gram of fat.

Although chestnuts can be boiled, I prefer roasted chestnuts for their greater intensity of flavor. Whole chestnuts are roasted in the shell. Before putting chestnuts in the oven, cut an X into the shell to allow steam to escape as the chestnuts roast. This is very important, as chestnuts not slashed will explode into a powdery dust. I've had firsthand experience with this.

Chestnuts are not easy to cut. One piece of advice <u>not</u> to follow is to slice the shell on the flat sides. Besides the fact that some chestnuts don't have a flat side, it is much easier to use that side to steady the nut on a cutting board while you slash the round side. Never hold a chestnut in your hand and try to cut it, for you are bound to hurt yourself. I've found that the best knife to use is a serrated bread knife. As I pull it across the shell, it grabs in and cuts through the shell with the least amount of effort.

Place the chestnuts in a single layer on a baking sheet, then roast them in a preheated 425 degree F oven for 20 to 30 minutes until the shells curl back from the X. Let them cool until you can handle them, but don't wait until they are room temperature because the bitter inner skin can be removed only while the nut is warm. If you have a lot of nuts to shell, take only a handful out of the oven at a time. Longer roasting won't harm the ones you get to later. Some chestnuts are harder to peel than others. Pass on the ones that are too frustrating. Store extra peeled nuts in a container in the refrigerator. Use them within 2 days of roasting.

Roasting chestnuts in the oven is a clean, consistent method of cooking them, but my favorite way is to put them in a pan over the embers in the fireplace. Invariably, ash gets on the nuts, one or two scorch, and I burn my fingers peeling them before they cool off. But somehow the flavor is richer, and peeling them doesn't seem like such a big chore.

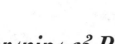

Parsnips & Pineapple

I love the sweet, pungent smell of parsnips. Pineapple, being both sweet and tangy, is a compatible partner. In this recipe, the two are baked together to bring out the full flavors of both.

SERVES 4 TO 6

4	parsnips (1 pound), peeled and cut into chunks	½ cup	water
1	carrot, peeled and cut into rounds	½ teaspoon	kosher salt
1 8-ounce can	unsweetened pineapple chunks or crushed pineapple packed in its own juice	¼ teaspoon	freshly ground pepper

1. Preheat the oven to 350 degrees F.
2. Put all the ingredients, including the pineapple juice, in a casserole. Stir to combine. Cover and bake for 30 minutes.

3. Puree or mash the ingredients before serving.

137 CALORIES PER SERVING: 2 G PROTEIN, 0 G FAT, 34 G CARBOHYDRATE; 254 MG SODIUM, 0 MG CHOLESTEROL

Layered Apples & Turnips

This recipe calls for baking varieties of apples because apples that are good for eating are not always good for cooking. For example, the McIntosh, a perfect eating apple, quickly turns to mush when heated. But a Rome will hold its shape much longer. All apples will soften and become applesauce if cooked long enough.

SERVES 4

2	apples, preferably a baking variety, like Rome or Cortland	¼ teaspoon	ground coriander
6	small turnips (⅓ pound)	½ cup	apple juice or apple cider
		¼ cup	walnut or pecan pieces

1. Preheat the oven to 350 degrees F..
2. Core the apples, then slice them into rings. Scrub the turnips clean, cut off the ends and cut the turnips into rounds.

3. Layer the apples and turnips in a 1½- to 2-quart casserole. Dust on the coriander. Pour in the apple juice. Cover the casserole and bake for 30 minutes.
4. Uncover the casserole, top with the nuts and bake for 10 minutes more.

108 CALORIES PER SERVING, 2 G PROTEIN, 5 G FAT, 17 G CARBOHYDRATE; 21 MG SODIUM, 0 MG CHOLESTEROL

Winter Squash

Winter squash are hard-shelled vegetables that come in a kaleidoscope of shapes, colors and sizes. Their flesh is usually warm yellow to deep orange-red in color (a clue to their high beta carotene content), and they cook up sweet and dense yet soft. Of the many varieties, the butternut and delicata are two of the sweetest. Acorn squash comes in sensible sizes and is mild in flavor. Hubbard squash, an old standard because of its excellent keeping qualities, is losing popularity because of its huge, knobby, irregular shape. Unless pumpkins are labeled "sugar" or "pie," they are best for jack-o'-lanterns, not for eating.

Peeling winter squash is difficult and can be dangerous because they are hard, round, and cutting into them with a knife takes strength. Luckily, if you need peeled, cooked squash, you need only cut them in half, scrape out the seeds and then bake them with apple cider at 350 to 400 degrees F for about 40 minutes. Or simply put the cut side down in the pan. Winter squash will bake faster and moister if covered during cooking. Once baked, the flesh is easy to scoop out.

There are times, however, when you want peeled, uncooked squash. Here are some hints that make working with these vegetables easier and safer.

Winter squash's hard, thick skin won't peel off with a vegetable peeler. Instead, use a large large chef's knife. When cutting any vegetable, it is best to have the food flat and secure on the cutting board. This is especially true for big, hard vegetables. If the squash rolls around, slice off a sliver of skin so the squash sits solidly on the board. Hold the vegetable firmly with one hand, placed on top of the squash and a bit to one side. Working from the top down toward the board, cut off the skin. Follow the shape of the vegetable as best you can, but don't worry if you cut off a tad more at the curves. If it is too difficult to cut straight down through the skin, use a slight sawing motion with the knife. You can cut fairly deeply (compared to peeling something like an apple) and not waste too much. Some squash are so oddly shaped that you might have to cut them into chunks before you peel them because the large chef's knife does not follow curves well. Never hold the squash in your hand while cutting. Always have it on the board, and always cut downward.

If all this seems like too much work, buy peeled squash. It is more convenient, although the selection is usually limited to butternut and hubbard and it will cost about 50 cents more per pound. If you miss having colorful whole squash on your kitchen counter, buy a few just for show.

Lemony Squash & Carrots

This is one of the simplest, quickest and prettiest ways to cook winter vegetables. Hard winter squash usually takes over an hour to bake, but when grated and sautéed, it takes less than one-quarter of that time.

SERVES 4

2 cups	winter squash, peeled and grated
1	small carrot, peeled and grated
1 tablespoon	lemon juice
⅛ teaspoon	kosher salt

¹⁄₁₆ teaspoon	freshly ground pepper
⅔ cup	defatted chicken or vegetable stock or water
1 tablespoon	minced fresh parsley

1. You can grate the squash easily in a food processor. You may grate it a day ahead of time and keep it in a container in the refrigerator.

2. Put everything but the parsley in a 10-inch non-stick sauté pan. Cook, covered, over medium heat for about 10 minutes until the vegetables soften. Stir occasionally

3. Add the parsley at the end of the cooking time.

54 CALORIES PER SERVING: 1 G PROTEIN, 0 G FAT, 14 G CARBOHYDRATE; 74 MG SODIUM; 0 MG CHOLESTEROL

Spiced Maple Pumpkin Mash

No recipe exemplifies autumn in New England better than this recipe. Like the vibrant and beautiful scenery, this dish is colorful and piquant. If sugar pumpkins are unavailable, any other winter squash will do.

SERVES 4

2- to 3-pound	pumpkin or winter squash, cubed (4 cups)
1 tablespoon	maple syrup
¼ teaspoon	kosher salt

¼ teaspoon	freshly ground pepper
1 cup	apple cider or apple juice
⅛ teaspoon	ground cardamom

1. Simmer all ingredients except the cardamom over low heat until the pumpkin is soft. This will take about 15 minutes.

2. Using a slotted spoon, remove the pumpkin to a bowl. Add the cardamom. Mash the pumpkin until it is smooth (a few lumps are OK). Pour in a little of the cooking liquid if necessary.

72 CALORIES PER SERVING: 1 G PROTEIN, 0 G FAT, 18 G CARBOHYDRATE; 128 MG SODIUM, 0 MG CHOLESTEROL

Winter Squash Gratin

The yogurt in this recipe is optional. Sometimes I want the slightly sour contrast to the squash's sweetness, and sometimes I don't. The yogurt also elevates the vegetables from the role of side dish to that of main course.

SERVES 6 TO 8

2 tablespoons	peanut or vegetable oil	½ teaspoon	basil
3-pound	winter squash, cubed (5 cups)	1 tablespoon	chives
1	red onion, chopped (1 cup)	½ teaspoon	kosher salt
3 cloves	garlic, minced (1½ teaspoons)	½ teaspoon	freshly ground pepper
2	medium potatoes, peeled and cubed (3 cups)	1½ cups	nonfat yogurt (optional)
½ teaspoon	marjoram	¼ cup	toasted pumpkin seeds or pepitas for garnish

1. Preheat the oven to 350 degrees F.
2. Stir together all the ingredients except the yogurt (if using) and pumpkin seeds. Transfer the mixture to a casserole. Cover and bake for 45 minutes.
3. Uncover and bake for 15 minutes more.
4. If you like the tang of yogurt and a dairy flavor, stir in the yogurt. Broil the casserole until bubbly and the edges begin to turn brown. This takes only a couple of minutes.
5. Garnish with the toasted pumpkin seeds.

205 CALORIES PER SERVING: 4 G PROTEIN, 5 G FAT, 39 G CARBOHYDRATE; 170 MG SODIUM, 0 MG CHOLESTEROL

Black Beans & Pumpkin

This is a wonderful accompaniment to roast chicken or grilled fish, but it also can be the focus of a meal when served with rice and a salad. It's colorful, full of flavor and a welcome alternative to mushy bean side dishes. If you can't find a sugar pumpkin, use another hard squash, such as butternut or acorn. Cutting winter squash can test a cook's patience (and muscles). See page 175 for some ways to ease the task.

SERVES 4

1 teaspoon	vegetable oil		2 cups	cooked black beans
1	small yellow onion, chopped (½ cup)		½ teaspoon	kosher salt
1 clove	garlic, minced (½ teaspoon)		½ teaspoon	ground cumin
1 cup	pumpkin, peeled and cut into ½-inch or smaller cubes		½ teaspoon	thyme
¼ cup	sherry		1 teaspoon	red wine vinegar
¼ cup	defatted chicken or vegetable stock or water		1	scallion, sliced

1. Heat the oil in a nonstick pan. Sauté the onion, garlic and pumpkin in the oil until the onion is golden.
2. Add the sherry and stock. Simmer until the pumpkin becomes fork tender (meaning a fork can easily slip into the flesh).
3. Add the beans, salt, cumin, thyme and red wine vinegar. Continue to simmer for 5 minutes more, until the beans are heated through.
4. Stir in the scallion during the last minute of cooking.

163 CALORIES PER SERVING: 8 G PROTEIN, 2 G FAT, 2 G CARBOHYDRATE; 241 MG SODIUM, 0 MG CHOLESTEROL

Homemade Pantry Staples

Most of the ingredients required to make the recipes in this book can be found fresh, bottled, canned or dried, but a few are best, or only available, if homemade. The following three recipes are for basic foods that complete a well-stocked pantry. With these, the creative cook can invent a meal in just minutes.

Roasted Garlic

Roasted garlic is one of those pieces of insider information passed on from cook to cook. But lately I've seen it on more and more restaurant menus, so I hope it will soon become common knowledge and everyday practice.

Raw garlic is sharp and pungent, and it is hard to take in large amounts. But when garlic is roasted, its flavor mellows, it puts out a sweet aroma, and it takes on the smooth texture of butter. A bulb of roasted garlic can boost creativity or turn a simple meal into a robust one. Spread the buttery cloves on crusty bread. Stuff chicken with it. Spread it on toast and top with sautéed mushrooms for a country sandwich. Puree it into a dip. Toss it with cooked pasta and roasted peppers.

1 bulb garlic

1. Preheat the oven to 350 degrees F. The temperature doesn't have to be exact. If you are cooking at 325 or 400 degrees F, just adjust the cooking time accordingly.
2. Select a large bulb of garlic with dry, papery skin and bulbous cloves. Rub the outside layer of skin off the bulb. Cut across the top of the bulb to expose most of the cloves. Don't cut off so much that you remove a lot of garlic. Don't worry about cutting down into the interior cloves.
3. Put the bulb in a baking dish. It is not necessary to grease or cover the pan. Bake for about 1 hour, or until the cloves become soft and spreadable.

Roasted Peppers

Charring peppers and then slipping off their skins imparts a smoky, complex flavor to these vegetables. Roasting also gives peppers a velvety texture that cannot be achieved by steaming or sautéing.

1 PEPPER MAKES ½ TO 1 CUP SLICED ROASTED PEPPERS

red or green bell peppers

1. Preheat the broiler.
2. Place the peppers on a baking sheet. Put the sheet in the oven. If you have a gas stove, you can roast the peppers individually over the burner. Hold them over the flame using long-handled tongs. The goal is to blacken the skin without burning the inside flesh. Pepper skins can char to a solid black and begin to peel away from the rest of the vegetable before the flesh is overcooked. Watching your peppers blacken requires some bravery, but peppers that do not roast to an ebony color are only steamed and difficult to peel.
3. As the peppers blacken, use your tongs to turn them over so that each side is exposed the flame. The amount of time it takes to roast peppers depends on the heat of your flame and how close the peppers are to it. It will usually take 5 minutes to char each side of the vegetable under the broiler.

4. Once the skins are blistered, put the peppers in a paper bag and fold over the top. Place the bag in the sink, as moisture from the peppers will make the bag soggy. Allow the peppers to cool. They will steam in the bag, and their skins will loosen.
5. With your fingers, pull off all the skin, even the skin that isn't black. Cut open the peppers and trim out the seeds, core and veins. You can slice the peppers or leave them whole.
6. Store the peppers in a glass jar in the refrigerator. If you wish, cover them with oil to prolong their shelf life.

Caramelized Onions

Don't be fooled by the short list of ingredients. A long, slow cooking in a touch of oil thoroughly transforms this basic bulb from a sharp, assertive ingredient into a sweet, complex relish. It is fine on its own as an accompaniment to grilled foods, but it also enhances many dishes, from leftover potatoes to Spicy Shredded Chicken (page 185) pita sandwiches. Perhaps my favorite is an open-faced sandwich with Roasted Garlic (page 179), Caramelized Onions and Thyme Mushrooms (page 171).

MAKES 1½ CUPS

1 teaspoon vegetable oil
3 medium yellow onions, thinly sliced (3 cups)

1. Heat the oil in a 10-inch nonstick sauté pan over medium heat. Add the onions, reduce the heat to low, cover and cook for 30 minutes. Stir occasionally. If the pan is too hot, the onions will turn dark brown quickly, so make sure the heat is reduced to low as soon as the onions are added. You can't start with low heat because, initially, the oil must be hot, though not sizzling.

2. The onions are done when they shrink to one-third their raw size and are golden brown.

3. Store them in the refrigerator for up to 1 week.

recipes

Tofu Burgers

Spicy Shredded Chicken

Topped Polenta

Chickpea & Pignoli Spread

Mushroom, Garlic & Onion
Open-Faced Sandwich

Crostini

Garlic Toast

Knish Dough

East Side Knish Filling

Classic Potato Knish Filling

Curried Potato Knish
Filling

Sandwiches

*L*unch often stymies people who are trying to switch to a
healthier way of eating. Gone are the luncheon meat
and mayonnaise sandwiches, the meatball subs and the
tuna melts. However, sandwiches are far from forbidden. In
fact, they have a lot of potential, with their healthy dose of
carbohydrate in the form of bread and the myriad fillings
that can be packed inside of them. This chapter has a selection of sandwich possibilities. There are others throughout
the book. After all, sandwiches are one of the best uses of
leftovers. Page 184 lists a number of recipes that can
become fillers or toppings for open-faced sandwiches.

An alternative to sandwiches are knishes. These are
dough-wrapped packages of hearty, spicy fillings. Tradi-
tionally filled with potatoes or kasha and served hot with
mustard from vendors' wagons on city streets, they adapt
well to home cooking and inventive treatments.

Lunches also can be salads, soup hot from a thermos, leftover lasagna heated in the microwave or nonfat yogurt, fruit and crackers. If you crave an old favorite, peanut butter and jelly is not out of the question. A sandwich on whole-wheat bread, with 1 tablespoon each of peanut butter and jelly is only 30 percent fat, which is well within the parameters of a healthy diet, especially if eaten along with a piece of fruit or a big salad.

Recipes that Make Great Sandwiches

Any leftover chicken makes a great sandwich.

Try mustard or chutney instead of mayo on the bread.

Fill a pita pocket with leftover Tandoori Tofu (page 104) and vegetables.

Roll Southwestern Black Beans (page 150) up in a flour tortilla, heat and eat.

Both tuna salad recipes, Tuna Salad with Capers (page 55) and Apple & Tuna Salad (page 55), go well between slices of whole wheat bread.

Put hot Pan-Cooked Fish Fillets (page 87) on bulkie rolls, and add lettuce and tomato. Use a dollop of nonfat yogurt if you miss mayonnaise.

Tofu Burgers

I don't eat hamburgers anymore, but I do want an excuse to eat catsup and relish on a patty on a bun. These tofu burgers taste good even without being covered with condiments. Think of them as a sandwich filling. My skeptical, hamburger-eating husband was surprised at how good they are and will eat them willingly as long as I don't say that they're hamburger substitutes.

Serves 4

1 pound	extra-firm or firm tofu
1 clove	garlic, peeled
1	egg
½ tablespoon	chives
½ teaspoon	oregano

1 tablespoon	soy sauce
½ cup	rolled oats
½ tablespoon	sesame seeds
¼ teaspoon	freshly ground pepper

1. Preheat the oven to 450 degrees F. Coat a baking sheet with a nonstick spray or line the pan with parchment paper.
2. Wrap the tofu in a clean kitchen towel. Squeeze out all the excess moisture. I twist the towel hard around the tofu because the less water, the better the texture of the burgers.
3. The ingredients can be easily mixed in a food processor using the steel blade. Mince the garlic first, then pulse in the rest of the ingredients.

If you're mixing the ingredients by hand, make sure the garlic is finely minced and the egg is lightly beaten before putting it all together. Handle it as you would meat loaf, by kneading it with your hands.
4. Using your hands, form the mixture into patties. Place them on the baking sheet.
5. Bake for 10 minutes. Turn over. Bake for 5 minutes more. You can reheat the patties in the microwave the next day.

232 CALORIES PER SERVING: 22 G PROTEIN, 12 G FAT, 13 G CARBOHYDRATE; 290 MG SODIUM, 53 MG CHOLESTEROL

Spicy Shredded Chicken

The seasonings in this recipe are fiery and complex. Tone it up or down with more or less cayenne pepper. Spicy Shredded Chicken has myriad uses. Serve it as a dinner entrée over brown rice, stuff it into a pita pocket for lunch, or serve it rolled up with black beans in a soft tortilla.

SERVES 4 TO 6

¼ teaspoon	ground cardamom		2 cloves	garlic, minced (1 teaspoon)
¼ teaspoon	ground cinnamon		1 tablespoon	lemon juice
½ teaspoon	kosher salt		1 pound	boneless, skinless chicken breasts
¼ teaspoon	freshly ground pepper		½ tablespoon	vegetable oil
¹⁄₁₆-⅛ teaspoon	cayenne pepper		1	small yellow onion, sliced
¼ teaspoon	ground coriander			(½ cup)

1. In a glass or stainless-steel bowl, combine the cardamom, cinnamon, salt, pepper, cayenne, coriander, garlic and lemon juice.
2. Cut the chicken into narrow strips 1½ inches long.
3. Toss the chicken in with the spices until all of pieces are evenly coated.
4. Marinate, covered and refrigerated, for 1 hour to 24 hours.

5. Heat the oil in a 10-inch nonstick pan over low heat. Cook the onion for about 10 minutes, until it is soft and golden .
6. Add the chicken, increase the heat to medium high and cook for about 5 to 7 minutes until the meat is white all the way through and the outside begins to brown. Stir frequently.

186 CALORIES PER SERVING: 30 G PROTEIN, 5 G FAT, 3 G CARBOHYDRATE; 307 MG SODIUM, 82 MG CHOLESTEROL

Topped Polenta

Ideal as a quick meal for one as long as the basic ingredients—tomato sauce in the freezer and squares of polenta in the refrigerator—are on hand. The recipe calls for sautéed mushrooms, but you could use zucchini, spinach, roasted peppers or any other vegetable. The tomato sauce contributes much of the flavor. It, too, can be varied according to the season or your mood.

SERVES 1

1	3- by 4-inch square polenta 🍴
1½ teaspoons	olive oil
3	mushrooms, sliced
½	small yellow onion, chopped (¼ cup)

½ cup	tomato sauce (see *Sauces & Salsas*)
1 ounce	mozzarella, Parmesan or feta cheese (optional)

1. Bake the polenta square at 425 degrees F for 5 minutes on each side. A toaster oven is perfect for this. Grease the baking tray or use parchment paper.
2. While the polenta is browning, heat the oil in a sauté pan and sauté the mushrooms and onion in the oil. Warm the tomato sauce.
3. The polenta is done when it is bubbling and the edges look crisp. Using a metal spatula, slip it onto a dinner plate. Top with the mushrooms and onion, then the tomato sauce.
4. If you wish, grate cheese on top. If you're using a melting cheese, like mozzarella, put it on the polenta during the last minute that it is toasting.

155 CALORIES PER SERVING: 3 G PROTEIN, 8 G FAT, 21 G CARBOHYDRATE; 827 MG SODIUM, 0 MG CHOLETEROL

🍴 page 134

Chickpea & Pignoli Spread

This is a takeoff on hummus, the popular Middle Eastern chickpea, garlic and sesame paste spread. Like hummus, it can be used as a sandwich filling, a dip or a cracker topping. It differs from hummus because pignolis, which are also called pine nuts, have a milder and slightly sweeter flavor than sesame seed paste.

Makes about 1¾ cups

2 cups	cooked fresh chickpeas, or 1 20-ounce can		3 tablespoons	lemon juice
2 cloves	garlic		1 teaspoon	kosher salt
¼ cup plus 1 tablespoon	pignolis		⅛ teaspoon	Tabasco or other hot pepper sauce
			2 tablespoons	water
			2 tablespoons	chopped fresh parsley

1. Start the food processor, then drop in the chickpeas and garlic. Process until they are minced. Scrape the sides of the bowl.
2. Add ¼ cup of the pignolis along with the lemon juice, salt, Tabasco and water. Process until a smooth paste forms.
3. Pulse in the parsley and the remaining tablespoon pignolis so that they are incorporated but large pieces of nut remain (about 4 pulses).

97 CALORIES PER SERVING: 4 G PROTEIN, 5 G FAT, 11 G CARBOHYDRATE; 540 MG SODIUM, 0 MG CHOLESTEROL

Mushroom, Garlic & Onion Open-Faced Sandwich

This recipe is so hearty and flavorful that not only do I eat it for lunch, but I've also served it for dinner, as well as in smaller portions as a first course. The type of bread you use is of great importance. A crusty loaf, chewy and filled with flavor, is ideal.

SERVES 2

⅔ cup **Caramelized Onions** ▦
       Thyme Mushrooms ☰

2 thick slices **good-quality, crusty bread**
6 cloves **Roasted Garlic** ▦

1. The onions and mushrooms need to be hot before constructing these sandwiches. If you're using leftovers (all the ingredients can be made ahead of time), reheat them. You can warm the onions in the microwave, but the texture of the mushrooms will be better if you heat them on the stovetop.

2. Toast or grill the bread. Put the slices on the plates that you'll be using. You won't be able to transfer these messy sandwiches from a serving platter to a dinner plate.
3. Squeeze the garlic out of the peels and onto the toasted bread. Spread it with a knife.
4. Top the bread with the onions and then the mushrooms. Serve immediately.

184 CALORIES PER SERVING: 7 G PROTEIN, 2 G FAT, 35 G CARBOHYDRATE; 313 MG SODIUM, 0 MG CHOLESTEROL

▦ page 181
☰ page 171
▦ page 179

Crostini

Crostini are slices of bread that have been grilled or toasted and then topped with a savory melange. They are finger foods at their best, although some are constructed so that a fork and knife become necessities. Good Italian bread is essential for crostini. It should have a crusty exterior and a soft middle. Don't use loaves that are too big around, or the middles will drop out when you add the toppings.

Toppings (choose one or more)

Tomato Olivada (page 113)
Marinated Tomato Salad (page 38)
Oven-Baked Ratatouille (page 90)
Roasted Tomato Sauce (page 113)
Roasted Garlic & Greens (page 169)

1 loaf   good-quality Italian bread, sliced thickly
freshly grated Parmesan cheese, crumbled feta cheese or grated low-fat mozzarella (optional)

1. Gather together the toppings you wish to use. If they are to be served warm, heat them.
2. Toast or grill the bread.
3. Mound on the topping of your choice.
4. If desired, lightly dust with cheese. Broil or heat until the cheese begins to melt.
5. Serve immediately.

Garlic Toast

This is not the garlic bread, slathered and softened with oil and butter, that is served in pizzerias and Italian-American restaurants. This is closer to a true bruschetta; it is a crisp and sharply garlicky slice of bread. Because there are only three ingredients, they all have to be of the best quality. This recipe requires a long, crusty loaf. I've had great success with French, sourdough and Italian breads.

SERVES 4 TO 6

1 long loaf   crusty bread, sliced
2 large cloves   garlic, crushed

1 tablespoon   olive oil (more or less depending on the size of the loaf)

1. Just before you are ready to eat, toast or grill the slices of bread.
2. As soon as they come out of the oven or toaster or off the grill, rub one surface of each slice with a clove of garlic. As the garlic falls apart and dries out a bit, switch to the next clove.
3. Lightly brush the garlicked side of the bread with olive oil.
4. Serve immediately.

203 CALORIES PER SERVING: 6 G PROTEIN, 4 G FAT, 35 G CARBOHYDRATE; 304 MG SODIUM, 0 MG CHOLESTEROL

Knishes

Knishes are street food, and even when served to guests in your home, they're not expected to be elegant little pastries. They're a great way for you to get experience putting fillings in dough because the end results are not supposed to be fancy. You're successful as long as you make them all about the same size and seal up the edges so that nothing leaks out.

Making Knishes

Have everything prepared ahead of time. Make the dough first, because it will need to chill in the refrigerator. When you are ready to roll out the dough and stuff the knishes, put everything that you'll be using on your work surface. Have a large, clean board ready for rolling out the dough. Have some white flour on hand to dust the area. Get out a knife to cut the dough. Have a couple of cookie tins ready. (You can bake the knishes on ungreased pans, but if the filling oozes out, it will stick. If possible, line the pans with parchment paper.) Bring over the filling (or fillings) in a bowl, with a tablespoon that you'll use for stuffing. Preheat the oven to 425 degrees F. Take the dough out of the refrigerator. You are now ready to roll out the dough. To do this, follow step 7 under the knish dough recipe on page 191.

There are several ways to fill knishes. For large knishes, cut the dough into 12 to 16 squares or rectangles. Precision will make for tidier packages, but if you can't get them exact, don't worry about it. Using the tablespoon and your fingers, drop the filling into the center of each rectangle. Bring the corners of the dough over the filling. Stretch them so that they come together in the center, then, with a twist, seal them up. Press the seams together tightly so that the filling is encased by dough.

For small knishes, divide the rolled-out dough rectangle into 3 long strips about 21 inches long and 3½ inches wide. With a sharp chef's knife, cut these into 3½-inch squares. Place the filling in the middle of each strip, then fold it as you would a large knish. Or place a small mound of filling in the center of each square, so that the dough can be folded over like a dumpling packet. To help seal the edges, brush a little water along the dough where it is pressed together.

Place the knishes on the baking trays. Bake small knishes for 12 to 15 minutes. Bake large knishes for 15 to 18 minutes. Do not overcook.

You can freeze knishes before baking if you wish. (Already cooked knishes do not freeze well.) Freeze them on the baking trays. Once they are frozen solid, slip them into a freezer bag and bake when needed. Bake frozen knishes at 400 degrees F for about 30 minutes. They can be microwaved, but the crust will be chewy. Toast them after microwaving to crisp up the crust.

Knish Dough

This is an easy low-fat dough. The trick is to refrigerate for at least one hour, preferably overnight before using. It rolls out smooth and even and doesn't stick to the board or pin. However, flours vary greatly in how much water they absorb and how they roll out, so the handling qualities of this recipe might vary. Also, if you don't have any experience with dough, you might need to practice a few times. But, once you get a feel for it, working with dough is fun.

MAKES 20 LARGE OR 40 TO 50 SMALL KNISHES

2 cups	unbleached white flour	1	whole egg
½ cup	whole-wheat flour	2 tablespoons	
¼ teaspoon	salt	plus ½ teaspoon	vegetable oil
1 teaspoon	baking powder	½ cup	cold water
2	egg whites		

1. Sift together the flours, salt and baking powder. Stir so that the two types of flour are well mixed.

2. In a separate bowl, beat together the egg whites, the egg, 2 tablespoons of the oil, and the water.

3. Pour the wet ingredients into the dry and quickly combine with a fork until everything is moist and a dough ball begins to form.

4. Knead the dough with the bottom of the palm of your hand, bringing the dough into your hand with your fingers. As with all pastry work, do this step quickly. Don't push so hard that you are squishing the dough against the side of the bowl. The purpose here is to make a semismooth ball of dough that is evenly moist, not to knead it as if it were a yeast dough.

5. Rub the dough with the remaining ½ teaspoon oil so that the whole ball glistens. Place it in a clean bowl, cover and put in the refrigerator for 1 hour or up to 24 hours.

6. When you're ready to work the dough into knishes, take it out of the bowl and knead it about five times to smooth it out.

7. Get out a large, clean board. To keep the board from slipping as you work, put a damp kitchen towel under it. Dust the board with white flour. Place the dough ball on the board. Using a lightly floured rolling pin, roll the dough into a rectangle. Work from the center out, using short, even strokes and pressing the dough outward. Lift and move the dough frequently to make sure it isn't sticking to the board. Keep the board consistently but lightly floured.

8. To fill the dough, follow the instructions on page 190.

74 CALORIES PER SERVING: 2 G PROTEIN, 2 G FAT, 12 G CARBOHYDRATE; 52 MG SODIUM, 11 MG CHOLESTEROL

East Side Knish Filling

Kasha is a heavy, assertive grain, but when combined with brown rice and sautéed mushrooms and onions, then tucked into a pastry pouch, it becomes a satisfying lunch. Small knishes are wonderful as hors d'oeuvres. Serve them warm with spicy mustard as a dip.

MAKES 16 LARGE OR 30 TO 40 SMALL KNISHES

1 teaspoon	vegetable oil	1 cup	cooked brown rice
2	medium yellow onions, chopped (2 cups)	1	egg white, lightly beaten
10	mushrooms, chopped	¼ teaspoon	kosher salt
1 cup	cooked kasha	½ teaspoon	freshly ground pepper
		2 tablespoons	minced fresh parsley

1. Heat the oil in a sauté pan. Sauté the onions and mushrooms in the oil until the onions become translucent.

2. Mix the onion and mushrooms with the remaining ingredients.

38 CALORIES PER SERVING: 1 G PROTEIN, 0.5 G FAT, 7 G CARBOHYDRATE; 35 MG SODIUM, 0 MG CHOLESTEROL

page 131

Classic Potato Knish Filling

This is the sort of knish sold by pushcart vendors in New York City—although the ones from the city probably have a bit more fat in them. My memories are of peppery knishes, and I use plenty of that spice here. You can reduce the pepper to ½ teaspoon if you're so inclined.

MAKES 20 LARGE KNISHES OR 50 SMALL KNISHES

1 teaspoon	vegetable oil	1 cup	low-fat milk
2	medium yellow onions, chopped (2 cups)	3 cups	water
3 large	Russet potatoes, peeled and quartered	1 teaspoon	kosher salt
		1 teaspoon	freshly ground pepper

1. Heat the oil in a nonstick pan. Sauté the onion until it is soft and golden.
2. Meanwhile, boil the potatoes in the milk and water for about 15 minutes until they soften.
3. Using a slotted spoon, remove the potatoes from the milk and drop them into a mixing bowl. Add the cooked onion, salt and pepper. Mash. Add the cooking liquid as needed to ease mashing and to get a moist and soft (though not wet and loose) consistency.

40 CALORIES PER SERVING: 1 G PROTEIN, 0 G FAT, 9 G CARBOHYDRATE; 100 MG SODIUM, 0 MG CHOLESTEROL

Curried Potato Knish Filling

This spicy, nontraditional filling will vary with the type of curry powder used. My recipe is based on a mild curry mix that is light on the chilies and cayenne. Use ½ tablespoon if your curry is hot.

MAKES 20 LARGE OR 50 SMALL KNISHES

2 large	potatoes		½ cup	fresh or frozen peas
1 teaspoon	vegetable oil		1	small carrot, peeled and chopped
2	medium yellow onions, chopped (2 cups)		1 teaspoon	kosher salt
			½ teaspoon	freshly ground pepper
2 cloves	garlic, minced (1 teaspoon)		1 tablespoon	mild curry powder

1. The potatoes don't have to be peeled before cooking. I peel potatoes only if they have tough, blemished or slightly green skin. Otherwise, I just scrub them well. Cook the potatoes using the method of your choice then mash them.

2. Heat the oil in a nonstick pan over medium-low heat. Sauté the onion, garlic, peas and carrots in the oil. Keep the pan covered between stirrings. Cook until the onion is soft, translucent and golden.

3. Stir the sautéed vegetables in with the mashed potatoes. Mix in the salt, pepper and curry powder. I find that a fork works best for this task.

33 CALORIES PER SERVING: 1 G PROTEIN, 0 G FAT, 7 G CARBOHYDRATE; 100 MG SODIUM, 0 MG CHOLESTEROL

recipes

Orange-Poppy Seed Corn Muffins

Blueberry Lemon Muffins

Ginger Carrot Muffins

Cornbread

Pumpkin Bread

Buttermilk Pancakes

Pecan Buttermilk Pancakes

Quick Breads & Pancakes

*Y*east breads are mysteriously alive doughs that pull the baker into conversation with them as they are worked. Quick breads are the opposite. They are carefully figured chemical equations. With precise measuring and efficient handling, they are transformed from batter into muffins, breads, cakes and pancakes. They take less time and involvement than yeast breads and yet produce some well-loved foods that fill the kitchen with homey aromas that speak of weekend mornings with friends, family and the Sunday paper. This sense of comfort and care extends even into time-pressured workdays. If you pull a home-made muffin out of the freezer, defrost it in the microwave and toast it for a minute, its smells and flavors transport you to a more relaxed time.

Baking Tips

Flours

Flours vary in the amount of gluten they contain. Gluten is a protein that makes yeast doughs elastic and light. But the same gluten can make pastries tough. Bread flour is high in gluten; pastry flour is low. All-purpose flours are a compromise and are adequate for both uses, though not superior for either. If you can purchase pastry flour for your cakes and cookies, do so. You will get easier-to-handle dough and crumbly, lighter desserts.

In whole-wheat flour, the germ and some of the outer bran layer remain after milling. Whole-wheat flour has a nutty flavor that works well in some dishes. It is heavier than white and makes a denser, chewier baked good. This can contribute body and substance to a recipe, but there are times when it is too much, so all white flour, or a combination of white and wheat is better. If possible, buy whole-wheat pastry flour. Second best is all-purpose whole-wheat flour. Don't use bread flour. Coarse whole-wheat flour is sometimes called graham flour. It is not a good choice for desserts.

White flour is sometimes bleached to look bright white. This is unnecessary. Buy unbleached white flour. Some natural food stores have unbleached white flour that has the germ added back in. This golden-flecked, nutritious flour tastes wonderful without being too strong or heavy.

Leavens

Baked goods lighten and rise when air bubbles are trapped in the dough. You can make this happen in a number of ways. Baking soda and baking powder, when combined with water and then heated, produce carbon dioxide, which pushes the dough up and out. Whipped egg whites trap air in their stiff structure, and when they are incorporated into a dough, they make an airy batter. Fat is used to separate grains of flour so that they can be moved by the leavens. Fat also keeps the dough soft and tender.

Baking soda needs an acid, such as buttermilk or molasses, to work. Double-acting baking powder does not need an acid. It starts reacting when moistened with any liquid and then produces more carbon dioxide as it is heated. The ingredients need to be in the right proportions; otherwise, the batter won't rise, it will fall or a residual taste of baking soda will remain. Measuring exactly is important, and sifting also is important, or you will have a clump of bitter leavening in one cookie and the other cookies will be flat. Baking soda and baking powder can be stored, tightly sealed, in a dark cupboard. They do age. Keep an eye on their expiration dates.

When egg whites are beaten with the wet ingredients, they provide some support and lift to the dough. For a higher and lighter dough, they are beaten separately and then folded into the batter. Whip egg whites in a clean glass or metal bowl. Do not use plastic. Any touch of grease will keep the eggs from stiffening. Egg whites change consistency as they are beaten. When they start to whiten and take shape, they are in soft-peak stage. Keep beating, and they will stiffen further, until a dollop of egg white holds its Hershey's Kiss shape. Further beating will produce dry egg whites, which look high and fluffy but are weak and will break down when baked.

Baking Pans

Dark, heavy baking pans and sheets absorb the heat of the oven, then slowly and evenly distribute it to the baked goods. Clear glass and tinny, warped metal pans cook foods quickly, and have a tendency to scorch. White pans reflect heat and will produce baked goods with lighter crusts.

Greasing the Pan

Do not use oil to grease pans because it will harden the crust and burn the outside of the baked goods. Greasing is best done with a saturated fat like butter or with a nonstick cooking spray. The sprays are good choices because they use only a small amount of fat to cover a large area. Nonstick pans are a possibility, but they need to be seasoned with grease occasionally, and I find that they work best with a light spray. Parchment paper is a white paper that bakeries use to line their pans. It is strong, even when wet, doesn't react with food and is absolutely nonstick. Because it is white, it lessens browning, especially of cookie bottoms. You can buy it in rolls, but I find the curled paper awkward. Bakeries use large, flat sheets. Try to convince your local bakery (or even supermarket bakery) to sell you some.

Handling Batters

Quick doughs are entirely different from yeast doughs. Whereas yeast doughs love handling, quick doughs need gentle, quick treatment. If air has been trapped in the batter with egg whites or with chemical leavens, any mixing risks breaking down the structure and toughening the dough. That is why dry ingredients are thoroughly sifted together and wet ingredients are mixed well on their own. Once combined, they are fragile and need to be handled accordingly. Mix the wet and dry ingredients with broad strokes of a rubber spatula. Turn the batter over, sweeping from the bottom of the bowl up to make sure no dry flour remains in the center. Do this quickly but gently and stop as soon as the batter is moist throughout. Leave it lumpy. If you try to beat the lumps out, the baked goods will be tough.

Orange-Poppy Seed Corn Muffins

These are not sweet breakfast muffins (although they do taste wonderful with jam).
They are more for an afternoon tea, or dinnertime breadbasket.

MAKES 1 DOZEN MUFFINS

1 cup	whole-wheat flour, preferably pastry flour	1½ teaspoons	poppy seeds
1 cup	unbleached white flour	1	orange
½ cup	cornmeal	1 cup	low-fat or nonfat yogurt
1 teaspoon	baking powder	2	egg whites
2 teaspoons	baking soda	3 tablespoons	vegetable oil
½ teaspoon	salt	⅓ cup	honey

1. Preheat the oven to 350 degrees F. Grease the muffin tin.
2. Sift together the dry ingredients. Stir until the two flours look like one.
3. This recipe requires 1 tablespoon of orange zest (page 127). Mince the zest.
4. Cut the orange in half and squeeze out the juice. Strain out the seeds and measure out ⅓ cup of juice. Put the zest and juice in a bowl. If you don't have enough juice, add prepared orange juice to make ⅓ cup.
5. Add the remaining wet ingredients to the juice. Beat until slightly foamy.
6. Pour the wet ingredients into the dry. Gently but quickly fold the two together until an evenly moist batter forms.
7. Fill the muffin cups about three-quarters full.
8. Bake for 25 minutes, or until the muffins are golden and firm to the touch.
9. Remove the muffins from the tin and cool them on a rack.

172 CALORIES PER MUFFIN: 5 G PROTEIN, 4 G FAT, 30 G CARBOHYDRATE; 266 MG SODIUM, 1 MG CHOLESTEROL

Blueberry Lemon Muffins

The white sugar in this recipe lightens and softens the texture of the muffins.
I also use honey to lend more complexity to the sweet flavor.

MAKES 1 DOZEN MUFFINS

1	egg white
1	whole egg
1 cup	nonfat yogurt
¼ cup	vegetable oil
½ teaspoon	vanilla
¼ cup	honey
⅓ cup	sugar
1 tablespoon	lemon zest

1 cup	unbleached white flour
1 cup	whole-wheat flour, preferably pastry flour
¼ teaspoon	kosher salt
1 teaspoon	baking soda
1 teaspoon	baking powder
1 cup	blueberries

1. Preheat the oven to 350 degrees F. Grease the muffin tin.
2. Beat together the egg white, egg, yogurt, oil, vanilla, honey, sugar and zest.
3. In a separate bowl, sift together the dry ingredients. Stir so that they are well blended.
4. Pour the wet ingredients into the dry. Fold them together with a rubber spatula until the batter is moist but still lumpy.
5. Stir in the blueberries.
6. Pour the batter into the muffin cups.
7. Bake for 25 minutes.

180 CALORIES PER MUFFIN: 4 G PROTEIN, 5 G FAT, 30 G CARBOHYDRATE; 161 MG SODIUM, 18 MG CHOLESTEROL

page 127

Ginger Carrot Muffins

These muffins have the sharpness of ginger and the sweetness of carrots. They are moist and light, but because of their low fat content, they go stale quickly. Eat what you want the day they are baked, then freeze the rest.

MAKES 1 DOZEN MUFFINS

1 teaspoon	ground ginger
1 cup	whole-wheat flour, preferably pastry flour
1¼ cups	unbleached white flour
¼ teaspoon	kosher salt
½ teaspoon	ground cinnamon
1½ teaspoons	baking powder
½ teaspoon	baking soda
¾ cup	buttermilk
3 tablespoons	vegetable oil
½ cup	honey
1	egg white
1	whole egg
1	large carrot, grated (1 cup)

1. Preheat the oven to 350 degrees F. Grease the muffin tin.
2. Sift together the dry ingredients. Stir until there aren't any spice streaks left in the mixture.
3. Beat together the buttermilk, oil, honey, egg white and egg.
4. Stir the carrot into the wet batter.
5. Stir the wet ingredients into the dry. Fold them together until the batter is moist but still lumpy.
6. Pour the batter into the muffin cups.
7. Bake for 25 to 30 minutes.

174 CALORIES PER MUFFIN: 4 G PROTEIN, 4 G FAT, 31 G CARBOHYDRATE; 145 MG SODIUM, 18 MG CHOLESTEROL

Cornbread

This easy-to-make recipe will have a distinct, rich, corn flavor if you use cornmeal that still contains the germ. This cornmeal needs to be kept refrigerated. For that reason, it is available only at natural food stores. It is worth the trip. For an easy variation on this recipe, add green chilies.

SERVES 12

1 cup	cornmeal
1 cup	unbleached white flour
1 teaspoon	baking powder
½ teaspoon	baking soda
¼ teaspoon	kosher salt
2 tablespoons	vegetable oil

1 cup	buttermilk
1	egg
¼ cup	sugar
4-ounce can	chopped mild green chilies, drained (optional)

1. Preheat the oven to 400 degrees F. Coat an 8- by-8-inch pan with nonstick cooking spray.
2. Sift together the cornmeal, flour, baking powder, baking soda and salt. Toss in any cornmeal that's too coarse for the sifter. Stir the dry ingredients until there are no streaks of white and yellow.
3. Whisk together the oil, buttermilk and egg. Beat in the sugar. Add chilies if desired.
4. Make a depression in the center of the dry ingredients and pour the wet mixture into it. Stir with a rubber spatula until the batter is evenly wet but still lumpy.
5. Pour into the pan. Gently spread the batter evenly across the pan.
6. Bake for 30 minutes until the top begins to brown and the center is firm.
7. Cool the bread in the pan for about 10 minutes before turning it out onto a wire rack. Or leave it in the pan.

125 CALORIES PER SERVING; 3 G PROTEIN, 3 G FAT, 21 G CARBOHYDRATE; 131 MG SODIUM, 19 MG CHOLESTEROL

Pumpkin Bread

This is one of the joys of autumn that can be made and appreciated year-round.

SERVES 12

½ cup	unbleached white flour
2 cups	whole-wheat flour, preferably pastry flour
½ teaspoon	salt
1½ teaspoons	ground cinnamon
⅛ teaspoon	ground cloves
¼ teaspoon	ground or freshly grated nutmeg
½ teaspoon	ground ginger

1 teaspoon	baking powder
1 teaspoon	baking soda
1 cup	pumpkin puree
3 tablespoons	vegetable oil
1 cup	honey
½ cup	buttermilk
1	whole egg
1	egg white

1. Preheat the oven to 350 degrees F. Grease 2 small loaf pans or 1 large one.
2. Sift together the flours, salt, spices, baking powder and baking soda. Stir until there are no dark spice streaks.
3. Beat together the remaining ingredients in a separate bowl.
4. Pour the wet ingredients into the dry. Gently but quickly fold the two together until a moist batter forms.
5. Pour the batter into the pan(s).
6. Bake the smaller loaves for 35 to 40 minutes and the large one for 50 minutes to 1 hour. If your oven heats unevenly, turn the pan(s) once during baking. The bread is done when the color becomes an even golden brown, it feels firm to the touch and the crack along the top looks baked, not raw.
7. Turn the bread out onto a cooling rack.

224 CALORIES PER SERVING: 5 G PROTEIN, 4 G FAT, 44 G CARBOHYDRATE; 209 MG SODIUM, 18 MG CHOLESTEROL

Buttermilk Pancakes

In my family, we've made a tradition of having a full breakfast on Sunday morning, and our favorite breakfast is pancakes. Sitting down together, reading the paper and eating "real" food combine to create a special family atmosphere. The time that it takes to put together the batter is minimal, and cooking in a nonstick skillet makes for easy cleanup. To make things even more convenient, I double the dry ingredients and freeze half so that I have a quick mix on hand.

MAKES 10 TO 12 PANCAKES

⅔ cup	whole-wheat flour, preferably pastry flour
1 cup	unbleached white flour
¼ teaspoon	kosher salt

1 teaspoon	baking soda
1	egg white
1	whole egg
2 cups	buttermilk

1. Sift together the dry ingredients . Stir until you can no longer see streaks of whole-wheat flour.
2. In a separate bowl, whisk together the egg white, egg and buttermilk.
3. Pour the wet ingredients into the dry. With a rubber spatula, stir the two together quickly. Make sure that you get all the flour off the bottom of the bowl but do not overmix. A lumpy batter makes for lighter pancakes.
4. Heat a nonstick skillet until a drop of water sizzles on it. If you're using an electric skillet (the best for this), keep it at 325 degrees F. If you haven't seasoned the pan for a while, use 1 teaspoon of oil. Drop batter onto the skillet. I use a ¼-cup measurer to make large pancakes about 4 inches across.
5. When the pancakes bubble in the middle, it's time to turn them.
6. Cook until the centers feel firm to the touch and the pancakes are light brown.

102 CALORIES PER SERVING: 5 G PROTEIN, 1 G FAT, 18 G CARBOHYDRATE; 193 MG SODIUM, 23 MG CHOLESTEROL

Pecan Buttermilk Pancakes

Pancakes are for breakfast, but they're also for lunch and dinner. Pecan pancakes are a special treat. One-half cup of nuts added to the recipe puts the fat content at less than 5 grams per pancake.

MAKES 10 TO 12 PANCAKES

1 recipe Buttermilk Pancakes
½ cup chopped pecans

1. Follow the directions for Buttermilk Pancakes. Add the pecans to the dry ingredients before adding the wet.

138 CALORIES PER SERVING: 5 G PROTEIN, 5 G FAT, 19 G CARBOHYDRATE; 193 MG SODIUM, 23 MG CHOLESTEROL

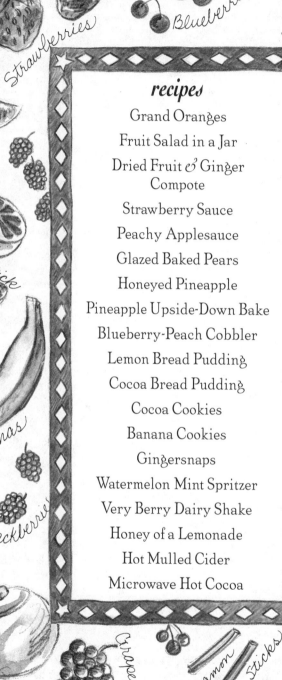

recipes

Grand Oranges

Fruit Salad in a Jar

Dried Fruit & Ginger Compote

Strawberry Sauce

Peachy Applesauce

Glazed Baked Pears

Honeyed Pineapple

Pineapple Upside-Down Bake

Blueberry-Peach Cobbler

Lemon Bread Pudding

Cocoa Bread Pudding

Cocoa Cookies

Banana Cookies

Gingersnaps

Watermelon Mint Spritzer

Very Berry Dairy Shake

Honey of a Lemonade

Hot Mulled Cider

Microwave Hot Cocoa

Desserts & Beverages

*f*ood is not only sustenance; it is also pleasure. And in no part of the meal is that more evident than in the dessert course. Desserts have one thing in common: they are sweet. When babies taste sugar for the first time, they smile, and we continue to smile over sweet things for the rest of our lives.

Desserts come at the end of the meal and are not meant to be a major provider of nutrients. But that doesn't mean that they can't fit in a healthy diet. I've left out light desserts that are mostly egg whites and sugar, because I personally don't like them. Desserts that are dense and decadent or soft and crumbly usually require butter to be successful. Because of this, you also won't find traditional cakes in this chapter. I've left out pies because good low-fat crusts can be tricky, and I want all my recipes to be perfect on your first try. The desserts in this book fall within the guidelines for eating well. They are low in fat and use wholesome, fresh ingredients. They contain fiber and nutrients. I can eat a large portion and still feel able to get up and be active. Although all are delicious sweet finales, none provide empty calories. But the true test of a dessert is whether you smile when you take your first bite. I believe that all the recipes here pass that test.

Sugar

These recipes mark the first time in many years that I have used white and brown sugar in my recipes. The sweeteners that I relied on the most in *For Goodness' Sake* were honey, maple syrup and concentrated fruit juices. The reasons that I avoided white sugar remain, but I have rationalized them as being less important than my need for a moderate amount of white sugar to cook with. Whenever a person chooses to put limits on what he or she eats, that person does so by sorting through desires, nutritional needs and personal philosophies. Since there aren't any clear rights and wrongs, it all comes down to weighing the information and making a personal decision. I hope that sharing mine with you will provide you with more food for thought about your own decisions.

I still prefer to use honey and maple syrup, and have local sources for both. The honey comes from the bees that live on the town's cranberry bog, and the syrup comes from sap that pours out of nearby maple trees. I like supporting local agriculture, and I like the flavors that are so tied to home. But maple syrup and honey (as well as molasses) have limitations in cooking. Their strong distinctive flavors can overwhelm delicate recipes. Baked goods made with these liquid sweeteners are heavier, stickier and more likely to burn, and they get stale and harden faster than those made with white sugar. Obviously, this limits the cook.

White sugar lends a neutral sweetness, helps incorporate air into fat to make lighter textures, tenderizes cakes by preventing their structures from becoming too rigid, retains moisture and is important in preserving food such as jams and jellies. When browned, it produces a rich caramel flavor of

use in both desserts and savory dishes. From the cook's vantage point, white sugar is hard to do without.

But cane sugar has a long past and current history of ecological disaster, enslaved workers and brutal working conditions. Additionally, sugar, which provides no nutrients other than calories, has become such a large part of our diet that other, more nutritious foods are being squeezed out. However, no sweetener has nutrients that count. Even honey and molasses provide little more than calories. The answer is not artificial sweeteners. Not only are their ingredients still being scrutinized for safety, but they don't help with weight loss. In fact, new data show that they might even make a person more likely to gain weight. Besides, they tend to be in processed products that are best left out of a heathy diet.

It turns out that almost 80 percent of the sweeteners consumed in this country are found in processed foods. Fourteen percent of America's sugar is used in the manufacture of cereal! I looked at my diet, which contains very few of these processed foods, and concluded that I am a minor supporter of the industry. When I learned that 40 percent of sugar comes from sugar beets, which do not share the same history as cane, I decided that a little white sugar in my home-baked goods was a compromise that I could live with. Many of my baked goods are better for it. Following are descriptions of the sweeteners used in this book.

White Sugar

White sugar is a crystalline sweetener that is 99 percent pure sucrose. No traces of its origins, either the sugar cane (a reed in the grass family) or sugar beet, remain. Stored in a tightly covered jar, it can last indefinitely. It attracts water, so keep it in a dry cupboard.

Other types of white sugar include powdered confectioners' sugar, which is used in unbaked goods where the grittiness of regular sugar would detract from the recipe, and superfine sugar, which dissolves faster in liquids than regular white sugar. Turbinado sugar is cane sugar that has been partially refined but still has some molasses clinging to the crystals.

Brown Sugar

During the process of making white sugar, the cane or beet juice is heated, clarified, strained, boiled and crystallized. Several times during this process, molasses, a syrupy by-product, is extracted. Brown sugar is white sugar that retains some molasses. It is made only from cane, since beet molasses is useful solely as animal feed. It is the molasses that makes brown sugar stick together. The molasses gives the sugar color and flavor, but contrary to popular belief, it lends only negligible nutrients. Light brown sugar is about 8 percent molasses and 92 percent white sugar. Dark brown sugar has more molasses. Some manufacturers take white sugar and add molasses back in to make brown sugar. That's OK. What isn't is the brown sugar that is actually white sugar with caramel coloring. It doesn't have authentic brown sugar taste. Brownulated sugar is brown sugar that has been crystallized to pour easily. Use light brown sugar in my recipes.

Store brown sugar tightly wrapped in a plastic bag. I use a chip clip to keep the bag tightly sealed.

Molasses

Molasses, a by-product of making sugar from cane, used to be clarified and lightened with sulfur, which imparted sulfur's unpleasant rotten egg aroma. Sulfured molasses is now rare. Blackstrap molasses is the last and most concentrated extraction of impurities from the cane in the making of pure sucrose. As such, it has the most nutrients, but it also has a harsh, bitter taste that makes it worthless as a cooking ingredient. Once touted as a health food, it actually isn't a rich source of nutrients, and its flavor limits its use to animal feed.

Honey

Honey, that sweet, golden nectar, is still produced solely by bees and not yet imitated by food scientists. Honey is very sweet and sticky, which makes it a desired ingredient in glazes and baked goods. Clover is a mild honey that is available in supermarkets. There are many other honeys, each reflecting the plants the bees have visited. Orange blossom or apple honey smells of orchards; wildflower honey is dark and complex. These and others are available locally from beekeepers and in specialty stores. Honey will crystallize if stored below 60 degrees F. To liquefy it again, simply set the jar in a warm-water bath. Crystallized honey is susceptible to fermentation by microbes, so smell the honey and make sure it is still in good shape. Honey sold in supermarkets has been flash-heated and filtered to delay crystallization. It also has a more neutral, uniform flavor. Do not feed children under the age of one honey, as it carries disease-causing spores against which the very young are not protected.

Measuring honey can be a sticky mess. It sticks to the cup, to the spatula and the bowl. To solve this problem, if the recipe calls for oil, measure it first, then use the same measuring cup or spoon for the honey. If the recipe is oil free, you might want to grease the measuring cup or spoon very lightly.

Maple Syrup

In the spring, amber-colored sap flows down the insides of sugar maple trees. Farmers tap the trees (some have permanent spigots in their bark) and collect the liquid. It takes a lot of labor and many logs to stoke the fire to boil down 30 to 40 gallons of sap into one gallon of syrup. As the sugars and amino acids interact and brown as the sap is boiled, the unique flavor of maple syrup develops. Syrup is graded. AA is the lightest in color and flavor. I prefer to eat and cook with grade B.

Maple syrup was one of the first artificial flavors invented, but the artificial stuff is still no match for the real thing. Please do not use substitutes in these recipes.

Grand Oranges

Grand Marnier is perhaps the best of the orange-flavored liqueurs. I use it here to make a sweet syrup to surround oranges. At the last moment before serving, you can add fresh raspberries to brighten this already pretty dessert. Leftovers will stay delicious for several days.

SERVES 10

8	oranges, preferably seedless
½ cup	orange juice
½ cup	water
2 tablespoons	sugar
1 tablespoon	honey

2 tablespoons	Grand Marnier or other orange-flavored liqueur
½ teaspoon	vanilla
1 cup	fresh raspberries or other delicate fruit (optional)

1. Peel the oranges (see below). Make sure you remove the bitter white pith. Slice the oranges into circles. Remove the seeds if there are any.
2. Bring the orange juice, water, sugar and honey to a boil.
3. Add the oranges. Bring the mixture back to a boil, then immediately take the pot off the burner. Let it sit for 2 minutes. Do not stir.
4. Using a slotted spoon, remove the orange slices to a bowl.
5. Stir the Grand Marnier and vanilla into the liquid. Return the pot to a full boil and keep it boiling until the liquid reduces down to ½ cup. This will take about 20 minutes. To test whether it is ready, pour the hot liquid into an ovenproof glass measuring cup. Return it to the pot if it has not reduced enough. By the time it boils down, the liquid will have become a thicker syrup.
6. Cool the syrup to lukewarm. Pour it over the oranges and chill.
7. Just prior to serving, add the raspberries if desired.

81 CALORIES PER SERVING: 1 G PROTEIN, 0 G FAT, 19 G CARBOHYDRATE; 1 MG SODIUM, 0 MG CHOLESTEROL

Cutting Round Fruits & Vegetables

*O*ranges, melons, winter squash, and other round fruits and vegetables that need to be peeled can be cut much faster and more efficiently using the following method.

As always, use a large cutting board and a sharp chef's knife. Cut a thin slice off each end of the fruit or vegetable. Set the fruit securely on one of the newly made flat surfaces. Hold the fruit steady with one hand. With the other, take the knife and, following the curve of the fruit, slice off the skin. When peeling an orange, cut all the way through so that you remove the white pith along with the skin and you are left with only the orange flesh. When you have cut around and down, turn the fruit over and set it on its other cut surface. Trim off any peel that you missed.

Fruit Salad in a Jar

My family and I eat at least twice as much fruit if it is cut up and put in a jar than if it is left whole, unwashed and unpeeled in the fruit bin of the refrigerator. So once a week, I buy a melon and whatever else is in season and looks good in the market. I take about 10 minutes to fill up a 2-quart wide-mouth jar with fruit salad. We eat it for dessert, breakfast, lunch and snacks.

Fruit salad will keep for up to 4 days as long as you use harder fruits like apples, grapes and melons. Soft or delicate fruits, such as berries, kiwis and bananas, can be added at the last minute. Always include a grapefruit or orange if you're using apples or pears. The citrus juice will prevent discoloration.

What follows is a general guide to making fruit salad. It is meant to be tinkered with according to your likes, dislikes and what is ripe and fresh in the market.

MAKES ABOUT 2 QUARTS

2- to 3-pound	melon	2	oranges
1 pound	seedless grapes	2	apples or pears

1. Cut the melon in half, scrape out the seeds and use a melon baller to remove the flesh. Or peel the melon, cut it in half, scoop out the seeds and cut the melon into cubes. Put the melon pieces in a large bowl. One melon yields about 3 to 4 cups. Watermelon is excellent in fruit salads, although the seeds can be annoying. To get rid of watermelon seeds, cut the watermelon off its rind. If it is a big piece of melon, do this in chunks. The seeds are not dispersed throughout the fruit, but grow in a line. Cut the melon straight through that line, exposing the seeds. Then cut off the section with the seeds. You can discard this or you take the time to pick the out the seeds.

2. Wash the grapes well, then pluck them off of the stems. Add them to the bowl. One pound makes about 3 cups.

3. Peel the oranges (page 208). Make sure you remove the bitter and unattractive white pith along with the peel. Slice the oranges into rounds or cut them into cubes. Pick out the seeds if there are any. Add the orange pieces to the bowl. Each orange yields about ½ cup.

4. Wash the apples or pears, then cut them into 4 or 8 segments. Remove the core from each piece. Cut the segments into cubes. Toss them with the rest of the fruit salad, making sure that they come into contact with the citrus. One apple produces about a cup of fruit.

65 CALORIES PER SERVING: 1 G PROTEIN, 0 G FAT, 16 G CARBOHYDRATE; 2 MG SODIUM, 0 MG CHOLESTEROL

Dried Fruit & Ginger Compote

Eat this in the morning with yogurt, for lunch, for dessert at dinner with frozen yogurt or ice cream, or all on its own. It remains fresh for up to a week if stored in the refrigerator.

SERVES 6

1 pound	assorted dried fruit, such as apricots, pears, raisins and prunes
1	cinnamon stick
2 slices	fresh gingerroot, each about the size of a quarter

¹⁄₁₆ teaspoon	ground cloves
	water

1. Put the fruit, cinnamon, ginger and cloves in a saucepan.
2. Pour in enough water to cover the fruit.
3. Simmer, covered, for about 1 hour. Stir occasionally.

4. Remove the cinnamon stick and ginger before serving. Serve hot or cold.

189 CALORIES PER SERVING: 2 G PROTEIN, 0 G FAT, 50 G CARBOHYDRATE; 6 MG SODIUM, 0 MG CHOLESTEROL

Strawberry Sauce

Pour this sauce over ice cream, fruit salad, yogurt, or just about anything else.

MAKES ABOUT 1 CUP

2 cups	strawberries
1 tablespoon	apple juice concentrate

1 tablespoon	honey
1 tablespoon	lemon juice

1. Put all the ingredients in a pot. Simmer until only the outsides of the berries soften. This takes only a minute or two. If the strawberries are not very flavorful, you might want to add more honey or apple juice concentrate. You can find apple juice concentrate in the frozen food section of the supermarket along with the other juices. Keep it frozen and spoon it out as you need it. You may use frozen berries. They do not have to thaw first, but the recipe obviously will take more time to cook if you put them into the pot frozen.

2. Strain the strawberries and liquid through a wire mesh strainer into a bowl. You can do this by pushing them with a wooden spoon, but it is best accomplished with a bowl scraper, which is a hard plastic semicircle. Straining the berries will remove their seeds and create a smooth sauce. At the end, remember to scrape what is clinging to the underside of the sieve into the bowl.
3. Serve reheated or chilled. This sauce stays fresh for 3 days in the refrigerator.

23 CALORIES PER SERVING: 0 G PROTEIN, 0 G FAT, 6 G CARBOHYDRATE; 1 MG SODIUM, 0 MG CHOLESTEROL

Peachy Applesauce

Spiced with cardamom, this unusual fruit sauce could be served with a light lunch of yogurt, cut fruit and granola or accompany meats. The sweetness will vary with the ripeness and variety of the peaches and apples, so season to taste.

The best tool to use when making applesauce is a food mill. This hand-cranked appliance pushes the food through small holes, which gives it an entirely different texture than a blender or processor. If you don't own a food mill and don't mind the work, you can try pushing the fruit through the holes of a wire sieve. Press it against the mesh with the back of a wooden spoon.

MAKES ABOUT 5 CUPS

1½ pounds	peaches		¹⁄₁₆ teaspoon	ground cloves
2 pounds	apples		⅛ teaspoon	ground cardamom
½ cup	honey		¼-½ cup	water
2	cinnamon sticks			

1. Wash the peaches, then remove the pits. This is an easy task if the peaches are a freestone variety, but a bit tedious if the flesh sticks to the pits. You can pit freestone peaches by running a knife around the equator, twisting lightly to pull the halves apart and then removing the pit. To pit other peaches, you have to cut the flesh cut from the stone. Use a sharp paring knife and do this over a bowl.

2. Quarter and core the apples.
3. Put the fruit and the remaining ingredients in a pot. Drier, older fruit will need the full ½ cup water. Otherwise, ¼ cup will be plenty. Simmer gently, covered, for 30 minutes. Stir once or twice.
4. Remove the cinnamon sticks.
5. Put the sauce through a food mill or puree in a machine.

158 CALORIES PER SERVING, 1 G PROTEIN, 0 G FAT, 41 G CARBOHYDRATE; 2 MG SODIUM, 0 MG CHOLESTEROL

Glazed Baked Pears

Pears are one of the few fruits that can be bought concrete-hard from the supermarket, then left to ripen on the counter to a juicy sweetness.

SERVES 6 TO 12

½ cup	apple juice
1 cup	honey
½ teaspoon	ground allspice

| ½ tablespoon | vanilla |
| 6 | pears |

1. Preheat the oven to 375 degrees F.
2. Whisk together the apple juice, honey, allspice and vanilla.
3. Slice the pears in half lengthwise. I like to leave the stem on one of the halves. It makes for a pretty presentation at the dinner table. Take a spoon (a grapefruit spoon works especially well) and scrape out the core and tough string.
4. Place the pears cut side down in a casserole. Pour the sauce over the pears. The type of baking dish will make a big difference in the outcome of this recipe. When I baked this in an enamel-lined cast-iron pot, the sauce caramelized into a sticky candy. But in a white porcelain baking dish, which reflects heat, the sauce bubbled and thickened slightly. The pears in the white dish also took about 7 minutes longer to bake. Both versions were yummy; just keep an eye on things.

5. Baking time varies with the ripeness of the pears. Rock-solid pears will take up to 45 minutes. For such pears, cover the casserole for the first 30 minutes. Ripe pears will take only 20 to 25 minutes. You can cook these uncovered. The pears are done when a knife can be inserted easily. (Try to do this test in an inconspicuous spot on the pear. Slash marks are unappetizing.) Or wait until their skins begin to crack.
6. Serve hot, with sauce poured over each portion. Leftovers are wonderful.

284 CALORIES PER SERVING: 1 G PROTEIN, 1 G FAT, 73 G CARBOYHYDRATE; 4 MG SODIUM, 0 MG CHOLESTEROL

Pineapple

Selecting an Edible Pineapple

*r*ipe pineapples are luscious, sweet, juicy fruits. Unripe pineapples are sharp, sour, tongue-smarting jokers. Picking a good one is a matter of knowledge and observation. A pineapple importer at a produce show showed me how to select a ripe one.

Pulling a leaf out of the top, picking a "male" over a "female" (there are no such divisions), equating ripeness with softness or going for the fruit with the most yellow will not lead you to a sweet pineapple. All those criteria are myths. Also, pineapples don't ripen at home. They get softer, which is nice, and their flavor blossoms at room temperature, but they don't get sweeter.

The most important quality a ripe pineapple has is aroma. An overripe pineapple will smell a bit fermented. An unripe pineapple will have no aroma at all. A ripe pineapple will give off a sweet, full pineapple odor. In the chill of a produce department, aromas are suppressed, so bring the fruit right up to your nose to test it.

Another supporting factor are full eyes (those dimples in the flesh). Eyes that are slightly weepy indicate a very ripe fruit, but beware of bruised or soft pineapples.

Store the pineapple at room temperature. Whole, uncut pineapples shouldn't be kept below 50 degrees F.

Ripe pineapple is a treat. I always check over the pineapples in the market, but I rarely buy them. I wait for the perfect one. For baking and fruit salads, I often use canned pineapple packed in its own juice. I don't use cans of fruit in heavy syrup because the sugar masks the pineapple flavor and renders it too sweet for most uses.

Cutting a Pineapple

*t*o cut a pineapple, begin by cutting off the skin the way you would any other round or oblong fruit or vegetable. First, cut off the top and bottom with a chef's knife. Slice off enough so that the fruit, and not only the core, is visible. Then stand it up on the newly made flat surface. Hold the pineapple with one hand. With the other, slice off the skin, following the curve of the fruit with your knife. Don't be concerned about the green remaining in the dimples. You can cut those off by using the tip of a paring knife. Cut the pineapple in half lengthwise and then into long wedges. Slice off the core using your chef's knife. At this point, you can slice the spears into triangles, leave them as is, or chop the fruit.

Honeyed Pineapple

Sometimes the easiest recipe can bring as much pleasure as the most complicated concoction. This dessert is a case in point. As with all simple recipes, however, the ingredients must be the best. Typical commercial clover honey is mild and bland, but most people living in the suburbs or the country have access to local honey. Even city dwellers can find interesting honey, as most specialty shops carry a selection of the amber sweetener.

SERVES 8

1 pineapple
¼ cup honey

1. Peel the pineapple, following the directions on page 213. Cut it into 4 wedges, then slice off and discard the core from each piece. Cut each section into narrower wedges or triangles. The pineapple triangles can be threaded onto skewers.
2. Put the pineapple in a glass or stainless-steel bowl. Coat it with the honey. Let it sit for at least 15 minutes, or up to several hours, before cooking.

3. Preheat the broiler. Line a baking pan with parchment paper. (This eases cleanup because broiled honey can really stick to a pan!)
4. Place the pineapple on the baking pan, then put it under the broiler. Cook for about 5 minutes until the edges turn light brown. Thick pieces can be turned once, using long-handled metal tongs.

71 CALORIES PER SERVING: 0 G PROTEIN, 0 G FAT, 18 G CARBOHYDRATE; 1 MG SODIUM, 0 MG CHOLESTEROL

Pineapple Upside-Down Bake

This recipe doesn't really fit into any category. It's not exactly a cake, and although I serve it right out of the baking pan as I would a pie, it is not one of those either. Neither is it a grunt, a buckle or a crumble. Whatever it is, it sure tastes good.

SERVES 9

1 20-ounce can	crushed pineapple packed in its own juice
1 20-ounce can	pineapple chunks, packed in their own juice
2 tablespoons	pineapple juice from the can
½ cup	honey
1 tablespoon	arrowroot
1	egg
¼ cup	vegetable oil
¼ cup	low-fat or nonfat yogurt
½ cup	low-fat milk
½ teaspoon	vanilla
1¼ cups	unbleached white flour
¾ cup	whole-wheat flour, preferably pastry flour
¼ cup	brown sugar
1½ teaspoons	baking powder
1 teaspoon	baking soda
⅛ teaspoon	kosher salt
½ teaspoon	ground cinnamon

1. Preheat the oven to 400 degrees F. Coat a 2-quart casserole or baking pan with a nonstick cooking spray.
2. Drain both cans of pineapple. Discard all but 2 tablespoons of the juice.
3. Combine the pineapple, juice and honey. Add the arrowroot. You don't have to sift it on, but you don't want to dump the arrowroot in all at once, or it will lump. Instead, cast it about and stir. Distribute the pineapple mixture evenly on the bottom of the casserole.
4. Combine the egg, oil, yogurt, milk and vanilla in a mixing bowl. Beat until foamy.
5. In another bowl, sift together the flours, sugar, baking powder, baking soda, salt and cinnamon. Stir until there are no dark streaks remaining.
6. Make a depression in the flour, pour the wet mixture in and fold the two together until there aren't any dry pockets. It should be evenly moist but still a bit lumpy.
7. Since the batter will be too thick to pour, you'll have to drop it by large tablespoonsful onto the pineapple. Spread it around with a plastic spatula until it is somewhat evenly distributed.
8. Bake for 30 minutes.

247 CALORIES PER SERVING: 4 G PROTEIN, 5 G FAT, 48 G CARBOHYDRATE; 147 MG SODIUM, 18 MG CHOLESTEROL

Blueberry-Peach Cobbler

Although this is a summer fruit dessert, it is also excellent when made with canned peaches and frozen blueberries. Just make sure that you buy peaches packed in light syrup or fruit juice and that you drain them well. Also, defrost the blueberries, or their chill will prevent the filling from being done at the same time as the biscuits.

SERVES 9

Filling

3 cups	fresh peaches, peeled and sliced or 2 16-ounce cans
3 cups	fresh blueberries, or 1 12-ounce bag frozen
1 tablespoon	lemon juice
¾ cup	brown sugar
2 tablespoons	arrowroot

Biscuit Topping

1 cup	unbleached white flour
1 cup	whole-wheat flour, preferably pastry flour
2 teaspoons	baking powder
½ teaspoon	baking soda
½ teaspoon	kosher salt
2 tablespoons	sugar
¼ cup	vegetable oil
¾ cup	buttermilk

1. Preheat the oven to 400 degrees F.
2. Stir together the filling ingredients. Put the mixture in an ungreased 8-by-8-inch pan (not glass).
3. Sift together the flours, baking powder, baking soda, salt and sugar.
4. Whisk together the oil and buttermilk. Make a well in the dry ingredients and pour the wet ingredients into the depression.
5. Using a fork, quickly mix the wet and dry ingredients together until the flour is moistened and lumps form. Create a ball of dough by kneading this with the palm of your hand (not your fingertips). Knead only until a rough ball forms.
6. Drop portions of the dough onto the fruit until the pan is covered. A few holes are OK. You can press the dough down slightly, but this dessert is supposed to look country casual.
7. Bake for 40 minutes until the biscuit browns.

295 CALORIES PER SERVING: 5 G PROTEIN, 7 G FAT, 57 G CARBOHYDRATE; 254 MG SODIUM, 1 MG CHOLESTEROL

Lemon Bread Pudding

Bread pudding is rustic in appearance and not the least bit pretentious, but it is light, creamy and refreshing. Bread pudding is soft on the inside and crusty on top. To achieve this texture, it is baked in a water bath, which is really very simple and does not require special equipment. The baking pan sits in a cushion of water in a larger pan. When filling the larger pan with water, remember that the water will be displaced when you put the pudding dish in it. The water needs to come only halfway up the smaller container's sides. When removing the pudding from the oven, be careful not to splash yourself with the hot water.

SERVES 6

2 cups	low-fat milk
1½ teaspoons	vanilla
⅓ cup	light brown sugar
2	egg whites
1	whole egg

⅛ teaspoon	kosher salt
4 slices	homemade-style white bread, stale or lightly toasted
1 tablespoon	lemon zest

1. Preheat the oven to 325 degrees F. Coat an 8-by-8-inch baking dish (or a 2-quart casserole) with a nonstick cooking spray. Partially fill a larger pan with water for the water bath. Put the larger pan in the oven. (It is easier to do it now than to try and move it when the pudding pan is in it.)
2. Beat the milk, vanilla, sugar, egg whites, egg and salt until foamy.
3. Tear the bread into 1- to 2-inch pieces. Stir them into the liquid mixture.
4. Stir in the lemon zest.
5. Pour the mixture into the pudding pan. Place the pan in the water bath
6. Bake for about 1 hour, or until the pudding sets and the top is light brown and slightly crusty.

142 CALORIES PER SERVING: 6 G PROTEIN, 2 G FAT, 24 G CARBOHYDRATE; 191 MG SODIUM, 39 MG CHOLESTEROL

page 127

Cocoa Bread Pudding

This pudding is smooth, homey and chocolaty. What more could you ask?

SERVES 6

2 cups	low-fat milk	⅛ teaspoon	ground nutmeg
3 tablespoons	unsweetened cocoa	3 slices	homemade-style white bread, torn into pieces
⅓ cup	brown sugar		
½ teaspoon	vanilla	1	whole egg
⅛ teaspoon	kosher salt	1	egg white

1. Preheat the oven to 325 degrees F. Coat an 8-by-8-inch pan or a 2-quart casserole, with a nonstick cooking spray, or use a nonstick pan. Metal or porcelain will work equally well.
2. Heat the milk. Whisk in the cocoa and sugar until there are no lumps of cocoa and the sugar is dissolved. Remove the pan from the heat.
3. Stir in the vanilla, salt, nutmeg and bread.
4. Lightly beat the egg and egg white. Stir them into the bread mixture.
5. Pour the mixture into the pan. Baking this in a water bath is optional, but it will result in a softer, fuller texture. See page 217 for information on using a water bath.
6. Bake for 50 minutes, or until the pudding sets.
7. Serve warm.

141 CALORIES PER SERVING: 7 G PROTEIN, 3 G FAT, 24 G CARBOHYDRATE; 177 MG SODIUM, 39 MG CHOLESTEROL

Cocoa Cookies

Eating these cookies is like eating bites of chocolate cake without the icing. I like them plain, but they also are very good with chopped pecans incorporated into the batter.

MAKES 2 DOZEN COOKIES

1 cup	whole-wheat flour, preferably pastry flour	½ teaspoon	sugar
		¼ cup	vegetable oil
1 cup	unbleached white flour	1 teaspoon	vanilla
2 teaspoons	baking powder	2	egg whites
¼ teaspoon	kosher salt	½ cup	honey
⅓ cup	cocoa		

1. Preheat the oven to 350 degrees F. Grease 2 baking sheets, or line them with parchment paper.
2. Sift together the flours, baking powder, salt, cocoa and sugar. Stir until no streaks of cocoa remain in the flour.
3. In a separate bowl, beat together the oil, vanilla, egg whites and honey until frothy.
4. Pour the wet ingredients into the dry. Fold it all together. Work quickly until a pastelike batter forms.
5. Drop tablespoonfuls of the dough onto the baking sheets. The cookies will spread slightly while baking.
6. Bake for 20 to 25 minutes.

83 CALORIES PER COOKIE: 2 G PROTEIN, 3 G FAT, 14 G CARBOHYDRATE; 53 MG SODIUM, 0 MG CHOLESTEROL

Cocoa

*f*or many, chocolate is nirvana. Others, less obsessed, still consider chocolate one of the necessary food groups. This pleasurable food comes from the nib of the cocoa pod. Fifty-five percent of the nib is cocoa butter, a rich, smooth fat. Luckily, the chocolate flavor is not contained in the fat, but in the other 45 percent of the pod. Cocoa powder is made from the solids left over after the cocoa butter has been extracted. Because of this fortuitous fact, fat-conscious cooks can still have chocolaty foods. Cocoa powder has all but 10 to 25 percent of the fat removed.

There are two broad categories of cocoa—Dutch-processed and regular. Dutch-processed cocoa is treated with an alkaline solution to raise its pH. This darkens the cocoa while at the same time making it milder and less bitter. It also improves the texture of the cocoa so that when it is mixed with a liquid, it lumps less. It is frustrating that few manufacturers state on their labels whether their product is Dutch-processed. This is especially important with baking, since Dutch-processed cocoa should be leavened with baking powder, not soda. Hershey's, the cocoa that many of us grew up with and love, is not Dutch-processed.

Cocoas vary. Like wine, cocoa has many varietals. Also like wine, soil, temperature and handling affect the final product. Harvesting and processing are all reflected in the flavor of the cocoa. This is one case where, up to a point, price reflects quality. I find the least expensive brands to be sharp and lacking in the round, lingering aftertaste of good chocolate.

Cocoa stored in an airtight container in a cool, dark place will last up to two years. Under less than optimum storage conditions, it is best to use it within a year.

Banana Cookies

I like chewy, flavorful cookies that aren't too sweet. The oats, ripe bananas and spices in these cookies suit me just fine. The secret to their success is to use ripe bananas.

MAKES 2 DOZEN COOKIES

½ cup	honey
½ cup	brown sugar
¼ cup	vegetable oil
1	egg
2 or 3	bananas, mashed (1 cup)
1 cup	whole-wheat flour, preferably pastry flour
1 cup	unbleached white flour

1 teaspoon	baking powder
½ teaspoon	kosher salt
1 teaspoon	ground cinnamon
¼ teaspoon	ground nutmeg
¼ teaspoon	ground cloves
1 cup	rolled oats
½ cup	pecans or walnuts, chopped (optional)

1. Preheat the oven to 375 degrees F. Grease 2 baking sheets, or line them with parchment paper.
2. Beat together the honey, sugar, oil, egg and banana.
3. Sift together the flours, baking powder, salt and spices. Stir to combine. Stir in the oats and (if using) nuts. Continue to stir until there aren't any streaks of spices or nuts.
4. Pour the wet mixture into the dry. Stir with a rubber spatula until the batter is evenly moist but still lumpy.
5. Drop the batter by large tablespoonfuls onto the baking sheets. The cookies will spread a bit so don't crowd them.
6. Bake for about 25 minutes until firm and golden. Rotate the baking sheets if the oven bakes unevenly.

120 CALORIES PER COOKIE: 2 G PROTEIN, 3 G FAT, 22 G CARBOHYDRATE; 58 MG SODIUM, 9 MG CHOLESTEROL

Gingersnaps

These crisp, spicy cookies are perfect with tea or a bowl of frozen nonfat yogurt. Despite the long list of ingredients, they are a snap to make. The flavor of ground ginger varies. Smell your ginger before you use it. If it doesn't have a sharp ginger aroma, discard it and buy a new bottle.

MAKES 5 DOZEN COOKIES.

1 cup	whole-wheat flour, preferably pastry flour		1½ teaspoons	baking soda
1½ cups	unbleached white flour		⅓ cup	vegetable oil
2 teaspoons	ground ginger		1	whole egg
⅛ teaspoon	ground cloves		1	egg white
1 teaspoon	ground cinnamon		½ cup	molasses
¼ teaspoon	kosher salt		½ cup	honey
			½ cup	brown sugar

1. Preheat the oven to 375 degrees F. Grease your sheets or line them with parchment paper.
2. Sift the flours, spices, salt and baking soda into a bowl. Stir until there are no spice streaks in the flour.
3. Combine the oil, egg, egg white and sweeteners in another bowl. Beat them with a mixer until the mixture is a little bubbly.
4. Pour the wet ingredients into the dry. Fold them together until the flour is completely wet and a batter forms.
5. Drop by full teaspoonfuls onto the baking sheets. The cookies will spread, so don't crowd them
6. Bake for about 6 minutes, or until the cookies are firm and begin to brown. Watch them closely as they cook. They go quickly from done to scorched. Remove them from the pans and cool them on racks. Store them in airtight bags.

53 CALORIES PER COOKIE: 1 G PROTEIN, 1 G FAT, 10 G CARBOHYDRATE; 32 MG SODIUM, 4 MG CHOLESTEROL

Beverages

It is not necessary to make beverages from scratch. Certainly there are plenty of bottled spritzers, juices, waters and teas capable of quenching a thirst without adding undue calories, fats or artificial ingredients. And yet there is something especially refreshing about a pitcher of homemade lemonade, a fizzy drink made with fresh fruit or a yogurt drink where you are the creative spirit behind the blender. Similarly, the aroma of hot mulled cider can set a cozy tone for an afternoon party.

Watermelon Mint Spritzer

In the summer, when heat wraps around you and slows you down, ice-cold drinks refresh and revitalize. During those days when even bottled fruit juices taste too heavy, I go for a watermelon spritzer.

SERVES 2

1 pound	watermelon
1 sprig	fresh mint (about 10 leaves)
1 teaspoon	lemon juice
¼ cup	seltzer or sparkling spring water

1. Cut the watermelon from the rind. Remove the seeds (page 209).
2. Liquefy the watermelon, mint leaves and lemon juice in the blender or food processor.
3. Fill 2 tall glasses with ice cubes. Pour half the puree in each glass.
4. Top off each glass with about 2 tablespoons of seltzer. This will make a pretty pink foam on the surface.

79 CALORIES PER SERVING: 2 G PROTEIN, 1 G FAT, 18 G CARBOHYDRATE; 13 MG SODIUM, 0 MG CHOLESTEROL

Very Berry Dairy Shake

I am always trying to get a young friend of mine to eat more fruits and to switch to low-fat milk. This shake was a big hit with him. The frozen berries give it the feel of a frozen dessert. The only drawback is that you must drink it right away. After refrigeration, it separates and gets grainy. Because of this, I usually share it with him.

SERVES 2

1 cup	low-fat milk
½ cup	low-fat yogurt
1 cup	frozen blueberries
1 cup	other berries of choice, such as raspberries or strawberries
2-4 tablespoons	honey

1. Puree all the ingredients in a blender. Add more milk if you want a thinner consistency. Start with 2 tablespoons honey and add more if desired.

222 CALORIES PER SERVING: 8 G PROTEIN, 3 G FAT, 43 G CARBOHYDRATE; 103 MG SODIUM, 9 MG CHOLESTEROL

Honey of a Lemonade

Think cold. Think ice clinking against the sides of a glass pitcher. Think sunny slices of lemon. Think tart citrus balanced with sweet honey. Think all this, and you have one of the best refreshers—lemonade.

SERVES 8

4	lemons, or 1 lemon and ¾ cup lemon juice	4 cups	cold water
¾ cup	honey		ice cubes
2 cups	warm water		mint sprigs for garnish

1. Wash one lemon well. (It is best if you can find an organic lemon.) Slice the lemon into rounds. Remove the seeds.
2. Put the lemon slices in a pitcher. Pour the honey and warm water over them. With a wooden spoon, stir the mixture until the honey dissolves in the water. Mash the lemon a few times to release the skin's flavors and some of the fruit's juice.
3. Pour in the cold water.
4. Juice the remaining 3 lemons. Each lemon should produce about ¼ cup juice. Or use prepared lemon juice. The best lemon juice is available in the freezer case of your supermarket. Add the juice to the pitcher. Stir to combine.
5. Chill the lemonade and serve over ice cubes. Garnish with mint sprigs.

103 CALORIES PER SERVING: 0 G PROTEIN, 0 G FAT, 27 G CARBOHYDRATE; 7 MG SODIUM, 0 MG CHOLESTEROL

Hot Mulled Cider

One of my favorite ways to make guests feel at home is to have a pot of hot mulled cider greet them as arrive. The aroma wafts through the house, giving it a relaxed, cozy ambience. For large parties, when I'm mulling a few gallons of cider, I take a whole orange, stud it with about a dozen cloves and let it float in the pot.

SERVES 8

½ gallon	apple cider	⅛ teaspoon	ground or freshly grated nutmeg
1	cinnamon stick	1 strip	orange peel, about 2 inches long
6	whole cloves		

1. Stir all the ingredients together in a large pot. Warm the mixture on the stovetop for about 15 minutes. Keeping the pot covered will reduce evaporation. However, I think the wonderful aromas that fill the house if the lid is left off are worth the loss of a little cider.

112 CALORIES PER SERVING: 0 G PROTEIN, 0 G FAT, 28 G CARBOHYDRATE; 17 MG SODIUM, 0 MG CHOLESTEROL

Microwave Hot Cocoa

I have fond memories of my father stirring hot cocoa in a double boiler on the stove top. I was about 6 years old, and I'd stand on my tiptoes to watch. It would take a while, and I'd be bursting with anticipation. I still like hot cocoa. These days, my husband makes it for me in the microwave, but it is just as good.

The type of cocoa used will make a tremendous difference in flavor and proportions of ingredients. Hershey's cocoa, with its sharper flavor, tastes a bit harsh compared to a Dutch-processed cocoa. I like my cocoa a little less sweet than most so I use 1 tablespoon cocoa to 2 teaspoons sugar. The addition of one more teaspoon of sugar will make a large difference. Not only will the cocoa taste much sweeter, but the sugar will increase the cocoa flavor and make the whole mug taste richer.

SERVES 1

2 teaspoons to 1 tablespoon sugar
1 tablespoon cocoa
1 cup low-fat milk

1. In a microwavable mug, stir together the sugar, cocoa and 2 tablespoons of the milk until everything is wet and well mixed.
2. Pour in the remaining milk and stir.
3. Microwave for about 2 minutes, or whatever works with your oven, until the milk is hot throughout but not boiling. Drink immediately.

162 CALORIES PER SERVING: 11 G PROTEIN, 4 G FAT, 25 G CARBOHYDRATE; 147 MG SODIUM, 10 MG CHOLESTEROL

Metric Conversion Guidelines

These guidelines were developed to simplify the conversion from Imperial measures to metric. The numbers have been rounded for convenience. When cooking from a recipe, work in the same system throughout the recipe; do not use a combination of the two.*

Metric Symbols

Celsius:	C
gram:	g
liter:	L
centimeter:	cm
milliliter:	mL
millimeter:	mm
kilogram:	kg

Length

IMPERIAL	METRIC
¼ inch	5 mm
⅓ inch	8 mm
½ inch	1 cm
¾ inch	2 cm
1 inch	2.5 cm
2 inches	5 cm
4 inches	10 cm

Volume

IMPERIAL	METRIC
¼ tsp.	1 mL
½ tsp.	2 mL
¾ tsp.	4 mL
1 tsp.	5 mL
2 tsp	10 mL
1 Tbsp.	15 mL
2 Tbsp.	25 mL
¼ cup	50 mL
⅓ cup	75 mL
½ cup	125 mL
⅔ cup	150 mL
¾ cup	175 mL
1 cup	250 mL
4 cups	1 L
5 cups	1.25 L

Mass (weight)

IMPERIAL	METRIC
1 oz.	25 g
2 oz.	50 g
¼ lb.	125 g
½ lb. (8 oz.)	250 g
1 lb.	500 g
2 lb.	1 kg
3 lb.	1.5 kg
5 lb.	2.2 kg
8 lb.	3.5 kg
10 lb.	4.5 kg
11 lb.	5 kg

Oven Temperature Conversions

IMPERIAL	METRIC
250 F	120 C
275 F	140 C
300 F	150 C
325 F	160 C
350 F	180 C
375 F	190 C
400 F	200 C
425 F	220 C
450 F	230 C
500 F	260 C

Some Common Can/Package Sizes

VOLUME		MASS	
4 oz.	114 mL	4 oz.	113 g
10 oz.	284 mL	5 oz.	142 g
14 oz.	398 mL	6 oz.	170 g
19 oz.	540 mL	7¾ oz.	220 g
28 oz.	796 mL	15 oz.	425 g

*Developed by the Canadian Home Economics Association and the American Home Economics Committee

Index

Page numbers in italic indicate photographs.

More Cookbooks from Camden House

FOR GOODNESS' SAKE
An EATING WELL Guide to Creative Low-Fat Cooking
By Terry Blonder
ISBN 0-944475-08-6 $14.95 paperback

RECIPE RESCUE COOKBOOK
Healthy New Approaches to Traditional Favorites
from EATING WELL Magazine
ISBN 0-944475-47-7 $18.95 paperback
ISBN 0-944475-48-5 $24.95 hardcover

THE EATING WELL COOKBOOK
Edited by Rux Martin, Patricia Jamieson and Elizabeth Hiser
ISBN 0-944475-22-1 $17.95 paperback
ISBN 0-944475-19-1 $24.95 hardcover

Steven Raichlen's
HIGH FLAVOR, LOW-FAT COOKING
ISBN 0-944475-31-0 $18.95 paperback
ISBN 0-944475-32-9 $24.95 hardcover

THE STONYFIELD FARM YOGURT COOKBOOK
By Meg Cadoux Hirshberg
ISBN 0-944475-13-2 $17.95 paperback

SIMMERING SUPPERS
Edited by Rux Martin and JoAnne Cats-Baril
ISBN 0-944475-69-2 $16.95 paperback
ISBN 0-944475-81-1 $21.95 hardcover

THE HARROWSMITH COUNTRY LIFE BAKING BOOK
Edited by Sandra J. Taylor
ISBN 0-944475-28-0 $18.95 paperback

Available at Your Local Bookstore

About the Author

*t*erry Blonder is a cooking instructor and food writer. She began her professional cooking career at the Pritikin Center, where the only oil allowed in the kitchen was used for sharpening knives. There, she learned to make the most of basic, fresh, seasonal whole foods, and to appreciate the flavors inherent in each ingredient. Since leaving the spa, she has worked in French restaurants and bakeries and brought these experiences into her own kitchen.

Blonder's first book, *For Goodness' Sake* (Camden House), was a James Beard Award nominee. Her articles have appeared in Eating Well, Harrowsmith Country Life and the Boston Museum of Science magazines. She has also taught cooking at Bread and Circus Wholefoods markets, in cardiac rehabilitation centers, through adult education programs and in fitness clubs. Terry Blonder lives outside Boston, Massachusetts.